RICE AND BAGUETTE

FOODS AND NATIONS is a new series from Reaktion that explores the history – and geography – of food. Books in the series reveal the hidden history behind the food eaten today in different countries and regions of the world, telling the story of how food production and consumption developed, and how they were influenced by the culinary practices of other places and peoples. Each book in the Foods and Nations series offers fascinating insights into the distinct flavours of a country and its culture.

Already published

Al Dente: A History of Food in Italy
Fabio Parasecoli

Beyond Bratwurst: A History of Food in Germany
Ursula Heinzelmann

Feasts and Fasts: A History of Food in India
Colleen Taylor Sen

Rice and Baguette: A History of Food in Vietnam
Vu Hong Lien

Rice and Baguette

A History of Food in Vietnam

Vu Hong Lien

REAKTION BOOKS

For my son Oliver D. Vu-Warder

Published by Reaktion Books Ltd
Unit 32, Waterside
44–48 Wharf Road
London N1 7UX, UK
www.reaktionbooks.co.uk

First published 2016
Copyright © Vu Hong Lien 2016

Printed and bound in China by 1010 Printing International Ltd

A catalogue record for this book is available from the British Library

ISBN 978 1 78023 657 5

CONTENTS

Introduction 7

ONE

From Molluscs to Venison *10*

TWO

Towards a Cuisine *24*

THREE

Agricultural Settlements, Animal Farms and Fisheries *41*

FOUR

The Chinese Millennium, 257 BCE–938 CE *60*

FIVE

Independence Food, 939–1859 *92*

SIX

The French Century, 1859–1954 *108*

SEVEN

Food at War *136*

EIGHT

From Traditional to Modern Vietnamese Food *162*

Timeline *230*
References *232*
Select Bibliography *237*
Acknowledgements *240*
Photo Acknowledgements *241*
Index *247*

INTRODUCTION

All living beings on earth share the same fundamental need: to eat for survival, be it by foraging, gathering or killing prey. However, it is how we as humans satisfy this need and what we do with food that set us apart from other creatures. We are the only species that knows how to farm and how to tame our sources of food. It has taken us hundreds of thousands, if not millions, of years to evolve from mere hunter-gatherers to agriculturalists, from eating raw molluscs to enjoying refined cuisines. Each individual or group has a different way of dealing with the need for sustenance, so the treatment of food can be a door through which to catch a glimpse into a people's culture, their view of life and afterlife, and their expectations, hopes and despair. To know what a people eats is to understand how its society works, why it goes to war or sues for peace. To understand how a group of people eat is to acknowledge how they both differ from and are similar to oneself.

The people of Vietnam have undertaken a long journey to arrive at the diverse food culture we know today, starting from the time when *Homo sapiens* first set foot on this coast of Asia and decided to settle, more than 70,000 years ago. The journey has been complex and full of surprises, but its destination is probably the most surprising feature of all. It points to the fact that if modern Vietnamese food had a voice, it would be bilingual, for it is the offspring of a marriage of convenience between a rice-based diet and a wheat-based culture. Today's Vietnamese cuisine is a mixture of French and Vietnamese dishes, adapted and modified to suit and complement one another.

This startling statement is bound to offend those who have always believed that Vietnamese culinary culture is subject to the palate of its Chinese big brother, considering that the Chinese colonized and occupied

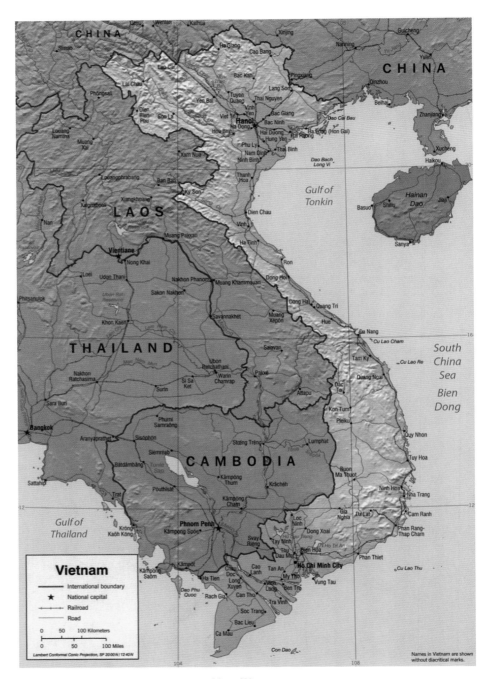

Map of Vietnam.

the original land of Viet (today's north Vietnam) for almost ten centuries, from 111 BCE to the middle of the tenth century CE. But Chinese cuisine, though important in Vietnam, exists as a separate tradition. It is a type of food for such important events as weddings and other landmark occasions. In contrast, when the French colonists brought their own cuisine to Vietnam in the second half of the nineteenth century, many of the dishes were instantly successful. The Vietnamese embraced them wholeheartedly, 'Vietnamized' them with local ingredients and happily consumed them as a natural part of their diet. Ragout, stuffed tomatoes, pâté, mayonnaise and so on were incorporated into everyday Vietnamese food, and each acquired its own local pronunciation and usage. Most remarkably, the Vietnamese loved the crunchy bread stick known as *baguette*. As *bánh mì* (wheat cake), it became the most cherished legacy of the French in Vietnamese cuisine. Having said that, as popular and cherished as *bánh mì* is, a square meal for most, if not all, Vietnamese people is still a meal with rice. Rice and its by-products have been around for millennia, since the prehistoric Việt lived on the deltas of the Hồng, Mã and Cả rivers. When they started eating the wonder grains they first found in the wild, their diet, lifestyle and social structure changed for ever.

Rice and Baguette is the story of what the Việt have eaten throughout history, and of why and how they eat certain types of food. It recalls the many thousand years of Vietnamese progress from mollusc-eaters to hunter-gatherers to agriculturalists. It tells of their struggle to tame nature and to adapt to it, and of their failures and successes in winning the most crucial element for life: food.

ONE

From Molluscs to Venison

Humankind has existed for millions of years, in different forms, but we became farmers only in about 10,000 BCE, when the last Ice Age ended and the earth gradually became warmer. In Vietnam, the new balmy climate allowed the cave-dwelling prehistoric Việt people to venture further afield to hunt, gather and try new types of food. In the course of these adventures, they discovered how to take the food sources home in order to experiment with growing or taming them. It was only in the twentieth century that we became able to date certain archaeological evidence with the help of modern technology. Traces found at various sites in the Red (Hồng) River delta in present-day north Vietnam show that the first rice agriculturalists could have existed in about 2000 BCE. This date coincides with that of various Vietnamese legends and is supported by later scientific analyses of rice grains and pollen. That is not to say that the prehistoric Việt did not know about rice and other agricultural products before then; it is just that archaeological evidence has not shown reliably whether the products they ate before this date were wild or domesticated.

In fact, the proto-Việt people might have known how to cultivate rice long before 2000 BCE, since it is generally believed that the ancient land of Việt included part of southern China. Archaeological sites in China have shown that rice was grown south of the Yangtze River from about 8000 BCE on. This area has now been accepted by many geneticists as the cradle of the rice variety of East and Southeast Asia, *Oryza sativa*. They have come to this conclusion by tracing biological components of today's varieties of rice grown in China, Thailand, Malaysia and Indonesia, with Vietnam being the land in the middle. It is not known exactly whether the concept and practice of domestication were transferred from China to Southeast Asia, or indeed how and when that would have happened, but if it did

Oryza sativa: rice plants.

happen it was most probably through immigration and perhaps trade. There is an 'if' here because, even now, scientists and researchers – even those of the same discipline – cannot agree on the origin of rice cultivation. Some believe that it was transferred from one region to the next; others argue that rice was domesticated independently in several centres throughout the world, perhaps as many as twenty. Southeast Asia, including Vietnam, is one of those centres. To illustrate this point, *The Cambridge World History of Food* notes that 'Initial selection and cultivation could have occurred independently and nearly concurrently at numerous sites within or bordering a broad belt of primary genetic diversity that extends from the Ganges plains below the eastern foothills of Himalaya, through upper Burma, northern Thailand, Laos, and northern Vietnam, to southwest and southern China.'[1]

From this evidence, it is logical to assume that rice was cultivated at least from the second millennium BCE in the Hồng River delta, either independently or imported. Once adopted, rice became the central ingredient of all meals in the land of Việt, and it remains so today. Not eating rice with a meal means we have not eaten, so the Vietnamese saying goes.

JOURNEY OF THE MOLLUSC-EATERS

Long before the appearance of rice and other agricultural products, wild or farmed, in the Vietnamese diet, prehistoric Việt people shared the diet of all their contemporaries, eating the products they found in the sea, in rivers and lakes, or in the mountains through which they passed during their epic journey out of Africa, beginning about 80,000 years ago. Archaeological sites along the continental coastline of the Arabian Peninsula, the Middle East and Asia, known as the Southern Route, show that these travellers ate plants, animals and marine products. We do not know exactly what other foods they ate, but we do know that they ate a lot of bivalve molluscs, cockles and snails, for they left numerous mounds of shells along their route during the 10,000-year journey from sub-Saharan Africa to the coast of today's Vietnam.

There the mollusc-eating habit continued: before moving inland to populate the land of Việt, they left several mounds of shells in Quỳnh Lưu (Nghệ An province), north Vietnam, and in Sa Huỳnh in today's central Vietnam.[2] Each mound is several metres high and hundreds of square metres in area. International and Vietnamese research during the late nineteenth century and throughout the twentieth showed that these mounds also contained human bones and teeth, and the bones of small animals. Using radiocarbon dating, it has been estimated that these relics have

Mollusc shells left behind by prehistoric Bắc Sơn people, c. 8,000 years ago.

Prehistoric necklaces made from discarded mollusc shells.
Shellfish was a staple food of the prehistoric peoples of Vietnam.

been around for tens of millennia. More evidence of what the prehistoric Việt ate during this time might have existed on the continental shelf off the coast of today's Vietnam, such as the bottom of Hạ Long Bay, which once linked northern Vietnam with southern China, or the ancient Sunda Continent, which joined south central Vietnam to the many islands of present-day Indonesia and Malaysia. This continent once stretched as far as what is now Bali, and included Java, Sumatra and Borneo; both parts were submerged during the last great melt, 8,000 years ago.

During the last Ice Age, a mild period was recorded at about 40,000–20,500 BCE, which affected Southeast Asia in a number of ways. The ice probably melted slightly, and its meltwater changed the shape of the Vietnamese coastlands, forcing groups of people living by the coast to move inland and upland, and to adapt their food cultures.[3] Most of these people moved up to high grounds in Lạng Sơn, by the border with today's China; to the hills of today's Vĩnh Phú province; to Mount Đọ in Thanh Hóa, further south; and on to the slopes of the Trường Sơn cordillera. The evidence they left behind shows that they progressed through several food stages, their diet changing according to the environmental conditions. Archaeologists have found more animal bones among the shells in the new high grounds settled by these people. The meat they ate then included wild pig, small animals and deer found in the high jungle. Molluscs continued to be their staple or perhaps even preferred food, however. The proto-Việt of this period used stone tools, perhaps to crack open shells or to cut meat. When their meals were over, they were happy enough to spend time making jewellery for themselves, using stone awls or sharpened animal bones to pierce the shells and stringing them together to make necklaces, bracelets and earrings.

During the earliest recorded period of Sơn Vì culture (21,000–9000 BCE), first found in today's Vĩnh Phú province, north Vietnam, the proto-Việt people lived in groups around a communal hearth formed by a large hole in the middle of a cave.[4] Animal bones and teeth and piles of crab claws and mollusc shells have been found scattered around the rims of such holes. The types of mollusc have been identified by Vietnamese archaeologists as freshwater cockles, marine scallops, clams and mountain snails; the last is a staple food still favoured by highlanders in the region.[5]

In 2012 and 2013 two of the latest finds uncovered in caves in the north and northeast of Vietnam showed that the proto-Việt lived there continuously for thousands of years, since about 6,000 years ago.[6] They left many mollusc shells, stone tools for cutting, pieces of jewellery, animal bones and human skeletons. Potsherds were said to be present among the artefacts, but the age of such pieces has not yet been ascertained. Further south, in Thanh Hóa province, 40 m (130 ft) above the ground, Vietnamese archaeologists found traces of groups of ancient people living in a cave called Con Moong. Their existence was traced back to the time of the Sơn Vì period, and the evidence showed that they had exactly the same eating habits as their fellow proto-Việt in the north.

In a series of excavations in that cave, starting in 1976, archaeologists found relics of a kitchen in every layer. Both freshwater and marine type of molluscs, such as those of the land snail *Cyclophorus*, the freshwater snail *Hybocistis* and the marine bivalve clam *Meretrix*, were found smashed, mixed with one another or encrusted with yellow soil.[7] These proto-Việt lived by hunting and gathering in the valley below their cave, which is now part of the Cuc Phuong National Park. The area is well known as a pristine forest with a rich variety of flora and fauna, some of which dates back to this time.

The proto-Việt of this period cooked their marine and freshwater products, and animal meat, directly over the fire, for at the bottom of the communal hearth were traces of ash mixed with animal bones and shells. The scorched bones had been cracked or smashed, presumably to get at the marrow. The people hunted a variety of animals, including deer, elephant, wild boar, wild cats, monkeys and foxes, and gathered crustaceans and molluscs along the coast, or from nearby streams and rivers. The remains suggest that they lived quite successfully by these methods. Sơn Vì

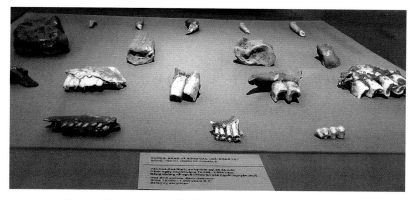

Bones and teeth from the Hòa Bình culture (12,000–10,000 BCE).

practices were the most widespread of all that are so far known in Vietnam, spread over 230 locations throughout the country and also occurring in Lang Rongrien and Moh Khiew in Thailand, and in southern China.

Overlapping and following this period is almost 10,000 years of the best-known segment of Vietnamese prehistory, the Hòa Bình culture, which dates from about 12,000 BCE to about 6000 BCE.[8] Archaeological evidence shows that by then the population of the Con Moong cave had increased three- or four-fold. By 7000 BCE, the Hòa Bình people of the cave had begun to venture down to the plain below, and started hunting more animals. They made more sophisticated stone tools to hunt, chop, crack and mash their food. One such tool – or, more accurately, set of tools – is still in use today throughout the world: the mortar and pestle. These familiar shapes grace the kitchen worktops of many households, and are used regularly in the most sophisticated restaurant kitchens and by the best-known international chefs.

Stone grinders, *c.* 6000 BCE, the forerunner of the mortar and pestle.

Face engraved on a cave wall in north Vietnam, 8000–6000 BCE.

Most importantly, during this period the proto-Việt learned how to grow root vegetables and some fruit; they also began to exchange products with people who lived near the coasts. The forests of Vietnam supported an abundance of wild hogs, deer, elephants, wild cattle and rhinoceros, so it can be assumed that the proto-Việt hunted them for food. By now, deer meat formed a large part of their diet. In caves in Nghệ An province, Vietnamese archaeologists have found large piles of animal bones consisting largely of deer bones (46 per cent), as well as cattle bones (24 per cent) and smaller numbers of wild-boar, monkey and rhino bones, mixed with numerous mollusc shells.[9] Further south, in Quảng Trị province, they have found a similar proportion of animal bones among the shells.

The Hòa Bình people showed a remarkable awareness of themselves and their environment. In a cave in Hòa Bình itself, they left pieces of stone engraved with animals and human faces. Engraved stones found elsewhere show that they appreciated certain plants enough to re-create them on stone. The leaves and branches engraved on these stones do not show what species they belonged to, but it is possible that such plants were used for food or medicine. It is most likely that the Hòa Bình people gathered fruit and nuts, much as their contemporaries did elsewhere.

Archaeological evidence also shows that during this period they grew certain types of plant and tamed animals such as dogs.[10] Traces of their primitive agricultural efforts show that they grew root vegetables, fruit trees and a form of rice.[11] The cultivation of rice, however, was not firmly recorded until about 2,000 years after the last date of the Hòa Bình. These farming activities show that they now stayed in one place, in groups or as small families among a larger group.

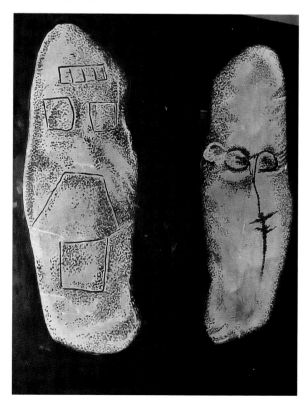

Plants and patterns engraved on stone, north Vietnam, 6000–4000 BCE.

The Arrival of Man's Best Friend

The taming of dogs has been explained by various researchers as the natural result of a sedentary life, when humankind began to live in settlements, and the ancient land of Việt is no exception. The availability of food waste, such as animal bones, in and near these settlements drew scavengers, including wolves. Over time, the proximity between wolves and humans made it easier for them to get to know each other and to accept each other's scents and habits. Such a coexistence was mutually beneficial, and so it was almost a natural next step for the wolves to come to live with those who fed them. The dog was the result of several stages of breeding and taming the wolf. Dogs were used as companions, possibly for food in lean times, or as helpers in the hunt thanks to their acute ability to track by scent, inherited from the wolf. The practice of using dogs in hunts continues today, albeit more for pleasure than out of necessity.

It is more difficult to tame other animals, especially shy herbivores such as elephants, cattle and deer. They would have been drawn to eat the grains and vegetation that humans grew in their settlements, but they shied away when humans approached, so hunting them for food must have continued as an important activity for the proto-Việt during this period, now with the help of their new best friend, the dog. The wild boar was also a scavenger, but it did not come near humans as the wolf did. Boar meat is tasty, however, so boar-hunting continued for the sedentary proto-Việt, as is shown by the regular appearance of boar bones in hearths. The wild boar was eventually domesticated, around 7000 BCE, to become the pig, the meat most commonly eaten by Vietnamese people today. Archaeological artefacts from this time show that, to enhance their hunting techniques, Hòa Bình people made better weapons, such as spears of bamboo and sharpened axes made of stone rather than pebbles, as previously. During this time, they also discovered how to make tools from sharpened bones, especially animal thigh bones.

The mild climate that followed the great ice melt of 8,000 years ago allowed grasses, herbs and many other kinds of vegetation to grow. Life became easier for herbivorous animals, including cattle, deer and goats, and they multiplied into large herds, making it easier for humans to chase and capture them. Such chases usually left the young animals vulnerable and more easily captured, to be raised in the settlements. Domesticated cattle and hogs appeared in about 7000–6000 BCE to become a more reliable source of food, instead of – or as well as – hunting and foraging.

Hunting and gathering equipment, *c.* 2000–1000 BCE.

Cattle were particularly useful since they became working beasts as well as being a source of meat.

Life must have been good for the proto-Việt, with domesticated plants and animals available on their doorsteps. They now had the time and inclination to make more sophisticated things with which to decorate themselves. Dried and weathered animal bones and elephant tusks now entered their artistic repertoire, and bone jewellery became as popular as shells. Fragments and even whole pieces of bone jewellery have been found at various sites throughout the land of Việt, along with those made from shell.

THE WINGED MEAT

The domestication of wildfowl that resulted in today's chicken happened separately and much later. Throughout most of the twentieth century, controversy surrounded the origin of the domesticated fowl, and two locations have been vying with each other as the original nest of the domesticated chicken: India and China. Neither won out: research published in 2008 by Uppsala University in Sweden established that the first chicken came from Southeast Asia.[12] By tracing the DNA of today's chicken throughout Southeast and East Asia, the researchers came to the conclusion that the newly tamed chickens were brought to other regions through trade, immigration and other human activities.

Jade pendants in typical Đồng Nai style. The Đồng Nai culture (*c.* 1500 BCE–500 CE) flourished in the area south of the central highlands, at the source of the Dong-Nai River.

The scientists argue that it must have been the human who transferred the chicken from region to region because this bird cannot fly any distance, even in the wild. The most a chicken can manage is to fly up a tree to escape a predator. It was this handicap that made it attractive to humans in the first place. The Uppsala researchers proposed that chickens might have been bred for other purposes at first, such as religious sacrifice or cockfighting, but in Asia, where people have no qualms about eating most things, it is likely that they were used primarily for food. Occasionally in the history of Vietnam, the chicken has been blamed for being the vessel for evil spirits, and thus killed, but such cases have been rare. The first domesticated variety of chicken is estimated to have appeared in Southeast Asia about 3000 BCE, much later than domesticated mammals. Other wildfowl species followed, and chicken, ducks, geese and pigeons entered the culinary repertoire of the Việt, valued as a food much more special than pork and served only on certain occasions.

International research has established that the availability of domesticated meat and plants helped the human population to grow. In Vietnam, as the number of inhabitants in the settlements grew larger, Hòa Bình people stopped sharing the large hearth. Instead, traces of much smaller hearths have been found in each place they were known to have inhabited. This suggests that as their population multiplied, the groups grew so large that one communal hearth was not enough to serve them all, and that they formed smaller groups who shared the same preferences, or clustered together as families. The hearths may be smaller, but animal bones and large numbers of shells are still present around the rims, along with traces of fire, wood and ash.[13] This shows that animal meat and shellfish were still the people's main food, and that they still cooked their food directly over the fire. Similar to those of their predecessors, Hòa Bình practices were widespread: 120 locations have been found so far in Vietnam, and many others in wider Southeast Asia, such as Cambodia, Thailand, Laos, Myanmar, Sumatra and even Australia.[14]

From this point, the proto-Việt progressed through different – sometimes overlapping – phases of development between 8000 BCE and 111 BCE, spreading from the upper Hồng River down to its delta and further south in central Vietnam, and even as far as Đồng Nai province in south Vietnam.[15] The three most populated deltas were those of the Hồng, Mã and Cả rivers, covering a geographical area that stretches from north of the present-day border with China down to the narrowest part of Vietnam, in Quảng Bình province.

In about 3000 BCE the prehistoric Việt still lived in caves dotting the hillsides, some 4–8 m (13–25 ft) higher than the surrounding plains.[16] The shells and animal bones and teeth they left behind show that they lived by catching freshwater molluscs, mountain snails and some marine molluscs, hunting wild animals such as tigers, elephants, monkeys and foxes, and raising cattle and smaller animals such as pigs. The presence of suckling-pig bones in their dwellings proves that they had raised enough domesticated pigs to be able to eat their young.[17]

Bronze agricultural tools, Đông Sơn period (1,000 BCE– *c.* 100 CE).

Primitive Statecraft and the Cultivation of Wet Rice

After a long period of fluctuation following the last great melt, seawater gradually receded from the coastlands of Vietnam, exposing large tracts of flat land that were suitable for agriculture. This must have enticed the proto-Việt down from the high ground. This period coincides with the legend of the origin of the Việt, in the tale of Âu Cơ and Lạc Long Quân, the mythical parents of all Việt people. Lạc Long Quân, the Dragon King and a great-great-grandson of the god-emperor of agriculture, came from the sea. He was a just king, who taught the Việt people to wear clothes, farm, learn good manners and respect family hierarchy.[18] He met and married Âu Cơ, goddess of the mountain. They lived on the high ground and had a hundred children. After a while, Lạc Long Quân took fifty of their children down to the plain towards the sea, his original domain, and Âu Cơ stayed on the higher ground with the fifty remaining children. The

Phùng Nguyên (2000–1500 BCE) cup showing typical swirling patterns.

legend may sound far-fetched, but it could be an embellished version of the move of some prehistoric Việt from the high ground to the coast in about 3000 BCE. Those who stayed on the high ground became the various ethnic-minority groups present in Vietnam today.

The period surrounding these developments, from about 4000 to 2000 BCE, was the most important stage in the development of the proto-Việt, and constitutes the end of their prehistory. Excavations by Vietnamese archaeologists have showed that people of this period did indeed move down from the high ground towards the sea to settle.[19] Artefacts they have uncovered show that the ancient Việt again changed their lifestyle and diet. On the plain, by the coast and the river deltas, they now used nets for fishing, among other activities. A large number of fishing-net weights made from stone and baked clay found underground along the coast have confirmed that they lived by net fishing and knew how to use clay.[20]

The area bearing the most obvious traces of these people is in Thanh Hóa province, at a site marked by a large mound of mollusc shells next to a stream that flowed down from the mountain into the valley. Many different types of artefact, such as stone tools, crude potsherds, animal bones and human skeletons, were also found there. The shells show that more than 60,000 years after settling in the land of Việt, the ancient inhabitants still ate many molluscs, despite having eaten animals and then grains and root vegetables for thousands of years.

Venison, however, lost its preferred position to pork, perhaps because the pig was more easily domesticated than the light-footed deer, and also because it would have been more difficult for the lowland Việt to find the latter on the plain. For those Việt who stayed in the highlands, barbecued wild meat, especially venison, has remained the preferred food to this day. By 3000 BCE they probably had chicken as well. The dog, unfortunately, still served the dual purpose of both meat and companion.

The pottery shards that date from about 3000 BCE are the most interesting finds from the site in Thanh Hóa, for they show that by this time the proto-Việt knew how to make containers out of clay, for cooking or storing their foodstuffs. It represented a leap in the way they dealt with food, and constituted a prelude to the period of semi-legendary, semi-historical nation-building of ancient Vietnam. This was when Vietnamese cuisine began to take shape and a rice culture began to appear.

TWO

Towards a Cuisine

The move of the prehistoric Việt people to the lowlands during the third millennium BCE marked an important point in their history: the beginning of several historical changes that shaped their lifestyle and eating habits. By stepping down from the mountains, the proto-Việt entered the period of their semi-legendary oral history; and by adopting a sedentary life on the plain, they moved into the first stage of their nation-building process and established a budding society. A settled lifestyle brought about long-term planning and organization, longer-lasting dwellings and expanding areas for agriculture and husbandry. With food more or less under control, and with more variety than ever, finding things to eat was no longer a pressing concern for the population. They turned to inventing different ways of dealing with food, investigating how to improve it and how to create foods for enjoyment, not just survival.

Temperatures in Southeast Asia fluctuated at this point, but within a reasonable margin, keeping Vietnam a land that was alternately tropical and temperate, as is shown by the presence of fern seeds found underground in several locations throughout the country. The changes in temperature affected the budding agriculture of the Việt to some extent. Pollen and seeds of certain products that grow in cooler or warmer climates have been found in alternate layers of soil at Phùng Nguyên sites (2000–1500 BCE), for example. This shows that as the climate changed, the products also varied, but the weather was not so extreme that a variety of agricultural products could not grow and spread. With both wild and domesticated plants and animals readily available, or perhaps even in surplus, the prehistoric Việt began to find ways to store, experiment with and preserve their food.

Before the Clay Pot

Before using clay to make pots and other food-related objects, the proto-Việt may have made use of what was available around them for their storage and cooking needs, such as hollow stone slabs, clam shells or bamboo tubes. The forests of Vietnam were full of the Asian plant bamboo, which was used widely for many purposes, from building houses and making furniture and weapons to weaving into baskets and shaping into kitchen utensils and cooking vessels. As did their neighbours on the Southeast Asian mainland, the ancient Việt may have used bamboo tubes for cooking and storing food. Many tribal groups living on the slopes of the Trường Sơn cordillera or the mountains of north and northwest Vietnam still cook food in fresh bamboo tubes over fire. The ancient technique is very simple, but the food is delicious, since whatever is in the tubes absorbs the fragrance of fresh bamboo as well as the other seasonings. Rice, meat and vegetables can all be cooked in these tubes without spilling or leaking, and are moist, succulent and fragrant. The use of bamboo tubes to cook rice was recorded later, in one of the most important Vietnamese semi-historical accounts, *Lĩnh Nam Chích Quái*.

Apart from using bamboo for cooking, the Việt highlanders also stored food and liquids in the tubes, sealed in the same way. The contents

Bamboo

Bamboo is a woody plant that grows straight up in clumps. The body of each plant is divided into sections about 30–50 cm (12–20 in.) long, marked by nodes, and some of the nodes are closed, providing each length with a natural stopper. To cook their food, Vietnamese tribal people cut tubes of bamboo at the nodes, taking care that one end has a closed node. After placing the food into the tube through the open end, the cook seals it with bunched leaves or herbs, and the bamboo tube is placed over or in the fire. Being a fresh material, bamboo burns slowly, so although the outer part of the tube becomes charred, the inside remains fresh enough to protect the food from scorching.

would stay fresh for at least a day, even in hot weather. The tubes were also portable on long trips, by attaching a string to both ends to form a loop that could be worn over the shoulder. The practice of keeping food in bamboo tubes was so popular among tribal people that they even raised and carried around chickens in this way, for a ready source of meat wherever they came to rest on a journey. The chick was put into a bamboo tube with its head and bottom sticking out at either end. It was fed as normal and excreted through the bottom end of the tube. As it grew, it took on the shape of the bamboo tube. Animal cruelty notwithstanding, this practice has been known at several locations in Vietnam, and the meat is seen as a highland speciality that dates back to prehistory.

The move down from the mountains made it difficult for the pre-historic Việt to find shelter, now that they no longer had readily available caves or stone ledges. Houses began to be built around this time, using bamboo for the structure and leaves to clad the roofs and walls. This prac-tice was noted by the French archaeologist and historian Henri Parmentier in 1918 as similar to that used for the houses of the Vietnamese highland people or the Malaysians at the time of his research.[1] Leaf roofs are still used by Vietnamese ethnic-minority people in the highlands today.

The Birth of the Clay Pot

During the period of transition between the highlands and the plain, the prehistoric Việt discovered a new material: clay. International researchers have argued that clay pottery was invented before agriculture in today's Middle East and elsewhere, but in Vietnam, so far, the earliest potsherds found have been dated only to this period. The pottery was intended to hold foodstuffs that could not be stored otherwise, such as liquids, small grains or food that was less solid than chunks of meat on the bone or mol-luscs in shells. Bamboo tubes, however convenient, were limiting as they did not allow large portions, or a degree of control over the adding of seasonings during cooking. Also, as the proto-Việt discovered the art of cooking, they may have wanted to experiment with different types of pots. Potsherds discovered at several sites in Thanh Hóa and Ninh Bình provinces in the twentieth century were one of the most significant finds in terms of understanding how the prehistoric Việt dealt with their food. Although the proto-Việt may previously have cooked their food in other ways than grilling or roasting it over the fire, pottery allowed them to become more adventurous in their culinary experiments. The clay pot made it possible to

Phùng Nguyên (2000–1500 BCE) clay cooking pot and stove.

season meat and fish in a more palatable and efficient way. It allowed them to put green vegetables and tubers in the same dish. Furthermore, the sizes of the pots made it possible to cook food in a quantity that suited them, for instance cooking in a large pot to feed the whole family.

It was only a matter of time before the proto-Việt found ways to make use of the abundance of clay in Thanh Hóa and Ninh Bình provinces. The pottery shards dating from about 3000 BCE found in caves inhabited by Hòa Bình people (c. 10,000–2000 BCE) and down on the plain in Thanh Hóa province show that the containers, pots and bowls they made were very simple. According to research by Professor Hà Văn Tấn of the Vietnamese Archaeological Department at Hanoi University, the clay was mixed with sand and laterite (a reddish clay found in topsoil), crudely shaped by hand and fired at a low temperature, resulting in thick-walled, grey pieces. Similar pottery was also found in Hải Phòng, bordering what is now Hạ Long Bay. These are so far the earliest pieces of Vietnamese-produced pottery to have been discovered.

During the next period, the Phùng Nguyên (2000–1500 BCE), techniques improved and fine pottery began to appear, fired at relatively high temperatures. The clay was mixed with fine sand and shaped on pottery wheels, producing thin-walled, smooth pieces in various shapes and sizes, each serving a different purpose: pots for cooking over the fire, urns and jars for storage, and bowls for serving food and drink. Pieces were round, square or even octagonal, with round or flat bottoms; further south, in Sa Huỳnh, central Vietnam, vessels in the style of flat-bottomed amphorae were more popular.

Life must have been good enough at this point for the proto-Việt to spend time and effort decorating their wares with S-shapes, swirling circles, dots and cord, comb and geometric patterns, some made by incision, others by indentation or slashes. Among the pottery shards and pieces from this period found at archaeological sites in Vietnam, small clay statues of cows and chickens have also been discovered, probably to show the humans' appreciation for their sources of meat. The many clay spools and shuttles also found at excavated sites have shown that the Phùng Nguyên people knew how to weave and make cloth.

Pottery vessels of this type are not limited to Vietnam, and potsherds found in western Malaysia, Thailand and Cambodia also show the same shapes and patterns. Some of the clay objects on display at the National Museum of Vietnamese History in Hanoi are particularly worth mentioning. These clay pots, which date from 2500–1500 BCE, were placed on or attached to clay tripods. It is obvious that they were meant to be placed over a cooking fire, or for a fire to be lit under them. It is particularly interesting that one piece, which dates from 2500 BCE, is crude in form and

Clay pot and tripod, Phùng Nguyên/Đông Sôn period.

Sa Huỳnh cup (1,000 BCE–200 CE).

material, but a later one, from about 1500 BCE, shows a marked improvement in technique and, uncannily, is very similar to the wares still in use in Vietnamese village kitchens today. A Vietnamese cup dated to the Phùng Nguyên period (2000–1500 BCE) on display at the British Museum in London shows a remarkably refined technique. The cup is in a highly fired terracotta colour decorated with a typical Phùng Nguyên swirling pattern. It is a noteworthy achievement of the prehistoric Việt in the Hồng River delta.

The variety of shapes and sizes of these clay pots and the abundance of potsherds give us an idea about the life of the proto-Việt during this period. The burning question is what they cooked in the pots, and how. The answer is as elusive as ever, considering the remote times we are dealing with, but we can at least guess how they ate their food. The plentiful supply of bowls of different shapes and sizes, some just right for holding in one hand, show that the proto-Việt no longer ate their food by gnawing chunks of meat off the bone, or slurping molluscs from their shells. They now placed their food in bowls, to serve and to eat from. Did they use something to scoop the food from the bowls, or did they use their hands? There is no evidence to help us to say for certain. However, the fact that they now knew how to weave and ate in a relatively orderly manner allows us to conjure up an image of groups of Phùng Nguyên people sitting together, wearing clothes, enjoying food cooked in clay pots and served in bowls. They also had refined cups to drink from, as the British Museum piece shows. It is the very image of a neat, well-fed, orderly and contented people.

Other artefacts found during the Phùng Nguyên period support this view, such as the abundance of stone and jade jewellery found at archaeological sites all over Vietnam. The pieces found in Bắc Ninh (north Vietnam), Tràng Kênh (Hải Phòng, north Vietnam), Sa Huỳnh (central Vietnam) and Oc-eo (south Vietnam) are truly beautiful. These necklaces, bracelets and earrings were made from different types of jade, and well crafted, to the point that they could easily compare with those made today. The crafting of beautiful objects that served no purpose for survival indicates a society well-fed enough to turn to artistic pursuits.

Plants and Vegetation

As for what the prehistoric Việt ate during this period, we do not know how they cooked or prepared their food in the clay pots but we do know what was available for them to eat. The modern process of using pollen to date plants and vegetation has helped international and Vietnamese botanists who specialize in the analysis of pollen to identify many types of plant food from the Phùng Nguyên period. Over many excavations in several parts of the country during the late twentieth century, they found traces of a large variety of vegetables. Pollen analysis showed that the proto-Việt ate plenty of greens, tubers, fruit and nuts, in addition to their traditional diet of meat, fish and shellfish. They had a form of peas or beans and lentils under the family of Leguminosae, mother to hundreds of varieties of bean, as well as nuts of the genus *Juglans*. The presence of the generic *Salix* meant that willow trees may have been around during this time, in the wild, where their catkins could be harvested and cooked as food. The willows also drew bees, and so honey may have been available during this time. Traces of another type of tree under the generic name *Carpinus* that date from this period could mean that the prehistoric Việt ate the larvae of some types of insect, too, since this type of tree is known as a food source for the larvae of winged insects of the order Lepidoptera (butterflies and moths).[2] This is hardly a surprise, for larvae, pupae, grubs and some types of adult insect are still eaten in Vietnam with everyday food. Some are even considered a delicacy, such as the coconut or palm grub of the Mekong Delta.

The tubers eaten by the prehistoric Việt of this period included taro and yam, two varieties that are considered among the oldest domesticated root vegetables in the world. In Southeast Asia, taro of different types was grown as early as 7,000 years ago.³ Yam was domesticated about 6,500 years ago, or perhaps earlier. Citrus fruit and various berries were also present in Vietnam during this period, including those with a hard or coarse outer shell but soft, juicy insides. The pollen of plants bearing certain types of large, multi-seeded fruit such as melon, watermelon and cucumber has been found in recent times by botanists, who have analysed it using modern methods and found that these species showed signs of having been cultivated by humans.

Recent archaeological and bio-archaeological research has shown that the banana was first domesticated in Southeast Asia, with the oldest traces dating from 8000–5000 BCE and found in Papua New Guinea. It was first mentioned in Vietnam in the semi-historical *Lĩnh Nam Chích Quái*, which was re-edited in the fifteenth century. According to this ancient text, during the time of the legendary Hùng kings (third–first century BCE) 'babies were put on banana leaves when they were born.'⁴ Banana leaves are next mentioned in legends attached to two ancient foods of the semi-mythical Hùng dynasties (*c.* 2879–258 BCE), *bánh chưng* and *bánh dầy*, in which they are used for wrapping the former. This is not to say that the banana did not make an appearance in Vietnam until then; it may have grown there for centuries, if not millennia, beforehand, but unrecorded.

It has been proposed that the banana tree was first domesticated for its leaves to cover shelters and for its fibres to be made into strings and ropes, since the fruit of the wild variety was small and filled with inedible seeds. Over a lengthy process of domestication, the fruit grew larger, and most varieties lost their inedible seeds to become the sweet fruit we know today. One variety of banana, however, retains its seeds inside the fruit. Each seed looks very much like a peppercorn, and remains inedible. Once domesticated the banana spread to other parts of the world, and more varieties became available according to regional preference. In Vietnam there are three main types: the long, yellow, sweet fruit called *chuối*; the shorter and fatter fruit with a brown or pink skin, *chuối tây* (probably a type of plantain imported into Vietnam later); and the royal banana, *chuối ngự*, a tiny, yellow, sweet fruit the size of a thumb. The royal banana is eaten as a dessert, but the other two can be used green in both savoury and sweet dishes. As a green fruit, the banana is starchy like yam, and can be braised, deep-fried in batter for dessert or wrapped in a cocoon of glutinous rice and shredded coconut to be grilled over a fire as a snack.

Although it is not grown on an industrial scale, the banana is probably one of the most useful plants in Vietnam. As well as its fruit, fibres and large leaves, the banana heart, which looks like a purple pointed cabbage, can be used; it is sliced finely and eaten on its own as a salad or added to a variety of dishes. Its crunchiness and slightly tart taste are much favoured as an addition to dishes such as paddy crab noodles. Green banana is often cooked with snails in a northern Vietnamese savoury dish called *ốc chuối*. This delicious dish also contains cubes of pork, onion and turmeric; the snails are a large type of paddy mollusc, *Pila polita*. When braised briefly, the green banana tastes more like a yam than a soft fruit. The dish is garnished with chopped garlic and *tía-tô*, a purple herb similar to the

Banana flower heart.

Japanese *shiso*. (It is this herb that makes the dish. Similar to its Japanese cousin, *tía-tô* is normally used to season fish or snail dishes, but is sometimes used with other herbs to complement grilled pork.) When its life is finished, the banana plant is chopped up and fed to pigs. Banana plants grow very easily in tropical climates and can be seen everywhere in the Vietnamese countryside today.

The mango is said to have been domesticated in Southeast Asia, notably Java and Burma, at least as early as 3000 BCE, before being transported to India to become a versatile and much-loved fruit. However, no record of it from ancient Vietnam has so far come to light. Nevertheless, it is unlikely that this fruit was absent from the country for long, since from the second century BCE people in the Mekong Delta traded with the Indian subcontinent and even further west to the Roman Empire. The mango could certainly have been grown in this region without being recorded.

Archaeological evidence shows that the watermelon has been cultivated in the Nile delta in northern Africa since the second millennium BCE. It is possible that its seeds were subsequently spread to other regions by birds, or perhaps the species existed simultaneously elsewhere; we cannot be sure. Its appearance in Vietnam has been dated to a period that coincides with the Phùng Nguyên era, according to Vietnamese oral history. In the version of the legend given here, the watermelon seed was found by an adopted son of a king from the semi-mythical Hùng dynasties (*c.* 2879–258 BCE). The story appears in more or less the same form but with different dates; some versions are dated to the third Hùng dynasty (about the end of the third millennium), while others, such as that in the Vietnamese official encyclopaedia, are said to have taken place during the seventeenth Hùng dynasty, in the latter half of the first millennium BCE.

Although the sweet pomelo and aubergine are known to have been domesticated in Southeast Asia, no pollen or seed from ancient times has so far been found in Vietnam. The aubergine, in particular, has been a familiar Vietnamese food since time immemorial, in different shapes and forms. Vietnamese aubergines are either small and round like a ping-pong ball (*cà pháo*), with a thin skin, or large, in the shape of a beef tomato (*cà bát*), with a thick, light green skin and many soft seeds inside. The small ones are often pickled while the large ones are braised by themselves or with meat and other ingredients. The long purple type that is seen more often in the West may have been imported to Vietnam at a later date.

The versatile bamboo contributed to the food intake of the prehistoric Việt by being available all year round as bamboo shoots, which may have

Legend of the Watermelon

A son of the Hùng king, An Tiêm, was a simple young man who did not value wealth as much as princes should, and so did not sufficiently treasure the gifts the king gave him. This attitude displeased the king a great deal, and he decided to send An Tiêm and his family to live in exile on a desert island off the coast of Vietnam. There the dispossessed An Tiêm lived a simple life with his wife and children, until one day he observed a bird dropping a piece of red and green fruit on to the beach. He collected the seeds from the fruit and planted them, and they grew into strings of vines, even on a patch of poor sandy land. The many fruits of these vines were huge and sweet, with a hard green skin on the outside but red on the inside. Realizing the value of the strange fruit, An Tiêm carved the location of his island on the skin of the fruit and sent them floating out to sea. It wasn't long before boats from afar began to stop at the island to buy the new fruit. When one of the fruits was offered to the king, An Tiêm's father, he liked the taste enough to ask about its origin. On learning that it came from the very island to which he had exiled his son, the king invited An Tiêm's family back and rewarded his son handsomely for finding a new fruit. Watermelon became a treasured fruit of the Hùng king and a source of wealth for the realm.

been sliced and added to meat or other ingredients in the clay pot to give the distinctive, enticing aroma and taste of fresh bamboo. They were preserved in brine or vinegar, or dried in the sun. The results tasted and smelled very different from the fresh version. Some Vietnamese prefer preserved bamboo shoots to fresh, for their stronger taste.

By combining the scientific analysis of pollen with the discovery of agricultural implements at archaeological sites and the observation of scorched swathes of land nearby, typical of a slash-and-burn agriculture, twentieth-century archaeologists came to the conclusion that the plants available during the Phùng Nguyên period might have been cultivated by humans from earlier wild species. To cultivate the land, the prehistoric Việt used a variety of agricultural implements that the archaeologists found in abundance: hoes, knives and axes, along with food-processing equipment such as a stone tool for mashing and grinding.

THE WONDER GRAIN: RICE

The origin of rice is still unresolved today, even though researchers have agreed that rice grains were initially gathered in the wild in tropical and subtropical regions. Rice was first used as a supplement to meat, fish, vegetables and shellfish. Once it was cultivated successfully, however, it gradually overtook other grains and roots to become the prehistoric people's preferred food. During excavations at a number of sites in the upper reaches of the Hồng River delta in north Vietnam in the 1970s and '80s, grains of rice were found among pineapple seeds, nuts, beans and bamboo sticks from the Phùng Nguyên period. At another site, on Hạ Long Bay, pollen from the modern Asian variety, *Oryza sativa*, was found. Putting the problem of origin aside, we can say that the Việt in this period had learned to cultivate rice in fields, and also grew a wide variety of root vegetables and other plants. These activities are mentioned in Chinese written history and recounted in Vietnamese oral history, and were later engraved on Đông Sơn bronze drums from the first millennium BCE.

THE BRONZE TIME CAPSULE OF ĐÔNG SƠN

The Đông Sơn period (1000 BCE–*c.* 100 CE) was the most significant time in the development of the early Việt after the Phùng Nguyên period. It was a time of rapid and intensive change following the discovery of copper and other metals to create bronze. Đông Sơn people lived slightly higher up in the hills of what is now Vĩnh Phú province, at the top of the triangle of land that slopes down to the Hồng River delta in north Vietnam.[5] Excavations by Vietnamese archaeologists beginning in 1959 covered a large area of this province. They found that the province was rich with many types of typical Phùng Nguyên artefact. This style of pottery decoration continued on the bronze objects made during the Đông Sơn period.

The proto-Việt of the Đông Sơn period were so enamoured with the new material that they made a large variety of bronze objects, big and small. Their techniques and artistry were so sophisticated that the Vietnamese bronze period has remained an enigma for researchers throughout the world. Questions have been raised about how the Việt came to acquire technology that represented such a leap forward, or whether the Việt

Bronze dagger, Đông Sơn culture.

themselves invented it, and if so what happened to the inventors and why the bronze objects ceased to be made. We are still speculating over how the proto-Việt came to achieve such a fine technique in such a short time. Most of all, researchers are still at loggerheads over what the Đông Sơn drums were for, or what message the images engraved on the drums were meant to convey.

There is no need here to attempt to decode the enigma of the Đông Sơn bronze drums, but by simply looking at the tympana of the oldest drums found so far, we can say that during the first millennium BCE the

Việt lived among deer and a variety of birds. One looked like a pelican and another, smaller bird was probably a type of chicken; there was also a long-tailed bird like a peacock or pheasant, and the largest type looked like an eagle. It is hard to imagine that during this time the Việt did not eat at least some of the many animals they illustrated.

The bronze drums and other objects of the period were so rich with images of life that we can treat each as a time capsule showing the lifestyle of the Việt during the first millennium BCE, and to some extent a menu of their food. Archaeological finds in the twentieth century supplemented this view by uncovering the types of agricultural implement they used and how they cooked and ate their food from this time onwards. From these finds and what is engraved on the Đông Sơn drums and other bronze objects of this period, it is startling to find that although three millennia have elapsed since the Phùng Nguyên–Đông Sơn time, the Việt still eat the same types of food, cooked in similar earthenwares in villages both on the plains and in the highlands.

Recent archaeological evidence on display at the National Museum of Vietnamese History in Hanoi shows that the Việt people started using stone hoes, axes and sickles for cultivating and harvesting, before adding

Bronze plough, Đông Sơn culture.

The Đông Sơn Bronze Drum

The tympana of the Đông Sơ'n bronze drum show that the Việt of this time certainly knew how to cultivate and process rice. Bands encircling the centre of the drum faces are engraved with the figures of men dancing and waving hoes, scythes and musical instruments, and of men and women with long hair pounding rice in stone mortars, a practice still followed by the tribal people of Vietnam.

bronze implements to their tool chest. They had also domesticated animals, judging by the engraved pictures of a pig and a goat being kept underneath houses. The bronze drums showed that the Việt lived in stilt houses of different styles made from bamboo and leaves, similar to the type of house we see in the highlands today. Also depicted on the drums were people going out to sea to fish, explore or wage war in solid and beautifully decorated boats.

Ngọc Lũ Đông Sơn drum face.

Living scenes engraved on the tympana of the Ngọc Lũ drum,
the most important bronze drum of the Đông Sơn period.

IN SEARCH OF A CUISINE

According to Vietnamese oral history, the overlap of about 1,500 years between the Phùng Nguyên and Đông Sơn periods was when a budding 'state' was created. It was the era of Hồng Bàng (Royal or Red Eagle), when the prehistoric Việt lived under the kingship of eighteen Hùng dynasties. The 'state' was called Văn Lang in later written history. This semi-mythical polity is said to have been located in the upper reaches of the Hồng River in present-day Vĩnh Phú province, about 35 km (22 miles) northwest of today's capital, Hanoi, and more or less where most Phùng Nguyên artefacts have been found so far. The match between artefacts and oral tales points to the existence of this state, or at least of an orderly alliance between tribes. Many Western researchers have seen the tales of the eighteen Hùng dynasties simply as legends, and viewed the match between artefacts and tales as the wishful thinking of the nationalistic Việt, who conveniently

Bronze water buffalo with a human rider, Đông Sơn era.

fill in the gaps to create a heroic past. We can only look at the example of the Hellenistic quest for Troy and conclude that sometimes legends can be proved to be fact through archaeological research. Gaps do exist in the establishment of the Hùng dynasties, but as more archaeological research is being conducted in peace-time Vietnam, more evidence may come to light to confirm the location and existence of these semi-historical dynasties. The existence of these thus deserves the benefit of the doubt.

During the last two millennia BCE, the Việt certainly ate many domesticated products, as well as some wild varieties of meat, fish and vegetables. This period was when agriculture brought an end to the nomadic life of hunting and foraging, and when the people chose to settle in one place to grow and raise their food. It was a decision that would change the lifestyle and the diet of the Việt and Vietnamese people for ever.

THREE

Agricultural Settlements, Animal Farms and Fisheries

The prehistoric period of the third millennium BCE corresponds with the mythical appearance of Lạc Long Quân (the Dragon King) in the land of Việt. As we have seen, Vietnamese oral history tells that he came from the sea, married the mountain goddess Âu Cơ and taught the Việt how to cultivate food, among other good practices. It is most likely that he was an immigrant – or that he represents many immigrants – possibly from southern China, such as the valley of the Yangtze River, where rice had been cultivated for millennia. Lạc Long Quân probably brought to the agriculturalists of Vietnam new techniques that had been practised in southern China. His association with agriculture was strengthened by the belief that he was a great-great-grandson of Shennong, the god–emperor of agriculture.

When Lạc Long Quân and Âu Cơ divided their children, fifty of them went down to the coast, and the remaining fifty stayed on the higher ground of today's Vĩnh Phú province. The latter formed the semi-mythical state of Văn Lang, ruled by the eighteen Hùng dynasties of the Hồng Bàng era, its 'capital' called Phong Châu or Mê Linh. The choice of location for this centre can be explained by the fact that the coastal land of north Vietnam was not as extensive then as it is today. The estuary of the Hồng River was probably still marshy as far up as present-day Hanoi, not suitable for any purpose other than wet-rice cultivation and fishing. The group of sons who followed Lạc Long Quân to the coast most probably became fishermen who used nets weighted with clay pieces, a tradition that is still followed along the coast of Vietnam today.

As the offspring of the Lạc Dragon King, the legendary Hùng kings ruled over a people referred to as the Lạc in Chinese written history. The earliest mention of the Lạc people dates from the reign of the Chinese king

Chuang or Chu (696–682 BCE). It was noted then that the Lạc people lived by cultivating rice in paddy fields, which they irrigated in a clever way to ensure a good harvest by controlling the water they directed from rivers and streams. The 'cleverness' observed here is the use of the tidal phases of the river. By digging ditches or canals that linked the river with the fields, and fitting them with watergates, the Lạc people could control the flow of water and drain their paddy fields when needed. Vietnamese archaeologists searching in this area in the late twentieth century found buried traces of the oldest type of rice in Asia, *Oryza sativa*.[1]

The presence of rice paddy fields has also been observed by international researchers in the southern region of China's Yangtze River, including the basin of the Pearl River, which is considered by some to be the cradle of rice cultivation in Asia. Paddies are easily created on hillsides as terraces, or beside water or on wet ground. Wet-rice cultivation is labour-intensive, because the fields must be irrigated constantly. Apparently, by knowing how to irrigate their paddies the Lạc people managed to grow enough food to survive comfortably, allowing them to stay in one place long enough to form villages and to multiply into ever-expanding groups. The many Lạc tribes of the upper reaches of the Hồng River then began to cooperate with one another through trade and the exchange of labour. They gradually evolved into an organized society around the strongest chief, whom Vietnamese oral history and Chinese written history call the Hùng king (*hùng* signifying a strong person).

According to Chinese written history – later reproduced in some of the earliest books on Vietnamese customs, such as *Linh Nam Chích Quái* or the fourteenth-century pro-Chinese account *An Nam Chí Lược*, and in later Vietnamese annals, such as *Đại Việt Sử Ký Toàn Thư* – the Hùng kings ruled over fifteen *bộ* (tribal lands or districts), where the Lạc people lived, in an undeterminable geographical area that may have included the two provinces of Guangxi and Guangdong in southern China and today's north Vietnam.[2] The southernmost border of the state of Văn Lang was shared with a 'state' called Hồ Tôn – said to be called Champa in Vietnamese historical records.[3] Each Lạc tribal group was ruled by a hereditary chief or military lord who was related to the Hùng king and was called Lạc Tướng.[4] The Hùng king was also assisted by a number of civil lords called Lạc Hầu.[5] Each Hùng king, meanwhile, ruled over his own *bộ* from his 'capital' in the centre.[6] He relied on the cooperation of the surrounding Lạc lords, who supported him and provided him with wealth and manpower.[7]

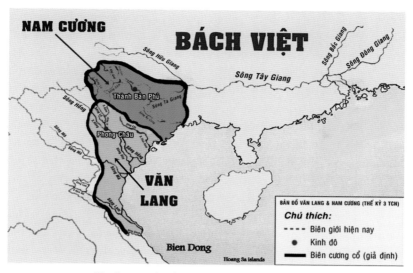

Văn Lang under the Hùng kings, 2879–258 BCE.

The Lạc people of Văn Lang were not the only tribal people to be living together in a form of society. Throughout the land of Việt, from the third millennium to the last quarter of the first millennium BCE, groups of tribal people lived in two other main centres: Sa Huỳnh in central Vietnam and Đồng Nai in the south. The groups followed a similar political system, living as tribes grouped around the strongest man, but each tribe functioned according to its own traditions. These three politico-cultural centres shared the same type of society based on agriculture, husbandry, hunting and fishing, and their people used similar agricultural implements, such as sickles, stone axes and knives. They worshipped the concept of life creation, represented by the *linga* cult in the centre and south of Vietnam and by the act of copulation seen on bronze statues decorating the lid of the Đào Thịnh bronze jar, which has been dated to the Đông Sơn era.[8]

The Lạc people followed a social system of sharing labour. The exchange of skills during this period turned the Lạc into a hierarchical 'state' with farmers at the bottom, rulers at the top and other classes in between. They supported and managed one another in a society that was no longer equal, but still stable and well-fed. This picture of life emerges in the engraved images on Đông Sơn bronze artefacts on display at the National Museum of Vietnamese History in Hanoi. According to these, Việt men and women wore their hair in high chignons, sometimes covered in rolled turbans. They wore clothes according to their social status;

many common men wore just a loincloth, while noblewomen wore open blouses over a bodice called *yếm* and a long skirt. Similar costumes are still worn by the Mường ethnic people today. Both men and women wore large jewellery on their ears, wrists, ankles and necks. They were fond of music and were often depicted playing instruments. Their bronze agricultural implements, such as axes and hoes, were elaborately carved with similar scenes of deer-hunting, music-making or dancing in feathered costumes. One surviving bronze axe shows a deer hunt with a dog. Many domestic tools and pots were made from bronze during this period to be used along with their earthen predecessors. Large ladles that date from this period suggest the use of large pots to serve a group of people eating together.

With the arrival of the Chinese in the mythical Văn Lang realm during the third century BCE, the Hồng Bàng era came to an end and the Việt lifestyle entered written history. The Chinese rulers gradually isolated the Lạc from the Sa Huỳnh and Đồng Nai peoples. Contact between the three groups, once regular, was now limited or even cut off entirely. The three regions continued to develop in different directions: the north of Vietnam became sinicized; central Vietnam turned to a new influence from India; and the Đồng Nai culture in the south expanded even further south and subsequently became a new culture, the Óc-eo (second century CE) of the kingdom of Funan, with links to Angkor in Cambodia. With these fresh influences, new foodstuffs and eating habits were introduced into their respective lands, and the three peoples gradually developed different cuisines with additions from imported tastes. Northern cuisine became blander than its cousins further south, where robust tastes and spicier dishes featured strongly and widely.

The element that still bound the three regions together, despite all the new imported tastes, was agriculture, with rice as the staple food. Each grouping used different techniques of cultivation and types of rice, for they had to adapt the grains to suit their local conditions. The northern and southern regions grew wet-rice suitable to their geography and water supply. In the central region of Sa Huỳnh – later known as Champa – people grew a different variety that required much less water, with better results and faster-maturing crops. They were so successful with this type of rice, later called Cham rice, that the species was imported into southern China by state decree, and into some areas of north Vietnam, to grow alongside wet-rice.

WET-RICE CULTIVATION

As we have seen from the various records discussed earlier, the Lạc people during the Phùng Nguyên–Đông Sơn period (2000 BCE–*c*. 100 CE) lived in houses on stilts and mainly by agriculture.[9] The fields in which they grew wet-rice were called *ruộng Lạc* (Lạc fields). They 'farmed by using knives, and planted rice by using water'.[10] The planting out of the rice seedlings had to be done at the right time to keep the seedlings fresh and plump, to ensure good rice, and to catch plenty of rain from the monsoon season. Without rain, it was much harder for the farmers to irrigate their fields. Keeping the fields well watered was back-breaking work and a sure sign of a good farmer. A flooded field kept out vermin and the types of weed that did not like water; the farmer would have to pull up other types by hand.

The harvesting of rice was another labour-intensive stage, as it was all done by hand. Many people from the community, or hired labour, were required to help the farmers, and they used knives, sickles and scythes. The cut stalks were tied into bundles and threshed in a kind of makeshift booth over a deep basket to catch the flying grains, which were then spread out to dry in the sun and pounded by mortar and pestle to get rid of the hard husks. The grains inside were rough and brown and still needed to

Rice planting on a woodblock print, Sinh village, central Vietnam, date unknown.

> ### The Cultivation of Wet-rice
>
> Cultivating wet-rice is a labour-intensive practice of two stages. Rice seedlings are first grown in nursery beds. Then, when the seedlings are tall enough to be transplanted, the floodgates of the paddy fields are opened to let in plenty of water, often to a level halfway up a person's calves. The rice seedlings are replanted quickly in straight rows in the flooded fields. It can take several days for all the seedlings to be planted, and it has been calculated that between twelve and fifty days of an individual's labour are required to transplant 1 ha (2½ acres) of rice land.

be polished to get rid of the bran before the farmer could finally get at the white grains. Rice grains, whether brown or white, could be used in many different ways, but the most popular was to boil them with enough water to soften and fluff out the grains so that they could be eaten as part of a meal.

In ancient Vietnam, rice grains still in their husks were dried on any flat surface in the village. The polished grains were usually stored in earthenware jars and urns with heavy lids to keep them dry and protect them from vermin. The discarded rice stalks and husks were used as fuel for cooking, and the bran collected from the brown rice during the polishing stage was fed to pigs. Another use for the husks was to mix them with salt and mud to preserve eggs. In modern times, rice is dehusked, dried and polished by machine, and the resulting grains are stored in sacks.

In some villages in northern Vietnam, there is a tradition of eating young rice, that is, before the tiny pods harden into grains. The practice is said to have come about by accident one year when the rain came early, before the rice was fully ripe. To salvage their crops, farmers harvested the rice prematurely; they ate some of the young rice and dried the rest to store. This type of soft young rice, called *cốm*, is light green in colour, delicately fragrant, and usually wrapped in lotus leaves to enhance the flavour. It later became a seasonal delicacy that could be softened further with sweetened water or eaten raw with banana or by itself. The leftover green rice was dried and stored. In the north, dried *cốm* was ground into a rough flour and used to make sweet cakes and puddings, or added whole to meat stuffing in braised dishes. Its unique fragrance added another layer of flavour to savoury dishes, usually braised

Green rice (*cốm*) on a lotus leaf, a traditional way to serve fresh green rice.

stuffed chicken, pigeon or duck – food for special occasions. When it was introduced to southern Vietnam, the dried *cốm* was softened with sweetened water and mixed with grated young coconut to make a delicious snack wrapped in banana leaves.

Wet-rice cultivation was hard and labour-intensive, but the farmers were often rewarded with an abundance of other types of food. A flooded field encouraged small and medium-sized fish, eels, snails, crabs and frogs, so by the time the rice was ready for harvest, the farmer would have collected plenty of these small creatures to eat. Field mice appeared when the water went down, and were particularly appreciated by rural people since their meat apparently tasted like chicken. Paddy crab was another type of food enjoyed not only by farmers but by almost everybody in Vietnam, including city-dwellers. The popular rural dish *bún riêu* (paddy crab noodle soup) appeared regularly at markets or street stalls from north to south.

In north Vietnam, the soup varies, sometimes being served with square pieces of rice pasta instead of noodles, to become *canh bánh da*, or without tomatoes but with yam pieces and morning glory leaves to eat with boiled rice. Another popular variety of *bún riêu* is served with extra snail or cockle flesh over rice noodles.

Paddy Crab Noodle Soup

Paddy crabs are usually small, varying in size between a one-euro coin and the British 50p piece, and most are dark green. For this dish, dozens of them are pounded into a pulp in a large mortar. The pulp is put through a sieve with water to separate the flesh from the hard bits of shell. The resulting paste is dropped spoon by spoon into a boiling soup made with fried tomatoes and chopped onion. When cooked, the crab flesh will float up to the surface in foamy patches. The soup now takes on the red colour of the tomatoes and the unique flavour of the paddy crabs. It is seasoned and served piping hot over white rice noodles and, depending on taste, with chopped vegetables, herbs and a further seasoning of a few drops of lime juice and slices of fresh chilli.

Bowl of paddy crab noodle soup – northern-style *canh bánh đa*.

Glutinous Rice

According to the *Lĩnh Nam Chích Quái*, the Lạc people cultivated both ordinary and glutinous rice, the latter of which they cooked in bamboo tubes or used to make rice wine. Ordinary rice, *Oryza sativa*, was taken for granted as the central ingredient of all Vietnamese meals. Glutinous rice or sticky rice, on the other hand, has been carefully recorded as a ritual food for both marriages and deaths since the time of the Hùng kings. 'For marriages, they offered each other salt as an engagement gift, and then killed cattle to celebrate the weddings. To mark their intention to consummate their marriage, the bride and groom shared some glutinous rice on their wedding night.'[11] For funerals and death anniversaries, cooked glutinous rice was put on the altar of the departed as a required dish. Both practices are still followed today. Over time, bridal sticky rice has been dyed red for good luck.

Two of the dishes that are said to date back to the time of the Hùng kings are still eaten today, during the Vietnamese Lunar New Year celebrations: *bánh chưng* and *bánh dầy*. The former symbolizes the earth as a large square slab of glutinous rice packed tightly in banana or other leaves and filled with mung beans and pork belly. *Bánh dầy* symbolizes the sky. It is made with a thick paste of glutinous rice powder and water shaped into a large round cake and steamed. The two cakes are always served together, the *bánh dầy* on top, because together they symbolize human existence on earth and beneath the sky.

Bánh chưng is still very popular today. The large version, about the size of a square book and weighing 1–1.5 kg (2–3 lb), is offered to welcome in the Lunar New Year. It continues to be offered during the next three days as a staple food, to eat with meat, fish and vegetable dishes, instead of boiled rice. The smaller version, about 10 cm (4 in.) square, is an everyday breakfast food or snack available at markets or street stalls.

The process of preparing *bánh chưng* is said to have remained the same throughout history, although its shape has changed according to the region. It stayed square in the north, but in the centre and south of Vietnam it became long and round like a large sausage and was called *bánh tét*. The ingredients vary, too, from sweetened mung beans to banana or coconut, but the most traditional *bánh chưng* is still a square slab filled with mung beans and pork. The ratio is around one cup of rice to one cup of cooked and mashed mung beans. This ratio, which varies from household to household, is important, and what makes the cake good or bad.

The Legend of *Bánh Chưng* and *Bánh Dày*

During the time of one of the Hùng kings — some say the third, others say the eighth dynasty — life was good and the realm was at peace. The Hùng king gathered his 22 sons together and told them that he would leave the throne to the one who would give him the best food on earth, by the end of the lunar year.

Twenty-one of the princes gathered rare plants and fruit, hunted elusive animals or netted impressive fishes. The 22nd prince, Lang Liêu, meanwhile, did not know what to do. He was poor; his mother had died when he was young, and he had no money to buy rare food. One day, as Lang Liêu sat worrying about what to do, he fell asleep and had a dream. In the dream, a sage appeared and told him: 'There is nothing more precious than rice. Rice is a treasure for the people. Nobody is ever tired of eating rice. If you use glutinous rice to make a square cake, fill it with good ingredients and then wrap it with leaves, it will be the symbol of earth. Then you grind the glutinous rice into flour, make it into a paste and shape it round, and it will be the symbol of the sky. You cannot go wrong with rice.' Lang Liêu woke up, did as he was told and made two types of cake, one square and wrapped in green leaves, the other round and left uncovered 'as white as the grains of rice that he selected'.

On the appointed day, the 21 princes brought in cart-loads of food, and spread them out before their father. The food on offer was indescribably rich, rare and enticing. In contrast, Lang Liêu offered only a humble tray, on which he placed his square green cake and round white slab of glutinous rice. The king was surprised and intrigued. When he started eating them, they were so delicious that he was greatly impressed. When told about the meaning of the rice slabs, he was convinced that he had found the right successor. Lang Liêu became the next Hùng king and ruled over a happy realm until he died.

Too much rice makes the cake heavy and tough, whereas too much mung bean will separate the whole mixture, causing the cake to fall apart when opened. For the centre of each *bánh chưng*, two generous strips of pork belly, marinated in fish sauce and ground black pepper, are enough. (Onion or spring onion is added to the filling in some regions.) The rice must be soaked overnight for even cooking. The wrapping leaves – banana leaves or a large leaf called *dong* (from the plant *Phrynium placentarium*) – are usually thoroughly washed and sometimes softened in hot water, so that they do not rip or break.

In villages in ancient times, the preparation of *bánh chưng* for the Lunar New Year was a communal affair and a festival in itself. During the day the village chief would kill a pig for meat, then the most skilful people would line up to do the wrapping – the squarer the *bánh chưng* the better. By the time the complex preparations were done, it would be late in the afternoon or perhaps early evening, so the cakes were probably cooked overnight in somebody's back yard. A group of people, usually young men and women, would volunteer to watch over the huge pot, feed the fire and boil extra water to add to the pot, keeping the water level above the cakes at all times. The excitement of the occasion, the thrill of being out overnight,

Bánh chưng wrapping session with *dong* leaves on a straw mat.

Bánh Chưng

Spread several layers of leaves on a flat surface. Pour on to the leaves one or more cups of rice, depending on the desired size, add a layer of mung beans, one layer of belly pork with onion, one more layer of mung beans and a last layer of sticky rice. Wrap the now huge mound tightly in its desired shape and tie with bamboo or other string to keep its shape. Pack the finished cakes into a large cooking pot the size of a barrel, full of water. The water level in the pot must be kept above the cakes, otherwise they will not cook evenly. Cook the large version for between eight and twelve hours to achieve the moist and succulent result that this food is famous for. For the small version, perhaps an hour or two is enough. Once cooked, press the slabs of *bánh chưng* slightly to get rid of extra water, and allow to cool. It is a time-consuming process that deters most home cooks; however, specialist food shops now offer several types of *bánh chưng* and *bánh dầy*.

A family session of wrapping *bánh chưng*.

Bánh dầy with a piece of pork sausage.

the cool air and the warm glow of the fire all added up to make the cooking of *bánh chưng* a great time for singing, storytelling and flirting.

The original version of *bánh chưng* is still popular, but the large *bánh dầy*, on the other hand, is not so well-loved today, perhaps because of its teeth-pulling stickiness. Its use is limited to temple offerings, ancestor-worship and ceremonies such as engagements or weddings. The smaller version, much softer but still slightly chewy, is much more popular. It is used to make a Vietnamese sandwich, with a slice of pork sausage (or anything else) between the pieces and two banana-leaf squares to protect the hand and make a convenient snack. It is still round, but only as big as a person's palm. It can also be deep-fried until golden, leaving the outside crispy and the inside soft and glutinous. Done this way, it retains the chewy quality that many Việt favour. The fried *bánh dầy* can be stuffed with fish, mushrooms or other ingredients according to individual taste or a restaurant's speciality. Another version of *bánh dầy* is even softer, rolled in cooked and mashed mung beans; sometimes it is filled with pork fat or more mung beans and fried onion.

RICE WINE

As well as being eaten, rice was the main ingredient for wine-making during the Hồng Bàng era, according to *Linh Nam Chích Quái*. Both varieties of rice were suitable, although, according to tribal tradition, rice wine made from the glutinous variety was more valuable than the other type. The highlanders of Vietnam still make this type of rice wine locally by cooking glutinous rice and drying it in the sun, then mixing the dried rice with a fermentation agent that they make from tree bark and spices. The mixture is put into earthenware jars, which are sealed with dried banana leaves, and left to ferment for a month. The resulting liquid is mixed with water and drunk through a straw, or sometimes through the nose for better flavour and a more dramatic effect.

In the third century BCE rice wine was mentioned in *An Nam Chí Lược* as the beverage offered by Zhao To, the king of Nan-Yueh, to a Han ambassador. By the second century BCE it had become the norm, for, according to both Vietnamese and Chinese historical records, when the Han came to conquer the land of Việt in 111 BCE, three Lạc lords came to offer the victor, General Lu Po-te, 1,000 measures of wine along with 300 head of cattle, among other things. Under Chinese rule, rice wine was often mentioned as the spirit the Việt liked to drink until they became completely drunk, or as a drink that was served on special occasions such as the New Year or other annual celebrations, including the mid-autumn festival.

TO EAT BUT NOT TO EAT

During the Hồng Bàng era, there was a custom sanctioned and adopted by the Hùng kings themselves: the chewing of betel. This practice started in the first millennium BCE and carried on unabated until the first half of the twentieth century, when it started dying out in the cities, although it lingers in rural areas. It was such a peculiar habit that throughout history the Chinese, French and many other observers have felt compelled to discuss it at great length. Betel is a non-food that many Việt liked to eat – without swallowing – to the extent that many were addicted to it. It was the equivalent of chewing gum, but involved more elaborate preparation and a much more dramatic performance by the chewer.

Betel is a heart-shaped leaf the size of a human hand. It grows on an evergreen vine belonging to the Piperaceae (pepper) family, and is indeed slightly peppery in taste. The betel leaf is used in many countries, especially in the Middle East and the Indian subcontinent, as a stimulant and medicine. The taste is so appealing that it can be addictive, especially when eaten with other ingredients. In Vietnam, betel leaves are usually combined with the kernel of the areca nut, seasoned with a touch of slaked lime and rolled up as a quid in varying designs. Traditionally, the art of rolling a betel quid was a measure by which a mother-in-law would choose a wife for her son. On the first serious meeting arranged by a marriage-broker, the young lady would be set the task of rolling a quid for her prospective mother-in-law, under that lady's watchful and critical eye. The resulting quid, whether plain or in the elaborate shape of phoenix wings, would have to be perfectly rolled, without bruising the leaf or spilling any of the ingredients. Whether the marriage could take place or not depended on what the prospective mother-in-law thought of the young woman's skill.

In the centre and south of Vietnam, a wad of shredded tobacco the size of a cherry would be taken with the betel quid for extra flavour. It would be placed at one corner of the lips, and the chewer would suck on the tobacco from time to time while chewing the betel. In rural areas or sometimes even in cities old ladies can still be seen squatting behind their wares at market, with wads of tobacco protruding from their mouths. Chewing betel produces plenty of saliva, while the chemical reaction between the leaves, the areca-nut kernel and the slaked lime turns the saliva bright red, staining the lips and teeth. The chewer has to spit the surplus saliva out from time to time, either into a spittoon or on to the ground. This appearance of spitting blood makes the performance fascinating or horrifying for those not familiar with the custom. The stimulant in the mixture produces a euphoric feeling or a sense of happiness, so it is no wonder that it can be addictive. After being chewed for a while, the betel quid is reduced to a small wad of flavourless fibres that the user spits out to make room for a new one. In one day, a person can use up to twenty betel rolls or even more.

Betel-chewing is not limited by social class, and until the mid-twentieth century even royalty did it. Evidence of this can be seen in the three pieces of equipment essential to the betel-chewer: a box to store all the ingredients and the tools for its preparation, such as a small knife for cutting the areca nuts or for shaping the leaves; the lime pot; and the spittoon. A royal betel box would be made of precious wood heavily decorated with mother-of-pearl, or custom-made in fine silver. Areca knives used by royalty would also be made of silver. Several royal betel boxes and lime pots are displayed today at various museums throughout Vietnam. Some royal ceramic lime pots were even made by famous French and British producers, such as the faience lime pot commissioned from the English firm Copeland & Garrett by Emperor Minh Mạng in about 1840; it is currently on display at the Museum of Royal Antiquities in Huế.

Betel-chewing is so compelling that the art of making travelling betel containers flourished in Vietnam during the nineteenth and part of the twentieth centuries, even though the travel might just be to visit a friend or relative near by. A travelling betel box could be made of any material,

The high art of betel quid rolling: a plateful of betel quids in phoenix style, usually reserved for important occasions. To make the phoenix, the betel leaf is cut in such a way that the resulting quid has wings.

Royal betel box in silver, made during the Nguyễn dynasty (1802–1945).

most commonly woven bamboo strips, wood or silver. Inside, it was divided into two layers: a deeper bottom layer for the areca nuts, knife and travelling lime pot, and a top layer in the form of a tray divided into compartments for the betel leaves, tobacco and other ingredients. The lime pot was the shape and size of a lipstick, with a short stick attached to the lid for scraping the lime; sumptuous versions would be made of silver or carved from ivory, while the poor made do with bamboo. Some travelling lime pots were tiny replicas of their owner's larger ones. Other betel-chewers preferred to carry a pouch containing ready-made quids. These pouches were made of embroidered silk or velvet for the rich, and plain cotton for the poor.

For a traditional engagement or wedding, betel leaves, areca nuts and a little piece of lime form part of the ceremony. Socially, the offer of a rolled betel quid to a stranger is seen as a gesture of peace and welcome. The custom has been noted several times in Chinese written history as peculiar to Vietnam. Historical records from the time of the Mongol invasions of Vietnam, in the late thirteenth century, also noted that chewing betel could ward off disease. Without chewing the betel, as the Việt did, Mongol troops succumbed to many tropical diseases, thereby weakening and eventually being defeated. Mongolian ambassadors sent by Kublai Khan and subsequent Yuan courts to the state of Đại Việt during the

The Legend of Betel-chewing

In common with many things in Vietnamese oral history, the custom of betel-chewing is an old one and emerges from a heart-wrenching legend. Once upon a time, under the reign of a Hùng king, there lived a pair of identical twin brothers called Cao Tan and Cao Lang. When their parents died, they became even closer to each other. Cao Tan eventually married a fine lady, while Cao Lang remained single. The three lived together, as is the custom in Vietnam, without any incident, until one day Cao Tan's wife mistook Cao Lang for her husband and embraced him. The mistake created such a rift between the brothers that Cao Lang left home. He wandered until his path was blocked by a large river. In desperation he sat down and turned into a boulder.

Meanwhile, Cao Tan was so sorry about the quarrel that he too left home, to look for his brother. When he arrived at the river, he sat down on the boulder to rest and to think sadly about his brother. Cao Tan turned into an areca tree growing next to the boulder.

It was now the turn of Cao Tan's wife to set out to look for her husband. She arrived at the same spot, sat on the boulder and leaned against the tree until she turned into a vine with heart-shaped leaves, twining around the tree trunk.

When the story was told among local villagers, they built a shrine by the boulder to commemorate the ill-fated trio. During the building works, a leaf of the vine fell on to the boulder just as a bird dropped a piece of areca nut on both. The spot turned red like blood. The villagers thought it was an omen, a demonstration of the heartbreak of the three unfortunate people. When the tale of the trio reached the ears of the Hùng king, he travelled to the shrine. There he picked a betel leaf, chewed it with a piece of areca nut and spat the remains on to the boulder. The spot turned red instantly. The king decreed that the mixture was a symbol of eternal love and loyalty, and allowed the villagers to grow more leaves and areca trees, and to collect lime from the boulder so that they could chew them together.

Lime pot of the second
Nguyễn Emperor Minh
Mạng (*r.* 1820–1841),
made in England.

thirteenth and fourteenth centuries reported that they were offered betel quids as a gesture of peace and friendliness by the Việt emperors.

The custom of betel-chewing even survived the takeover of the land of Việt as a Chinese colony for more than a millennium, from 257 BCE to 938 CE. The Việt people who emerged at the end of the colonization period were very different from their ancestors under the Hùng kings, having acquired many Chinese habits and tastes; but, oddly enough, betel-chewing remained a Việt custom.

FOUR

The Chinese Millennium, 257 BCE–938 CE

The idyllic Hồng Bàng era came to an end in 257 BCE, when the Lạc people became subjects of the Chinese leader Thục Phán, formerly a prince of the Shu kingdom, one of the realms fragmented by conflict in China. Thục Phán's ancestors had fled to the Chinese–Viet border and taken refuge with the Âu or Ou tribe at what is now the border with Vietnam, and in 257 BCE he became their leader. It was said that he took over the Lạc people because the Hùng king at the time was complacent and too busy drinking wine to defend his people from Thục Phán's army. Under Thục Phán, the realm was called Âu Lạc to signify the mingling of the Lạc with the newly arrived Âu people. Âu Lạc was in turn conquered by another Chinese king, Zhao To of Nan-Yueh, in 207 BCE.[1] Even then, the Lạc society was preserved almost unchanged, with Lạc lords now acting as local officials of the new king, who ruled from Guangdong.

The Chinese occupation of the Hồng and Mã river deltas isolated the north of Vietnam from the other two regions, which later became known as Champa (central Vietnam) and Funan (the Mekong Delta). Each region developed in its own way and absorbed different political, cultural and culinary influences to become very different from the others. Champa and the Mekong Delta were gradually taken over by the Việt under the Nguyễn from the sixteenth century onwards. The separation of north Vietnam from the rest of present-day Vietnam made it distinctively more Chinese, both politically and in culinary terms, and it was in the north of Vietnam that the Chinese millennium made its earliest, deepest and longest-lasting mark.

Under Zhao To, the realm of Âu Lạc was divided into two prefectures, Jiaoche and Jiuzhen (Giao Chỉ and Cửu Chân). Giao Chỉ incorporated the land around the Hồng River delta, and Cửu Chân that of the Mã

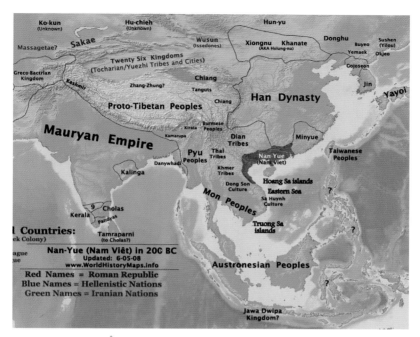

Nan-Yueh and Âu Lạc, two political entities that became one under Zhao To,
first king of Nan-Yueh (r. 203–137 BCE).

delta, further south.[2] Both were governed by legates appointed by Zhao
To, with the responsibility of controlling trade routes and commercial
activity. The Lạc lords answered to them but governed their own people,
who still farmed wet-rice and other agricultural products. They now paid
taxes to the new authorities, the Chinese rulers.

The Chinese province of Nan-Yueh, located in what is now Guangxi
and Guangdong and with a climate similar to that of northern Vietnam,
probably grew products familiar to its Vietnamese subject peoples, so we
may assume that food varieties and cooking methods changed little in
northern Vietnam during this period under Zhao To and his appointed
legates. Certainly, if they did it was not recorded. More profound and
permanent change came in 111 BCE, when the Han conquered Nan-Yueh
and took over the former land of the Việt.

Việt Cuisine under the Han

The Han (206 BCE–220 CE) ruled from present-day Xian in northwestern
China and appointed governors to administer the former Âu Lạc, which
they divided into three districts: Giao Chỉ, Cửu Chân and Nhật Nam

Seal of the kings of Nan-Yueh (203–111 BCE).

(Rinan). As we have seen, Giao Chỉ and Cửu Chân made up the kingdom of Âu Lạc; Nhật Nam was previously unknown until it appeared in Han texts, but is thought by historians to have been further south than the others, beyond the Hoành Sơn massif.[3] A commercial centre named Luy Lâu was created in today's Bắc Ninh province, about 30 km (20 miles) northeast of Hanoi. This town featured largely in international trade during the last three centuries BCE and at the beginning of the Common Era. It served as a gateway for influence and products from the world at large to enter the land of Việt, and vice versa. Vietnamese archaeologists have uncovered many traces of the first Han occupation of Vietnam on this site. The Han to Tang layer of soil (206 BCE–906 CE) has yielded artefacts belonging to many nationalities, ranging from Chinese to Indian to Middle Eastern.[4]

The Âu Lạc social system was kept more or less the same, but, thanks to Han record-keeping, we know a little more about the products the Việt grew and ate. The *Book of Han*, a Chinese historical record covering the period 206 BCE–23 CE, meticulously recorded details of local products and of the tribute the Việt were obliged to pay to the Han. According to the fourteenth-century *An Nam Chí Lược*, which was partly based on that book, the Lạc people were required to send to China pearls, ivory, rhino horn, spices, coral, pheasants and rare birds such as peacocks and their feathers.[5]

The supply of salt, another important product, was controlled by a state monopoly in early Han China. In Vietnam, it was made by evaporating seawater, or – more commonly – in salt fields on the coast. Seawater was channelled into large fields, dammed by earthen banks, and left to evaporate in the sun. The salt grains were then raked up and purified before use. Being a thin strip of land bordering the South China Sea (in Vietnamese Biển Đông), the land of Việt produced ample salt this way, both for local

Model of a house in Vietnam under the Han (III BCE–544 CE).

consumption and to send as tribute to China. This availability of salt made it possible for the Việt to produce many salted products, from vegetables to fish to other ingredients they found in the wild.

Honey and beeswax were also noted as tribute from the Việt under the Han. The spices the Han required, meanwhile, were ginger, turmeric and galangal, a root of the ginger family. All three were used to season food, and as medicines. Both ginger and galangal were used by the Chinese and the Việt as remedies for stomach problems, or for more serious diseases, such as dysentery and cholera. They were also added to food to balance out 'cold' ingredients. Ginger, in particular, was considered to have a warm quality. By adding ginger to 'cold' ingredients, the cook balances out the *yin-yang* quality of the dish. Turmeric was used for its healing quality, among other functions. According to *An Nam Chí Lược*, galangal was also an ingredient of the fermentation agent used to make Vietnamese rice wine.

The districts of Giao Chỉ and Cửu Chân were known as the home of several animals that were unfamiliar to people from northern China, where the Han held court. One of these was the gaur or Indian bison, known in Vietnam as *bò tót* (wild variety: *Bos gaurus*; domesticated as *Bos frontalis*). The gaur – a large type of cattle that looked like a water buffalo but had more in common with the cow – was another product sent as tribute to China during the second and third centuries CE. By the fifth century CE it had been joined by another exotic animal from Vietnam, the white deer.

Collecting sea salt from salt fields on the coast of Ninh Hòa, south central Vietnam.

One of the delicacies mentioned in several historical Chinese and Vietnamese documents written during the Han occupation was ant larvae, which is perhaps the equivalent of caviar today. In Han-occupied Giao Chỉ and Cửu Chân, ant larvae were served as a sour, fermented paste or salted and left to ferment whole. Chinese officials were alerted to this dish, but it is not known if they were advised to try it or to avoid it. These expensive larvae still grace tables in some countries, including Mexico, Colombia, India, Myanmar and Thailand.

RICE UNDER THE HAN

Rice cultivation underwent a dramatic change during the first century CE, as is recorded meticulously in Chinese documents and later reproduced in Vietnamese histories. The records started with the appointment of a Han governor, Hsi Kuang (Tích Quang), sometime during the first years of the Common Era. According to his biography, he made the Việt adopt Han customs and manners.[6] However, his own actions could not compare with those instigated by an official that he himself appointed to the district of Cửu Chân in 25 CE, Jen Yen (Nhâm Diên). According to Han records, Jen Yen noticed on his arrival that the local Việt preferred to hunt and fish, instead of growing rice. He soon ordered them to give up this traditional way of life and concentrate on growing rice. Han accounts say that he taught the Việt to grow rice, but this is obviously an exaggeration, or a misinterpretation of his policies, since we know from archaeological finds that the Việt people knew how to cultivate wet-rice in the Hồng River delta as early as the first millennium BCE.[7] What Jen Yen did was to introduce the iron ploughshare pulled by water buffalo into the Việt's process of cultivating rice. He also imposed a policy favouring rice-growing, perhaps to feed the increasing number of Han settlers in Vietnam. The policy was a success, and the district under his care was able to produce enough rice to supply both Giao Chỉ and Cửu Chân from then on.[8]

RICE NOODLES

A by-product of rice that came into Vietnam during the Chinese millennium was the rice noodle, which the Việt called *bún* or *bánh phở* depending on the method of production and the size of the strands. Controversy over the origin of rice noodles is still unresolved, but most historians agree that they were invented in southern China either under the Han or much later,

Rice noodle strands.

during the Northern and Southern dynasties (420–589 CE), and then imported into Vietnam and other Southeast Asian countries. Whatever the case, rice noodles came to stay in Vietnam during the Chinese millennium. Over the years they took on a completely different role and assumed their own identities as bases for many different Vietnamese dishes. The number of ways the Việt use these rice noodles surpasses their functions in China and elsewhere in Southeast Asia. Over time, they have become the most important ingredient in many snacks, breakfast dishes and occasional foods from north to south. The Việt produced these noodles locally, and very rarely – almost never – used the dried versions that are available worldwide today.

WATER BUFFALO

The water buffalo is one of the endearing symbols of country life in Vietnam, domesticated many thousands of years before the arrival of Jen Yen in Cửu Chân. An image of a water buffalo cast in bronze and dating from the Vietnamese Bronze Age is known to depict a domesticated animal by the fact that a human is riding it. One of the regions credited with the domestication of this ancient beast is the Yangtze River delta, where wet-rice has been grown for up to 7,000 years. Many water-buffalo bones have been found there. It is known that the animal was used to pull ploughs (it still does to this day, although in some regions machinery has replaced it); it may also have been used as a source of meat by the time Jen Yen arrived in the land of the Việt, although it has never been as popular as pork, beef or chicken.

Another nourishing product of the water buffalo, milk, was never consumed by humans in ancient Vietnam. Milk has been valued and used extensively in the West, in Central Asia and in other parts of Asia such as India and northern China, but it is thought that cow, buffalo and goat milk was not used in Vietnam until the mid-nineteenth century, when the French arrived, since the hot, humid climate very quickly rendered it unsafe to drink. Over time, many southern Chinese and Vietnamese developed the well-known syndrome of lactose intolerance that persists to this day. Until the mid-nineteenth century Vietnamese babies were breast-fed and/ or given the watery part of soft-boiled rice until they could start eating solid food.

WHEAT

While Vietnamese products were sent to China as tribute during the Chinese millennium, the import of Chinese products and cooking methods into Vietnam was much more intense and extensive. Over ten long centuries, many waves of immigrants and refugees arrived from all over China, each wave prompted by war, political upheaval or court rivalry. Meanwhile, Chinese officials and soldiers continued to be dispatched to Vietnam to administer the land, to collect taxes and tribute, and to keep the peace. Both officials and immigrants brought with them their own foods, and some were unknown to the Việt, such as wheat, millet, barley and, perhaps, soybeans.

Wheat, in particular, has been grown in northern China since 4000 BCE, and has for millennia been as much a staple of the diet there as rice is for the southern Chinese and Vietnamese.[9] The northern Chinese expatriates must have found rice lacking, just as a southern Chinese or Vietnamese person would find wheat heavy on the digestion. Wheat and its by-products were probably imported into northern Vietnam early in the Chinese millennium. Over time, they became important to Chinese cuisine in Vietnam, but they have never become a staple part of the Vietnamese diet. Chinese yellow noodles, steamed buns and wheat pasta sheets (*won ton*) feature prominently in many Chinese dishes in Vietnam today,

Won-ton soup, a famous legacy from the Chinese millennium.

some 2,000 years later, still as Chinese food. The Việt enjoy eating these wheat dishes, but only occasionally, perhaps as snacks or street food. Won-ton soup is a favourite snack of many Vietnamese. As well as being offered in restaurants and from market stalls, it is sold in the street by men who push their carts around while calling their wares. More often, the presence of a Chinese noodle and won-ton cart is announced by a boy walking ahead of it clicking two pieces of wood together in a unique rhythmic click-clack that can be heard streets away. Buyers hail this boy

Bánh bao, a steamed dumpling made of wheat flour.

and place their orders, and the bowl(s) of noodles or won ton are brought to their doors.

Fresh or dried wheat noodles are consumed in Vietnam in as many ways as in China, in soup and shallow- or deep-fried with a variety of ingredients. Similarly, Chinese won-ton dumplings are served in soup or deep-fried. They have also remained distinctively Chinese, though. Apart from noodles and won-ton soup, Chinese food has always been reserved for special meals, eaten only on important occasions such as weddings or to celebrate the passing of an exam or a landmark birthday. This highly valued cuisine tops the list of the three best things that a Vietnamese man could wish for in life, it is said – along with French housing and a Japanese wife.

Pau or *bao* is another wholly Chinese wheat product that has been adopted as a favourite Vietnamese snack while still existing as part of a Chinese dim-sum meal. The Chinese stuffed this steamed bun with meat, onion and Chinese sausage (*lap cheong*), but the Việt fill it with all kinds of things, according to the cook's fancy. *Bánh bao*, as it is known in Vietnam, is not usually made at home, but is bought from street vendors or shops. The Chinese version is valued more, but is less popular because of the higher price. The *pau* is one of the many ordinary Chinese dishes left behind after the Chinese millennium that the people in Vietnam now take for granted as a snack.

Roast Meat

Another type of Chinese food much loved by the Vietnamese came during the Chinese millennium: roast meat. Although as a dish this has always been treated as Chinese, in both its ingredients and its method of cooking, many Vietnamese have forgotten its origin, and it is often taken for granted and made as a treat or on special occasions.

Chinese roast meats, such as crispy pork, *char siu* (barbecued pork), roast chicken and duck, have come to occupy a central position in popular Chinese cuisine in Vietnam, unrivalled by any local imitation. Roast meat is something the Việt insist on buying from Chinese shops. The secret is in the five spices or more used to marinate the meat; the proportion and combination of spices are always a secret of the house. Although this aromatic concoction is readily available as five-spice powder and is used in some Vietnamese dishes, it remains authentically Chinese, and an ingredient that will make a dish Chinese, not Vietnamese. The next crucial element in the popularity of these meats is the way they are roasted, something

Chinese *lap cheong*, a wind-dried sausage made of pork or pork liver,
pork fat, herbs and spices.

the Việt and many other peoples have never mastered, even with modern
technology. The secret is in the shape of the oven and the temperature.
Recently, the most famous chefs in the UK have tried to roast duck the
Chinese way, with mixed or poor results.

SUN AND WIND-DRIED MEAT

One of the most familiar Chinese foods today is the Chinese sausage, *lap
cheong*, which can be found in all Chinese or Southeast Asian supermarkets.
It was imported into Vietnam sometime during the Chinese millennium
and became an adopted food, still wholly Chinese but accepted as part of
a Vietnamese meal. *Lap cheong* is made with pork meat and pork fat, or
pork liver and pork fat. The pieces of meat or liver are marinated overnight
in salt, sugar, spices and rice wine. The wine is important as a preservative,
and the type and grade of the wine determine the quality and price of the
sausage. The marinated pieces of meat or liver and fat are stuffed into processed pork intestines to form strings of sausages, which are hung to dry
in the sun for a couple of days. They are then moved to a shady place to be
wind-dried for a further week or two. The result is a string of wizened red
or brown sausages that can be kept for months.

The Chinese sausage is usually fried or steamed, and is a favourite with
the Việt, either on its own with rice or sliced with other ingredients as part

of a dish of fried rice. It is one of the required dishes for a special-occasion meal. From the mid-nineteenth century it became a favourite filling for a length of French baguette, for breakfast or as a snack.

Other wind-dried meats that are popular with the Chinese, such as flat or pressed duck or belly pork strips, have never been liked by the Việt, although it is not clear why. These meats can be found hanging outside any Chinese shop, but they have never been part of a Vietnamese meal, ordinary or otherwise.

PRESERVED EGGS

Eggs have been preserved in both China and Vietnam for centuries, if not millennia, but it is not known if the practice was imported into Vietnam during the Chinese millennium. There are many types of preserved egg, but the two most common are the salted egg and the jelly black egg, the latter of which is known as the 'century egg' or the 'thousand-year-old egg'.

Salted eggs are made with chicken and duck eggs and, more rarely, quail eggs; the quail version is more popular for special occasions. The eggs are soaked in brine or packed individually in damp, salted charcoal powder and placed in an earthen jar or vat for several weeks to absorb the added ingredients. This type of egg must be boiled before it can be eaten. Despite its charcoal cocoon, the cooked and peeled egg is creamy white

Century egg, a Chinese preserved egg.

Century Eggs

The century egg is made by coating a whole raw egg with a mixture of clay, salt, ash, quicklime and rice chaff and leaving it to mature for several weeks. A chemical reaction between the ingredients cooks the egg, so there is no need to cook it again. The peeled egg is transparently dark brown or black, with a jelly-like consistency, and the yolk is greenish yellow. The taste is slightly salty but with a flavour of sulphur or ammonia, prompting the misconceived rumour that it is made by soaking the egg in horse urine.

---

and the yolk is a bright orange-red; it has a salty taste. One version of the salted egg was the marbled egg. Although processed in the same way, the egg was first tapped slightly to crack its shell into fine patterns. After boiling, the peeled egg would be decorated all over with a mosaic pattern. Unlike the Chinese, who ate both salted egg and century egg with their breakfast rice porridge or as part of an omelette, the Việt preferred to eat the salted egg with rice and the century egg on its own as a special hors d'oeuvre for family celebrations. In a male-orientated society like that of Vietnam, the eggs would be eaten by the men with their aperitif of rice wine or other alcoholic drink, before they joined the rest of the family for the main meal.

Over the course of the Chinese millennium, the intense assimilation process overseen by Chinese officials like Hsi Kuang and Jen Yen turned ordinary people in Han-occupied Vietnam into a docile race, as the fourteenth-century An Nam Chi Luoc tells us, quoting Han documents: 'The men worked in the fields or attended to commerce. The women raised silkworms and wove cloths and silk. Their staple diet consisted of pickled vegetables, fermented fish and marine products.' From this, it can be assumed that meat had become scarce or too expensive, and that they had to find alternative foods to supplement their rice diet. For this purpose, many Việt developed the arts of pickling, salting and fermenting the meagre ingredients that were available to them, to make them tastier and to stretch them further.

The Vietnamization of Chinese Ingredients

During the Chinese millennium, while prepared Chinese food stayed Chinese, raw ingredients such as shiitake mushrooms and black fungus were incorporated into many Vietnamese dishes, not for every day but to add something extra-special. The soybean, on the other hand, has been accepted into Vietnamese cuisine and is processed into many dishes, whether fresh or as fermented bean paste, salted beans or ground bean powder. The most remarkable soy product to be imported from China into Vietnam during this millennium must be tofu. It has become so well integrated into Vietnamese cuisine that its roots have been completely forgotten. It is thought to have become popular through Buddhism, which was introduced into Vietnam in about the fifth century CE either from China through occupation, or from India through trade via the commercial centre Luy Lâu. The teachings of the Buddha prohibit the killing of all living things, including animals and insects, so many Buddhist Việt turned to an alternative source of protein for survival. If that was so at first, however, the taste of tofu is pleasant enough for it to be appreciated on its own merits, and it quickly became one of the few Chinese ingredients to be wholly adopted into Vietnamese cuisine from high to low. From its very first appearance, it was embraced with gusto, and it is now a staple food for Vietnamese rural people, who find meat too expensive, and for many city-dwellers who simply find it good to eat. This versatile product – which can be cooked in many ways, in both savoury and sweet dishes, and especially in vegetarian dishes as a meat substitute – is a smooth paste of varying grade and consistency, and is produced easily from processed soybeans. The softer and smoother the slab of paste, the more soy it contains.

Tofu is rarely made at home. The buyer goes to the market or to the house of tofu to choose the type they prefer. The firm type is for frying, the less firm type is for soup or light braising and the softest version is used for dessert. Thick soy milk is steamed in a pot until it is cooked to a milky, jelly-like consistency. To serve the dish, a flat, thin spoon is used to scrape up the surface of the tofu mass into wafer-thin slices, and a syrup of palm sugar and ginger is added to the bowl of tofu slices since, by itself, tofu has no flavour at all, apart from a slight fragrance of soy. Dessert tofu is eaten hot or cold and is very popular with both children and adults.

Tofu's lack of strong taste makes it an ideal base to absorb the flavour of added ingredients, as with plain boiled rice. There are too many ways

Fermented tofu, a favourite food of monks and vegetarians. It is highly pungent but considered delicious by many in Vietnam, China and Southeast Asia.

to cook tofu to be listed here, but, in general, tofu is boiled, steamed or fried. It can be added to soup, steamed with other ingredients such as fried mushrooms and onion, or eggs, or deep-fried into crispy golden cubes to be garnished with spring onion. Fried tofu is most likely to be eaten on its own with rice and fish sauce or soy sauce. Leftover fried tofu can be braised quickly in water and fish sauce, and seasoned with spring onions or tomatoes (or both) to become stewed tofu, another favourite dish among the Việt. Tofu is usually eaten fresh – the fresher the better – but several dry versions exist, as sheets or rolls to be used in vegetarian dishes.

Fried Tofu

Fresh tofu is sometimes criticized for being too bland and slimy. Frying it adds an unexpected dimension to the texture, rendering the outside crispy and the inside soft with a delicious fragrance of soy.

I large box or 2 small boxes of fresh tofu, medium-firm grade
45 ml (3 tbsp) light olive oil or sunflower oil
4 spring onions, trimmed and finely chopped

Cut the tofu into 3-cm (1-in.) cubes and leave in a sieve or colander for about 10 minutes for any excess moisture to drain off, or dry the cubes one by one with kitchen towel. Heat the oil in a frying pan until it is almost smoking and shallow-fry the tofu over a high heat, turning until lightly golden all over. The tofu cubes will make a hissing noise and may splatter a bit. The cooking has to be done with the utmost care. The high heat is necessary to achieve a golden crispy skin on the outside of the cubes. Scoop the tofu out, drain on a piece of kitchen towel, then transfer to a serving plate. Quickly stir-fry the chopped spring onion in the hot oil, then scatter it over the tofu cubes and serve. Non-vegetarians can dip the tofu cubes into a bowl of neat or diluted *nước mắm*; vegetarians should use soy sauce instead.

Another way of processing tofu is by fermenting it to become *chao* in Vietnamese. For this, cubes of fresh tofu are seasoned with salt, vinegar, chilli, sesame oil and other ingredients, depending on who's making it, and left to ferment. The soft, pungent result can be eaten on its own with plain boiled rice, or with soft rice porridge (congee) for breakfast, or mashed up to season other foods, or used to flavour or coat meat, fish and vegetables. It can also be mixed with lime juice, sugar, chilli and garlic to make a dipping sauce for boiled vegetables or pork or fried tofu. Fried crabs with a sauce of fermented tofu (*cua xào chao*) or roast chicken rubbed with fermented tofu (*gà nướng chao*) are two favourite dishes among the Vietnamese.

SOY SAUCE

The soul of Chinese food, soy or soya sauce, is another of the chief products of the soybean. It is made from the boiled beans, which are left to ferment with roasted wheat, salt and water. The fermenting agent is a fungus or mould. The resulting liquid is siphoned off to become soy sauce, and the remaining paste is fed to animals. Soy sauce was first produced in the third or second century BCE in China, so it was inevitable that it travelled with the Han settlers to Vietnam around the same time or soon after. It became an important condiment in Vietnam, not just for seasoning Chinese food, but for marinating some Vietnamese meats, such as pork, to give a sweet taste that becomes caramelized during cooking. Soy sauce is also used extensively as a condiment for vegetarian dishes, since it is free from meat and fish. It is available in several different grades, according to thickness and salt level. The taste has changed little over the centuries, if not millennia.

SESAME SEEDS

Sesame seeds and sesame oil are two more Chinese ingredients that took up residence in Vietnam during the Chinese millennium. Sesame oil is not widely popular among the Việt, and indeed it is hard to find Vietnamese dishes seasoned with or fried in sesame oil, for its distinctive taste and flavour instantly turn the food Chinese. (Oyster sauce has a similar effect.) Sesame seeds are another matter, though. Dry-fried or roasted, they form an important part of rural meals and are a staple food for vegetarians. They are eaten regularly by monks and nuns in Vietnamese temples, and are usually served as a coarse powder mixed with salt and eaten with plain boiled rice. Roasted whole sesame seeds may be sprinkled over a sweet dessert to add another layer of flavour.

LUXURY FOOD

At the other end of the culinary spectrum is the luxury food that the Chinese millennium introduced into Vietnam. Elite or imperial Chinese food existed to serve Chinese courts and rich people, and over the country's lengthy dynastic history, many luxurious dishes were created solely for the purpose of impressing emperors and their courtiers. Many seem strange and excessive now, but in their own times they represented the height of sophistication, and were aspired to by people in Chinese colonies, such as Vietnam during the Chinese millennium. Later on, even after Vietnam had become independent, its courts and its rich, powerful or titled people still embraced these dishes to show off their status and wealth. The rarer the ingredients, the richer and more important the host would seem. These dishes do not depend for their taste on the main expensive products themselves, but on supplementary ingredients. Swallow's or swift's nest and shark's fin are examples of this.

By itself, the palm-sized nest naturally made by the swift using its saliva is tasteless, but used in a soup or a steamed dessert it became the best of all luxury foods in Vietnam, just as it had been in China. It is not known exactly when in the Chinese millennium the bird's nest became important in Vietnam, but the name itself has become synonymous with the highest honour an emperor could bestow. As well as being served to esteemed guests such as visiting ambassadors, it was given as a reward to those who did well by the court, such as victorious generals, trusted mandarins and newly qualified doctors of literature. Such celebratory events, when guests were invited by the emperor to partake in a rich array of dishes, including swift's nests, were known as *Ban Yến*. Any Vietnamese royal banquet would follow a strict Chinese order of dishes, usually consisting of eight rare

Peacock food decoration. Royal food was usually decorated with carved vegetables or fruits in the shapes of birds, animals, flowers or fabulous animals such as phoenixes and dragons.

products called *Bát Trân*. Eight is a lucky number for the Chinese, since it is very similar in sound to the word for 'prosper'. The eight set dishes varied, but all included rare and unusual ingredients. Those served to a visiting Qing ambassador to the Nguyễn court in the nineteenth century consisted of the following:

Nem công – Peacock meat
Peacock *nem* is a precious dish because the peacock is a precious bird symbolizing beauty and pride. Peacock meat is generally believed to be an antidote to poison, and so it is always included in a banquet as a safety measure.

Chả phượng – Phoenix patty
Chả is a fried or grilled patty of minced meat or fish, usually mixed with other ingredients. Pheasant is used in this dish, since the fabled phoenix does not exist.

Da tây ngưu – Rhinoceros skin
The Chinese value the rhinoceros for its strength and perceived virility. In this dish, a small square of soft skin found under the arms of the animal is stewed with other ingredients to create a rare dish that symbolizes power.

Tay gấu – Bear's hand
The bear represents untamed power, and its powerful hands are particularly valued.

Gân nai – Venison tendon
The deer is one of the fastest animals on earth. By eating the tendon of its leg muscles, it is believed that this quality will be absorbed into the system.

Môi dười ươi – Orang-utan's lips
The significance of this dish is unknown, but it is believed to have been extremely tasty and worthy of a royal table.

Chân voi – Elephant's foot
The elephant is a strong and noble beast. Stewed elephant foot is thought to impart its strength to the eater.

Yến sào – Swallow's or swift's nest
The rarity of these nests and the peril faced by the nest-harvesters made this a precious dish for the royal banquet.

LONG BRAISING

The Chinese millennium did not just leave the Vietnamese with new ingredients and Chinese dishes; it also left new ways of cooking food. The northern Chinese brought into Vietnam the technique of long braising, in which meat or fish is stewed for hours to become soft and succulent. In southern China and Vietnam before the arrival of the Han, stir-frying, grilling quickly over charcoal or very quick braising were the norm, for economic reasons. Fuel such as wood and charcoal was expensive, and long cooking particularly so, considering that the Việt ate at least two hot meals a day. Except on special occasions, such as the cooking of *bánh chưng* during the Lunar New Year, having a pot on the fire for a long time was considered wasteful and a luxury that could be ill afforded. In northern China, long braising must have come about for another reason: to keep the fire going for heat during winter months.

One enduring long-braised dish is duck with medicinal ingredients (*vịt tiềm*). The Chinese believed that food had *yin* and *yang* qualities and that those must be balanced in a dish, or across a range of dishes, in order to keep the eater healthy. This duck dish was created for that purpose, quite apart from its unique taste. A whole duck or just the legs are marinated in a mixture of soy sauce, spices such as cinnamon, star anise, cloves and ginger, and medicinal herbs. The whole duck can also be stuffed with a rich mixture of minced pork, shiitake mushrooms, glutinous rice and nuts, such as gingko or lotus nuts. After being braised in a clay pot over a low heat for several hours, the duck becomes succulent and its skin turns dark brown from the marinade. The flavour is strongly medicinal, not in a bad way, but it can be off-putting for some. At some point the Việt modified this dish by substituting green young rice (*cốm*) for the glutinous rice, and seasoning it with fish sauce. Stuffed duck is served on special occasions such as the anniversary of the death of an ancestor, or as part of a banquet.

Another version of long braising is steam braising, which is even more special than the pot-braising method. For this, a whole small chicken, of a special variety called *gà ác*, is crammed into an individual steam cup the size of a coffee mug, with all the required Chinese medicinal ingredients. A lid is put on and the cup is cooked in a bain-marie, with water reaching

Nguyễn royal steam cup. Steamed or braised food is considered an extravagance in Vietnam due to the length and the cost of fuel it takes to cook the food. Individual steam cups are the most extravagant of all. The Nguyễn emperors had these cups made at the imperial kiln of Jingdezhen. They are now coveted collectors' items.

about halfway up the cup. After several hours the chicken, including its bones, softens and would fall apart were it not for the tight fit of the cup. The idea is to keep all the juices in the cup, to intensify the flavour. This type of steam-cup chicken was a favourite of the rich and of royalty, for it was believed to render the eater more virile. It also gave rise to an entirely new type of lidded ceramic cup. The Vietnamese Nguyễn emperors of the nineteenth and twentieth centuries had many of these cups made to their own designs by the Jingdezhen imperial kilns in China.

Tea

It may have been a coincidence, but at about the same time as Buddhism arrived in Vietnam, during the fifth century CE, a revolutionary product also entered the country: tea. From being a drink taken for health and to quench the thirst, tea took on a cultural role sometime during the Chinese millennium. The preparation of tea was elevated to an art during the eighth century under the Tang in China. It was an art of the gentle people that was greatly admired by the Việt, who, by then, had been under Chinese rule for 900 years.

In Vietnam and China, the way a man prepared his tea would be a sign of his breeding, and would show whether he was a gentleman, a scholar or someone from a more humble background. The male gender is used here on purpose, for a Vietnamese high-born or learned man would prefer to make his tea himself, to keep it pure and not 'tainted' by feminine hands at certain times of the month. At court, when maids or the emperor's favourite ladies made tea for him, they would be carefully checked by palace eunuchs first to make sure they were 'clean'.

To make his tea, a gentleman would need a ceramic or porcelain tea set. Even more refined people would use a tea set of tiny earthen cups and

Individual teapot and charcoal stove, tea-making tools of the scholar-gentleman, *c.* 19th century.

an equally tiny earthen teapot, since the unglazed but polished clay was preferred to enhance the flavour of the tea. Boiling water would first be poured into the empty teapot, rinsed around to warm up the clay and then poured away, before tea leaves or buds were added and more boiling water poured into the pot. While the tea was brewing, the tiny cups were warmed in the same way. The tea was then poured into the warm cups to be drunk scalding hot; lukewarm tea would be severely frowned on and ultimately rejected.

At first, tea was imported from China, but it was later grown in the Vietnamese provinces along the Chinese border, on higher ground along the Trường Sơn cordillera, and in north and central Vietnam. Over time, each variety of tea acquired its own regional reputation. Imported Chinese tea has always been a favourite among the Việt, but for some the Vietnamese regional varieties rank higher in taste and strength. It is not known when other flavours, such as jasmine, chrysanthemum or lotus, were added to tea leaves, but these varieties seemed to be the most favoured in towns and cities in Vietnam. People in rural areas, on the other hand, prefer fresh tea leaves or tea buds for their refreshing quality.

COOKING UTENSILS

Two cooking utensils that are associated closely with Chinese food all over the world are the wok and the chopstick. Both were late additions to the Chinese food repertoire, so it is unlikely that they were used in Vietnam during the Chinese millennium. The wok has never been a favourite cooking utensil in a Vietnamese kitchen, because of its awkward size. It has always retained its identity as a 'Chinese frying pan' (chảo tàu). Chopsticks made their appearance under the Han as cooking utensils, but were adopted as acceptable table tools only under the Ming (1368–1644); they may have been made obligatory in Vietnam during the Ming occupation, as part of an intensive assimilation programme for the Việt. Chinese-style cooking pots, kettles and various other implements, on the other hand, were introduced into Vietnam during the Chinese millennium to complement the existing clay and iron pots.

As the Việt were drawn more and more deeply into the Chinese sphere during the Chinese millennium, the production of ceramics flourished, both for the table and for export. Over time, Vietnamese ceramic dinner services became more sophisticated and more beautifully decorated, with a variety of glazes. By the end of the Chinese millennium, Vietnamese ceramic tableware could compare with that made in some parts of China, Thailand and elsewhere in Southeast Asia. Ceramic kilns first established under the Han in and near Luy Lâu were uncovered by archaeologists in the twentieth century.

The utensils that have been found show that during the Chinese millennium and afterwards, wine still featured prominently in the life of the Việt. Archaeologists have unearthed many types of ceramic wine bottle and cup made during the Chinese millennium in Vietnam. Rice wine continued to be a favourite drink among Vietnamese men, who preferred its rough and strong taste to the more refined versions. It is also a ritual drink, offered during ceremonies such as weddings or when praying to the ancestors. For weddings, it is offered with betel and areca nuts.

CHINESE FOOD IN THE SOUTH OF VIETNAM

While the northern Vietnamese became accustomed to both northern and southern Chinese ways during the Chinese millennium, the central and southern regions of Vietnam were open to Indian and Khmer influence through trade and, less so, immigration. As the regions absorbed outside culinary influence from different sources, they developed their own distinct local foods. Central and southern Vietnamese food acquired a richer and spicier taste, owing to influence from India and the Khmer kingdom. Curry, for example, was strictly a southern phenomenon in Vietnam until at least the sixteenth century.

EAST–WEST TRADING UNDER THE HAN

The first centuries of the Chinese millennium in Vietnam coincided with the wane of ancient Greece and the rise of the Roman Empire in Europe. Both of these European empires have been documented as trading partners of Han China, first by land via the Silk Route and later by the maritime route via the Arabian peninsula, India and Malaysia with stopping points in Vietnam before reaching China. The expansion of trade between East and West encouraged the exchange of ideas, religions and, more importantly, food products between the two continents. These new ideas and new foods eventually reached Southeast Asia, via Vietnam, the most immediate southern colony of China.

The Silk Route was an extensive ancient network of more than 6,000 km (3,700 miles) of roads linking Mediterranean Europe with northwestern

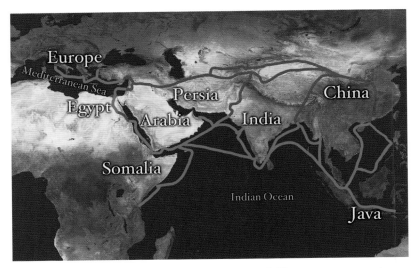

Map of the Spice/Silk Route, Graeco-Roman period. The route was a network
of roads linking Europe with Han China, starting from about 300 BCE,
and was used until the mid-15th century CE.

China, where the capital Chang An (today's Xian) was located. Over this
network, merchants of various nationalities and nomadic people moved
their products back and forth: silk from China, spices from India, agricultural products from both Europe and India to China and back. It
was an intense exchange that was first fostered and protected by Greece
and Han China. When the Romans defeated the Greeks in 30 BCE and
became masters of the Mediterranean region, they continued to trade with
China and, by association, Vietnam, which existed then as Giao Chỉ and
Cửu Chân. Archaeological artefacts found in northern Vietnam during the
nineteenth and twentieth centuries strongly attest to such trade.

Silk and later spices were a craze in the Roman Empire, and the profits
associated with the trade in these coveted products were such that international merchants doubled their efforts to bring them back to Rome from
India and China. The possibilities of trade were greatly expanded with
the establishment of the maritime route, starting around the beginning of
our Common Era. This route continued to be used during the following
centuries, and was described elaborately by Marco Polo in his *Travels* of
the fourteenth century. Polo's description of his return journey to Venice
from China at the end of the thirteenth century is still the most detailed
account of this route, even though doubt has been cast on his credibility
and his position at the court of the Mongol ruler Kublai Khan. The route
was again described in detail in the fifteenth century, as part of an account

of the travels of Admiral Zheng He, who went to collect tribute from the countries along the South China Sea and the Indian Ocean, even as far as Africa, for the Ming.

The East–West maritime route was a long one, hugging the coast of the Arabian Peninsula, the Indian subcontinent, Malaysia and Vietnam, before reaching Hangzhou and Guangzhou, the main silk-producing regions of China. The presence of Roman coins bearing the image of Antoninus Pius at Óc-eo in the lower Mekong Delta, near what is now the border with Cambodia, is firm evidence of the existence of East–West maritime trade in today's Vietnam during the time of the Han.[10]

In 166 CE a group of ambassadors from the court of Marcus Aurelius were recorded as stopping in Giao Chỉ on their way to the Han court.[11] Such stops usually lasted not a day or two, but much longer, since travelling in ancient times was slow and difficult, and ships were obliged to wait for the right monsoon winds. Each stop offered a chance to rest, but was also a commercial opportunity. In the inevitable interaction between visitors and locals, products from both sides were traded and techniques of production learned and reproduced.

In the second century CE, during the Chinese millennium in Vietnam, the maritime route and its stops were carefully mapped by Claudius Ptolemy, a great Greco-Egyptian geographer, mathematician and astronomer, among other things (although Ptolemy's map has been criticized by

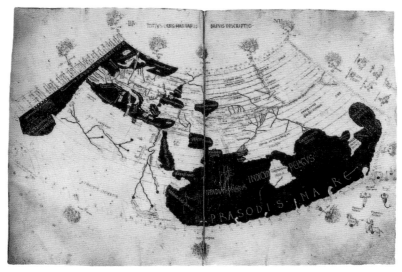

Ptolemy's map of the world, taken from his *Geography* (c. 150 CE) and reproduced in a 15th-century manuscript.

many as inaccurate because of his mapping methods).[12] A copy on display in the National Museum of Rome shows that most Roman, Greek and Arabic ships stopped at two places in Vietnam: Óc-eo in the Mekong Delta and Cattigara, which could be today's Hải Phòng.[13] While accepting Óc-eo as a point of access to the ancient kingdom of Funan, today's Mekong Delta in Vietnam, Ptolemy's critics have questioned the location of Cattigara, identifying it variously as Guangdong in China or several other sites in eastern China and Southeast Asia. However, it is most likely to be present-day Hải Phòng for two reasons. One is that the maritime route between the coast of north Vietnam and southern China in the second century CE was treacherous with huge submerged rocks that were not cleared until 868 CE, under the Tang.[14] Traders tended to avoid it, using the land route instead, or to risk travelling much further out in the open sea, off the east side of Hainan Island, a treacherous venture in different ways.

The second reason is that during the second century CE, the Han traded through their commercial centre at Luy Lâu in Vietnam, which has been described by Europeans as a Chinese or Asian entrepôt. This so-called Nan-Hai trade was by way of the South China Sea, and flourished to the extent that the route became a well-worn thoroughfare.[15] The way by sea into Luy Lâu was via Hải Phòng or one of the main Hồng River estuaries around it. The uncertainty over the sea route is caused by the fact that some

Óc-eo bronze figure. Óc-eo was a major East–West trading post of the lower Mekong delta that existed from the beginning of the common era until *c.* 7th century CE.

A collection of Óc-eo jewellery made of glass beads and precious stones.

branches of the Hồng River have changed course near the coast over the centuries. From Luy Lâu, ships could travel up to southern China through a riverine system, or by well-travelled roads. Guangdong was relatively close to Luy Lâu. The international controversy over the identity of Cattigara, however, was still unresolved at the time of writing.

A Tale of Two Fish Sauces

Amid these intensive East–West trading activities, a significant food product was born or became prominent in both the Roman Empire and Vietnam: fish sauce, called *garum* in Latin and *nước mắm* in Vietnamese. The uncanny resemblance of these condiments begs the bold question whether the Romans learned to make their fish sauce in Vietnam during the intensive trading period of the first and second centuries CE, or whether it was the other way around.

Garum, also called *liquamen* or *muria* (a lower-grade version), was a popular Roman fish sauce made by adding salt to fish entrails or whole fish such as mackerel or anchovy, and leaving the mixture to ferment for one to three months in earthen vats in the sun. The result was a two-part liquefied fish, a paste at the bottom and a top layer of amber liquid. *Garum* was the liquid part of the fermented fish mixture. It was siphoned off,

Roman *garum* amphorae from Pompeii, *c.* 1st century CE.

stored in amphorae and used to season food during cooking, and also as a table condiment. Herbs or other ingredients were sometimes added to the fermented mixture to make it an exclusive house product of the maker. The most valuable *garum* was made with mackerel. The bottom paste, called *allec*, was valued by the poor as a substitute for *garum*, which they could not afford. The pungent smell of the liquid was widely discussed among learned men of the Roman Empire. Some, such as the philosopher Pliny, praised its aromatic flavour as pleasant enough to drink, while Plato was known to have called the product 'putrid'.[16]

Garum was valued highly by the Roman elite, who loved it so much that they built *garum* factories in many places throughout the empire: along the Mediterranean coast, in Italy itself and in Roman colonies, such as Gaul and Spain. Among these, the most famous site of *garum* production was surely Pompeii, the city tragically destroyed by the eruption of Mount Vesuvius in 79 CE. Amphorae containing traces of *garum* have been unearthed by archaeologists in Pompeii over the years, the latest in 2008, when they used the traces of *garum* in an amphora to date the eruption more accurately. Other evidence for Pompeii's status as thriving *garum* production site is anchovy bones, mosaic pictures and stacks of amphora stands bearing traces of the condiment. Historians have also identified a man named Umbricus Agathopus as the owner of the best *garum* shop in Pompeii before the destruction of the city. So far archaeologists have not found any traces of an actual factory in Pompeii, prompting the conclusion that the factories must have been placed outside the city because of the strong smell.

Recipes for many Roman dishes favoured by the elite specify *garum* or *liquamen* as a required ingredient. One such recipe, for lamb stew, was written by the renowned gourmet and food writer Marcus Apicius in the fourth or fifth century CE: 'Put the pieces of meat into a pan. Finely chop an onion and coriander, pound pepper, lovage, cumin, *liquamen*, oil and wine.'[17] Some recipes also spoke of *garum* being mixed with wine, herbs and other ingredients to make a dipping sauce or condiment for the table. *Garum* survived the collapse of the Roman Empire, but could not withstand the tide of fashion; by the tenth century it had disappeared from the European culinary repertoire.

On the other side of the world, according to the *An Nam Chí Lược*, the Việt under the Hùng kings, during the first three millennia BCE, hunted and fished and knew how to use salt to season their food and to preserve their catch. During this period they also began to develop the fish sauce that eventually became the soul of Vietnamese food: *nước mắm*. 'They used fish and shrimps to make Nước Mắm, and seasoned their food with ginger roots.'

The process of making *nước mắm* is the same as that for *garum*, except that the Việt use whole small fish such as anchovies or any fishy product, such as the worm known as *rươi*. It is not recorded whether they made a version with fish entrails alone, like *garum*. However, we do know that the small fish were not gutted, so the entrails would have been included in the fermentation process. The method of production varies slightly from centre to centre, but the general idea is to ferment fish and salt in the sun. In the distant past, earthen vats would have been used; today it is more likely to be barrels. Some factories now use wooden barrels imported from the wine trade in Europe. The liquid was siphoned off into smaller earthen containers called *tin*, which look like flat-bottom amphorae, their lids sealed with hardened clay. Today it is kept in bottles and plastic containers, the *tin* having disappeared except in the rural depths of the country. Anchovies were most commonly used, followed by other varieties such as sardine or mackerel; salmon is the latest addition to the variety of fish sauces available today.

To make *nước mắm*, the fish is stacked in thick layers in a barrel, at a ratio of three parts fish to one part salt, one layer of fish to one layer of salt, until the barrel is full. No other ingredient is added at this stage. The barrel is closed and left to ferment in the sun or in the heat of the hangar-like factories. After a month or two, the mixture has liquefied and can be

Óc-eo ceramic bottles and vases, *c.* 1st–7th centuries CE.

collected through a small tap at the bottom of the barrel. The first-press *nước mắm* is a rich, golden liquid, not too salty, but sweet and only slightly pungent. It is the best type, and is reserved for the owners of the factory and their friends. More salt is then added to the barrel for the mixture to ferment further until it produces a second press, which is still valued as luxury-grade *nước mắm*. Each time the liquid is collected, more salt and now also water are added to the barrel to produce more fish sauce; each addition of salt and water produces a lower-grade sauce.

As in Pompeii and elsewhere in the Roman Empire, the making of fish sauce is such a smelly affair that the factories are confined to certain areas outside the town or city centres. In Vietnam, the three best-known *nước mắm* locations are Phan Thiết on the south central coast and the islands of Cát Hải in the north and Phú Quốc, off the lower Mekong Delta, in the Gulf of Siam. All three have been important points on the East–West maritime trade route since the beginning of the Common Era. Phan Thiết was well-documented as a stopping point in the Cham kingdom of Panduranga, until the land was absorbed into Vietnam. Cát Hải is near the estuary of the Hồng River, gateway to Luy Lâu. Phú Quốc is off the coast of Óc-eo, a recognized trading centre during Roman times and one of the two trading centres in today's Vietnam that Ptolemy identified in his map. All this still leaves the question whether, since fish sauce has existed in Vietnam since sometime in the second or third millennia BCE, it travelled west from Vietnam to Rome on the East–West maritime route, or was imported into Vietnam during these trading stops.

No doubt the origin of fish sauce will never be conclusively known. It remains an enigma for us to ponder as we taste the food of Vietnam. No matter where it has travelled to or from, as far as Vietnamese food is concerned, *nước mắm* is the reigning culinary queen, the backbone of the cuisine, the aroma that presides over all Vietnamese dishes. It is what makes a dish distinctively Vietnamese.

FIVE

Independence Food, 939–1859

In the year 938 CE, the Việt people rose up and won their independence back from the Chinese. It was the beginning of a millennium of self-rule under a series of Việt dynasties, interrupted only by a brief occupation by the Ming in the early fifteenth century.

Very little is known about food during these dynasties, since the annals recorded only events that concerned the courts and natural disasters that befell the Việt people, not what they grew and ate. However, from the reported conflicts and calamities, we can see that rice continued to be central to the Vietnamese diet, for the lack of it during these times caused serious social upheaval and even civil war. Locusts, hailstones, drought and floods were all noted from the time of the first independent Ngô dynasty (939–65) to the last Nguyễn dynasty (1802–1945).

To ensure a good rice crop was therefore extremely important to whoever held power. After a patchy period of living independently from the Chinese, but peppered with internal conflict, a new dynasty, the Lý (1009–1225), came to power. They immediately looked for a unifying factor to keep the nation together, and they chose Buddhism. By then one of the three most important religions of Vietnam, along with Taoism and Confucianism, Buddhism was now elevated by the Lý to a national religion. It was not a surprise choice, for the first Lý emperor began life as an orphan raised by monks. Many temples and pagodas were built throughout the land under the Lý, and it was considered an honour for men to shave their heads and become monks.

The sacred flower of Buddhism was the lotus, and its by-product, the lotus seed or nut, became a favourite food among the Việt people. The lotus flower and its seeds were not unfamiliar to the Việt: they had very probably been grown and used, mainly by the elite, during the

Láng pagoda, built in the 11th–12th century under the Lý dynasty.

Chinese millennium, the flower as a symbol of purity and the seeds as a calming medicinal ingredient. The lotus was probably brought into northern Vietnam during the fifth or sixth century, following the arrival of Buddhism, either by Chinese settlers and monks or by visiting traders and monks from India. Under the Lý, the flower became widely available thanks to Buddhism's new popularity. With the court actively promoting the religion, lotus flowers were grown everywhere, from royal lakes

Terracotta lotus, architectural decoration, Lý dynasty (1009–1225).

Dried lotus seeds without their green skins.

A fresh lotus cone and its young pods.

to humble village ponds, in and near the Buddhist temples and pagodas that were being built at a frenzied pace. The flower and its seeds grew and spread quickly in any type of fresh water, and were harvested in the summer and early autumn.

Lotus seeds form when the flower grows old and its centre turns into a round, spongy upturned cone 6–10 cm (2–4 in.) in diameter that looks like an old-fashioned shower head in both shape and size. (In fact, the Vietnamese word for 'shower head' translates as 'lotus cone'.) Within the lotus cone are several holes containing green pods, each of which contains a soft seed the size of a peanut. The seeds were harvested by prising the green pods out of the cone and peeling them open to reveal a soft, creamy-white nut with a bitter green stem in the middle that was removed before eating. The stems were saved and dried in the sun to be used for medicine, while the seeds were eaten raw or used in cooking. Surplus seeds were dried in the sun and strung together like necklaces for easy storage.

Similar to the banana, every part of the lotus plant had its own useful function. The whole flowers were reserved for the altar, the petals were used to flavour tea and the seeds were a luxury ingredient in both savoury and sweet dishes; they could be part of a soup, a stuffing for meat, a paste for cakes or used on their own in a vegetarian dish. The porous stem of the plant was also useful as a medicine or eaten braised or cold in a salad, and the large, fragrant leaves were used to wrap savoury cakes or fresh green rice, to provide extra flavour.

Vegetarian Cuisine

Another effect of Buddhism on Vietnamese food under the Lý was a new respect for vegetarian cooking, which eventually turned into a separate cuisine in Vietnam. The killing of living things is forbidden in the Buddha's teachings, so Vietnamese vegetarian food is strictly vegan and is seasoned with salt and soy sauce, rather than the traditional fish sauce. With many temples being built throughout the country, and the rise of devout Buddhism as a virtue for all, vegetarian cooking quickly became the norm, from humble temple to royal table. It swiftly became a culinary art that delighted people of all classes, for the finished dishes were very similar to their meat counterparts, in both taste and appearance. The vegetarian 'fish' and 'chicken' looked exactly like their meat counterparts, but were made entirely of tofu and/or vegetables such as radishes, bamboo shoots, yam and mushrooms, wrapped into the shape of the meats using dried tofu sheets that had been softened in water. Dried tofu rolls were also softened and cut into pieces to be cooked in the same way as chunks of meat, seasoned with soy sauce instead of fish sauce. Just a few of the many popular vegetarian ingredients were sweet potato, banana, squash, pumpkin, bamboo shoots, mushrooms, lentils and other pulses.

At the highest level, vegetarian food occupied its own position at the royal table, since even royalty was obliged to be abstemious at least twice a month according to Buddhist regulations, on the first day and at the middle of the lunar month. Before performing solemn ceremonies, emperors were also required to abstain from impure ingredients, and so could eat no meat or other animal products for at least a day beforehand. All these requirements elevated vegetarian cuisine to a high art. In the nineteenth century, for example, vegetarian dishes were regularly required at the royal table of the Nguyễn emperors, all of whom were devout Buddhists and so preferred to eat vegetarian food once or twice a month. For the royal table, each dish was cooked to perfection and presented just as royally as meat and fish dishes at other times. On special occasions, such as the anniversaries of the death of their ancestors, the Nguyễn royal family offered their guests a vegetarian banquet consisting of dishes that looked and tasted like their meat and fish counterparts.

For ordinary people or in rural areas, vegetarian food was simply rice with tofu, which might be fresh, dried or fermented. In many cases, a vegetarian meal consisted of just rice and no meat, but with roasted sesame seeds, chopped peanuts and a wide variety of green vegetables instead. Pickled vegetables were also popular. Temple banquets, which were served at funerals, death anniversaries or prayer ceremonies, consisted of at least eight vegetarian dishes, usually four plates and four bowls.

The Lý and the Specialized Market

One of the biggest decisions made by the first Lý emperor was to move the capital back to the site of the old citadel of La-Thành or Đại La-Thành, built by the former Tang military governor Gao Pian (Cao Biền) in the ninth century CE, and to rename it Thăng-Long (it is now Hanoi). The first independent Việt emperors had chosen to rule from different places, such as the old citadel of Cổ Loa, across the Red River, or Hoa Lư, far southeast of Hanoi, to show their disgust at the Chinese occupation.

The return to Thăng-Long in the eleventh century drew thousands of traders to a large area outside the royal citadel, stretching from its eastern wall to the bank of the Red River. Traders and village artisans picked their spots and displayed their wares, and that, in turn, drew more traders from the surrounding area and even from China. Over time, so many trades and traders were involved that each profession occupied its own street, turning the area into a busy market that was later called the 36 Streets, where everything was available. The street names reflected the products on sale. Chicken Street was where live chickens, ducks, pigeons and other birds were displayed in their cages; Sugar Street specialized in cakes and sweets; Cotton Street offered clothes, sheets and blankets. There was even a Sail Street, which specialized in the repair of sails for the trading junks that docked at the river port on the eastern side of the market.

As well as the permanent shops, farmers from the suburbs or even further afield came to sell fresh produce on the pavement or at street corners. These groups of daily traders formed a series of small pop-up markets that lasted only a couple of hours, while the produce was still fresh. Over time, these pop-up markets became a fact of life for the people in Thăng-Long. The specialized streets and their accompanying mini-markets continued throughout subsequent centuries, under different dynasties.

Even with such a plentiful supply of fresh produce on their doorsteps, nothing could be more important to the people than rice, and the Lý emperors never forgot that. To ensure a steady supply, they created a system of farms manned by soldiers who took turns as farmers when the country was not at war.

For millennia most of the rice of northern Vietnam had been grown in the Red River delta, but the area was prone to flooding, which could destroy the crops at any time. To prevent this, the Lý established a polder system to regulate the flow of water at the delta. Even then, it was inevitable that occasional periods of serious famine were recorded under the Lý, when bad weather got the better of human effort, such as the earthquakes of 1179 and 1180 and flooding in 1180. 'These were dire times for all . . . The people did not have enough food and famine was widespread . . . almost half of the population died from hunger' in 1181. Hunger continued to be a major problem for the Việt in the following decade. Drought, earthquakes, hailstorms and typhoons occurred almost every year. In 1199 a great flood 'destroyed most of the rice crops, and once again, many Việt people starved to death'.[1]

The rulers of the next dynasty, the Trần (1226–1413), were even more cautious than the Lý in the effort to maintain a steady supply of rice. Not only did they maintain the soldier/farmer tradition, they also created a special ministry to deal solely with the maintenance of dykes and polder. Polder corvée became a duty for all able-bodied male citizens, to be performed at least twice a year as a form of poll tax. At the same time, princes and princesses were given land outside the capital, Thăng-Long, to farm for themselves so that they could earn an income from selling their produce. The policy worked well until the invasion of the Mongols from Yuan China. After several decades of good living, the Việt were again subjected to famine. Although they ended in failure, the three Mongol invasions directed by Kublai Khan (in 1257–8, 1283–5 and 1287–8) destroyed Vietnam's infrastructure. The polder system that protected Thăng-Long and regulated floodwater in the Red River delta was seriously damaged, exposing the agricultural plains to frequent floods.[2] With state resources depleted, the damaged polders were left neglected. Irregular distribution of water brought years of crop failure for all, from princes to paupers. Flood and drought became 'a monotonous feature in the annals of the post-Mongol decades, and almost annual calamities by the middle of the fourteenth century'.[3] Widespread hunger was noted on several occasions during this period, and was particularly serious in 1290, when people 'died on the streets' and 'parents sold off their children for rice.'[4]

The poor harvest in the princely estates around the capital turned into a war of words at the Trần court, with courtiers blaming one another for the nation's disasters. The weak court eventually collapsed in 1400 and a usurper, Lê Quý Ly, later called Hồ Quý Lý (r. 1400–1413), took over. This in turn brought in the Ming from China, with the excuse that they had to restore order and return the throne to a legitimate Trần heir. The Hồ usurper succumbed to the superior power of the Ming, and the country was once again occupied by China, albeit only briefly, from 1407 to 1427.

FOOD UNDER THE MING OCCUPATION

As with the Han, life under the Ming was recorded in Chinese historical documents that were extracted by Vietnamese annals in later centuries. These notes give us a glimpse of how the Việt lived and ate in the fifteenth century.

Under the Ming, salt became a state commodity, and no citizen was allowed to sell it privately.[5] A salt tax was imposed and the production of salt was supervised strictly by officials. Any salt that was gathered had to be declared and the tax paid before the producer could sell it, provided they had official written permission to harvest it in the first place. Any traveller

Japanese maritime map of trade with northern Vietnam, 17th century.

was allowed to carry a maximum of three bowls of salt and a small bottle of *nước mắm*.[6] Pepper was another tightly controlled commodity, and was grown in many parts of Vietnam under the Ming. We do not know when the cultivation of pepper began, but it was noted in the Vietnamese annals that it was harvested on the fourth moon of 1418 and handed over to an official from China, and that more pepper was grown after that.[7]

The Ming occupation ended in 1427 after a prolonged war led by the Vietnamese nobleman Lê Lợi, which almost failed when his troops suffered terrible hunger and were forced to eat their elephants and horses. Lê Lợi eventually asked for a truce, which allowed him to take his troops back to their home villages to farm the land and recover their strength. They went on to win back the land of Việt from the Ming. Lê Lợi became Emperor Lê Thái Tổ (*r.* 1428–33), the founder of the Lê dynasty (1428–1527 and 1593–1801). One of his first decrees sent a large part of his army of 250,000 men home to farm their land.[8] Even this policy, however,

The Lê court of the 17th century.

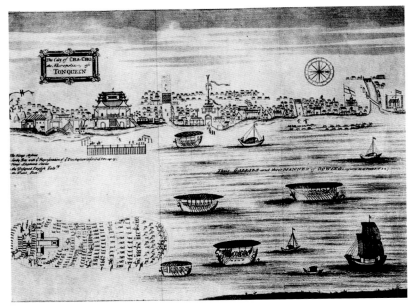

Market scene of Thăng Loing in 1685.

could not save the population from hunger caused by natural disasters such as drought and earthquakes, which started in 1448 and continued into the next century. Each time, paddy fields were destroyed and many people starved to death.[9]

Under the Lê, commerce flourished in Thăng-Long, and trading was busier than ever. The 36 Streets area expanded, and commercial vessels came and went regularly at the river port. The Lê were renowned for their statecraft and social organization. One area that received their special attention was the recruitment of mandarins through exams. Until the thirteenth century, court officials and local bureaucrats had been selected from the nobility. The system was expanded to ordinary men during the rule of the Trần so that talented commoners could be selected to deal with the difficult and volatile Mongol envoys that noblemen were not able or willing to face. The exam system was further expanded under the newly independent Lê, with great success. It represented an opportunity for young men from rural areas to win a coveted position, an honour that would benefit not just their own family but everybody in their village. However, this great opportunity brought with it a culinary side effect: mock food.

If vegetarian food imitated meat and fish, this was not food at all; it was wooden fish. The story of the wooden fish is often told to mock stingy people from certain poor regions of Vietnam, but it had a practical origin and reflected the shame the Việt people felt if they let others know how poor they were. The mandarin recruitment exams took place every one or three years in the cities, so it was important but costly for men in remote villages to travel to take the exams, often requiring several days of riding or walking and camping along the way. Even after they had arrived, many camped near the exam hall to save money.

Dried fish, *mắm*, rice, fish sauce and pickled vegetables were packed for the journey, and – since they camped in close quarters – each scholar could see what the others were eating at meal times, which were usually served outside their tents, each by an accompanying servant boy. The poorest scholars, who had already gone to such large expense for the journey itself, could not afford even dried fish with their rice, so they packed a wooden fish to save face. At meal times they would dip it into a bowl of

Lord Trinh's palace. The Trinh were the real power behind the Lê emperors.

nước mắm and pretend to eat it, although they were really eating just rice and drops of sauce. After every meal, the fish would be surreptitiously washed and stored for the next time. If the scholar passed the exam, the wooden fish would be forgotten. If he failed, the fish would be put away until it was required at the next round of exams.

In the middle of the sixteenth century civil war flared between the Lê court (backed by the Trịnh lords) in the north and the Nguyễn lords in the south. It lasted on and off for the next two centuries, and consecutive battles seriously disrupted the supply of food. Some periods of fighting lasted for several years, either in the north of the country, where Thăng-Long was, or in the south, in the provinces now known as Quảng Trị and Thừa Thiên.

The pressure of the northern army on the Nguyễn forced them to move steadily south, to take over first the Cham land and then the Mekong Delta from the Khmer. From then on, the Nguyễn developed the former Cham land, today the site of Hội An in central Vietnam, into a busy port, where ships from both Asia and Europe came regularly to trade.

Along with the movement south, many Việt settlers came to stay in the newly acquired land. They were traders, soldiers and followers of the founder of the Nguyễn dynasty, Lord Nguyễn Ánh (later Emperor Gia-Long), who was fighting to wrest the throne from his rivals in the north. The new Việt settlers soon acquired culinary habits and dishes from the local Chams and Khmers, most notably the use of spices and various

Ships docking at Hội An during a voyage to Nguyễn Cochinchina, 1792–3.

The Nguyễn's southern push, a movement that started in the 16th century and eventually absorbed the kingdoms of Champa (central Vietnam) and Zhenla (Mekong Delta).

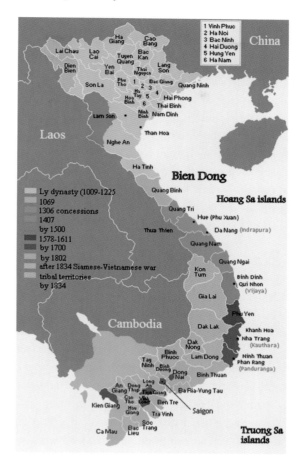

curries. Many other Cham and Khmer dishes may have been included in Vietnamese southern cuisine at the time, but the most recognizable legacy was the fermented food.

Mắm nêm was a typical Cham food that entered southern Vietnamese cuisine during the Nguyễn Southern Push. The Cham belonged to a race that had more in common with other Southeast Asian people, such as the Malay, than with the Vietnamese in the north. They lived in a string of kingdoms hugging the coast of Vietnam, from the present-day province of Quảng Trị to that of Bình Thuận. One by one, these kingdoms were conquered and annexed into Vietnam, but not before they had acquired their own distinct cuisine, influenced by India and elsewhere, including Java. Cham food is very much like that of Cambodia, Laos and northern Thailand. It is sweeter and spicier than northern Vietnamese food and uses many different types of *mắm*, one of which is *mắm nêm*. This fermented paste is made with salt and marine shrimps in a different way from the Vietnamese *mắm tôm*, and has a completely different flavour and smell, owing to the different spices added during the much longer fermentation process. It can be used on its own or as a condiment to flavour other dishes.

Another *mắm* that may have been a Cham product is *mắm ruốc*, a similar paste made with ground small shrimps and salt and left to ferment for days until it changes from purple to red. It is a famous condiment of central Vietnam, the former Cham land, and is used to season many dishes; it can also be eaten in its own right with raw vegetables, herbs and boiled pork. *Mắm ruốc* is a vital ingredient in the central Vietnamese noodle dish *bún bò Huế*.

Further south, the Mekong Delta once belonged to another kingdom, called Funan in Chinese historical documents. Funan existed at the beginning of our Common Era, but is thought to have been absorbed into the Khmer kingdom sometime during the sixth or seventh century.[10] By 1779 the entire Mekong Delta had become Vietnamese territory through a series of wars and land cession. Like the Cham, the Khmer in the Mekong Delta used a lot of *mắm*, and they transferred their taste for it to the Việt sometime during the eighteenth century, when large numbers of Vietnamese came to settle there. The most famous Khmer *mắm* is *mắm pò hóc*, which is made with fermented fish in yet another way. Unlike the traditional Cham and Khmer dishes that were absorbed into Vietnamese cuisine, this *mắm* was not so popular with the Vietnamese, for reasons that are unknown, but it was a favourite food among the Cham and the Khmer in the Mekong Delta.

Curries were another addition to the southern Vietnamese table during this period. With influences from India and Cambodia, the cuisines of central Vietnam and the Mekong Delta have a stronger taste, since they involve spices such as cardamom, cinnamon, star anise, clove, ginger, turmeric and ground coriander. Coconut milk and coconut cream were added liberally to many dishes. Most Cham and Khmer people in central and southern Vietnam were either Muslims or Hindus, so their food was strictly dictated by their religion. As a result, fish, goat and chicken were more popular than pork and beef. Unlike the people in the north of Vietnam, they ate a good deal of curry in a style similar to that of Thailand or Malaysia, with plenty of coconut milk.

Along with the adoption of some Cham and Khmer dishes into the Vietnamese diet in the Mekong Delta, a new type of Chinese food entered

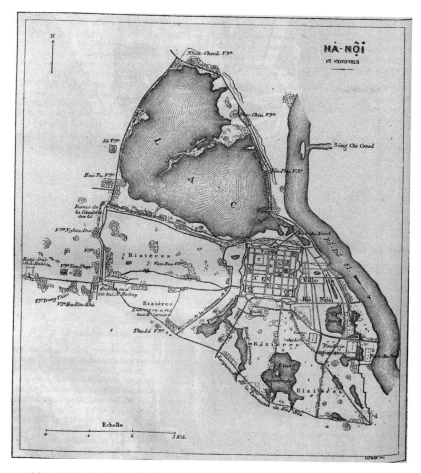

Map of Hanoi, 1873, with the 36 Streets clearly marked to the northeast corner.

the region by way of some 3,000 refugees who arrived from China in 1679. These were Ming loyalists (Minh Hương) who had escaped from Qing China when the Ming dynasty collapsed. They came to settle in the area around present-day Saigon or Ho Chi Minh City, in Mỹ Tho in the upper Mekong Delta and in Hà Tiên in the lower Mekong Delta. The Ming loyalists were particularly industrious, and turned their adopted sites into thriving market towns. They grew vegetables on an industrial scale and exercised their remarkable trading skills to buy and sell both local and Chinese products back and forth. They gradually expanded their communities to become neighbours of the local Khmers and the Việt settlers, to whom they brought their diverse Chinese cuisine, from Chiu Chow (Teochew) to Fujian, Hainanese and Shanghai specialities.

The ship *Yun-nan* docking at the port of Hanoi, 1891.

Later, in the seventeenth and eighteenth centuries, they established a wholesale market next to the Việt enclave in Saigon, selling products such as game, rare plants, vegetables, herbs and spices from the highlands and their own farms into international maritime trade. Their agricultural products and other trading activity contributed a great deal to the southern economy and helped to turn the Mekong Delta into an important agricultural region in Vietnam. That, in turn, transformed the area we know today as Saigon into a major trading port from the eighteenth century onwards.

The Trinh–Nguyễn civil war continued, however, with fierce battles, some of which lasted for years. The Việt people again suffered famine caused not only by the fighting, but by natural disasters (drought and flooding that caused great famines virtually every year from 1595) and by widespread banditry perpetrated by hungry hordes roaming the country looking for food.[11] The situation lasted to a greater or lesser extent until 1802, when the last dynasty, the Nguyễn, won a total victory and took over.

The victory of Lord Nguyễn Ánh (the first emperor Gia-Long) did not come easily. He and his troops suffered periods of extreme hunger during the late eighteenth century, while fighting. In a series of running battles up and down the Mekong Delta and in the Gulf of Siam, the Nguyễn forces were forced to eat tree roots to survive. Later, they managed to hold the delta, surviving thanks to the newly established military plantations and the region's plentiful supply of fresh produce. By the nineteenth century commercial activities were still going strong in the 36 Streets, which were maintained as a network of specialized shops and street markets.

SIX

The French Century, 1859–1954

After nine centuries of developing and settling into a recognizable pattern, Vietnamese cuisine went through a dramatic and profound change in the second half of the nineteenth century, following the arrival of the French. The astonishing feature of this culinary transformation is that it happened voluntarily, rapidly and wholeheartedly, in spite of the tense political situation and the hostility in Franco–Vietnamese relations.

The French military intervention in Vietnam began in 1859, after several years of sporadic clashes between the navies of the two countries. The French saw their interference in Vietnam as an attempt to secure better treatment for French and Spanish Catholic missionaries and trading rights at a number of Vietnamese ports. The Confucian Nguyễn court (1802–1945) in the royal capital, Huế, viewed the presence of the European priests and their preaching about a Lord in Heaven as a challenge to the emperor's celestial mandate, as Son of Heaven in the eyes of his citizens. Both views must be put in the wider context of Western presence in China and other parts of Asia, with the British in India, Hong Kong and Singapore, the Dutch in Indonesia, the Portuguese in Macao and the Spanish in the Philippines. The Nguyễn refused both French demands. After each refusal, the French navy bombarded the coastal cities near Huế and then left, only to return for more of the same.

The impasse lasted until February 1859, when a joint French–Spanish naval force left the central region to attack the southern city of Saigon. The city succumbed quickly and in February 1860 was declared an open port by Admiral François Page of the French fleet. By March 1862 the French had won four of the six provinces of south Vietnam, forcing the Nguyễn court in June 1862 to sign a treaty that ceded to France three eastern provinces, in

The French capture of Saigon in 1859, from the 23 April 1859 edition of *L'Illustration*.

return for the fourth. However, in 1867, under heavy military pressure from the French navy, the remaining provinces were ceded to France, making the whole of south Vietnam a French overseas territory. The cession was later formalized in another treaty signed in 1874.

After another ten years of heavy fighting in north and central Vietnam, the country succumbed altogether and was placed under French rule according to the last and most comprehensive treaty, of 1884. The south was confirmed as French-owned Cochinchina, while the remaining land of Vietnam was divided into two regions governed by different authorities: Tonkin or Bắc Kỳ in the north, under the French, and the Nguyễn court in the centre, called Annam or Trung Kỳ. Both regions were put under French 'protection'. From 1887, all three regions of Vietnam were integrated into the wider French territory known as L'Union Indochinoise, which also included Cambodia and Laos.

The different statuses of the Vietnamese regions made it difficult for Việt people to cross regional boundaries, since complicated travel papers were required. Most people in each region thus turned inwards and developed lifestyles that were distinctively different from one region to the next. As for food, the vocabulary of ingredients also varied from region to region, especially in the southern provinces, which had been a French territory the longest. The southerners now had a repertoire of Vietnamized French ingredients with which the other two regions were still unfamiliar. The differences became more pronounced by the time the French left, in 1954, to the extent that one of the first cookbooks published in Vietnam

The port of Saigon in 1866.

in the 1950s devoted several pages to a glossary of ingredients in regional languages so that cooks from all three regions could find the ingredients for the dishes without mishap.

FOOD IN COCHINCHINA

Being the first part of Vietnam ceded to France, Cochinchina began to be developed in earnest even before the treaty of 1862 was signed. Almost on the heels of the military, many French commercial companies set sail for Vietnam. Saigon at the time was a shabby but thriving river port, threaded with canals bordered by little houses of timber and thatch. Catinat was the main street to the dock and later became the main street of the city, and a convenient thoroughfare for the loading and unloading of cargo. By 1864 the first commercial brick house in town was Maison Denis Frères, a luxury emporium that offered both French and English products shipped from the company's headquarters in Bordeaux. The commercial strategy of the Denis brothers was two-pronged: to import foreign food and wine into Vietnam, and to export rice and other agricultural products to Hong Kong and China. It was a resounding success that encouraged others to follow. French enterprises such as the shipping company Messageries Maritimes and an abundance of French products, such as milk, butter, cheese, coffee, chocolate and charcuterie, soon arrived in Vietnam. All these products left a deep impression on the Vietnamese, who had not been exposed to such alien delights before.

One of the early commercial ships docking in Saigon, 1888.

As the number of French grocers in Cochinchina grew, so did the number of Vietnamese who had acquired a taste for French food. By the end of the nineteenth century, demand for butter, condensed milk and cheese had gone through the roof, a surprising fact given that dairy products had not previously been part of the Vietnamese diet. Nevertheless, after two decades under French rule, many Vietnamese in the south had taken to all three products – on offer from the French at a high price – as

The French import–export company Denis Frères was the first commercial establishment in the French colony of Cochinchina. The poster is about the company's operation in the whole of French Indochina but the dragon logo at the lower right corner signified that it was meant for Vietnam.

if they had been born eating and drinking them. The process of absorption was repeated in the north of Vietnam later, and, last, in the central region, where imperial power was still nominally present.

DAIRY PRODUCTS

The assimilation of dairy products may not have happened immediately after the French arrived, but when it did, it was a case of 'love at first bite' for many Vietnamese, and the products are still cherished to this day. One of the most coveted dairy foods from the period was the salted butter Beurre Bretel, which came in an iconic red-and-gold tin. It was the ultimate luxury for the many middle-class families enthralled by its deeply buttery smell and salty taste. The delightful combination left a lasting impression on the palate of generations of Vietnamese, to the extent that even in the United States and Europe today, where fresh butter is cheap and widely available, many Vietnamese still search high and low and even online for this butter.

Bretel butter was made by Maison Bretel Frères in the Manche region of northern France. As a newly established dairy in 1865, Maison Bretel may have taken a little while to penetrate the Vietnamese market, but once the butter arrived in the country, it never left. The texture is soft and spongy and the butter does not need to be refrigerated, making it ideal for the tropical market. Bretel's dairy products have won many awards in France and these are proudly displayed on the labels; the top of the butter tin is decorated with a curving string of round gold medals similar to Vietnamese gold coins. The image prompted the Việt to call the butter *bơ đồng tiền* (coin butter), a name that remains to this day. For the less well-off Vietnamese, who could not afford real butter, margarine was available, which they called butter as well through their Vietnamized pronunciation of *bơ* or *bứa* (for *beurre*).

The next longest-lasting French product in Vietnam is the soft cheese called Laughing Cow (*La Vache qui rit*). It is also just as popular today as it was during the French century. This cheese, made by the French firm Fromageries Bel, is another wonder dairy product: it does not need to be refrigerated, and yet it does not melt or become sticky in the hot, humid climate of Vietnam. It is still a favourite of Vietnamese adults and children alike, and is considered so iconic that successive Vietnamese national airlines have served it as part of their in-flight meals, both on domestic and international routes. Other types of butter and cheese, such as Claudel

butter and Gruyère cheese, became available at the turn of the twentieth century, but Beurre Bretel and the Laughing Cow remained the first loves of many Vietnamese. Condensed milk followed suit; in fact, it may have been introduced at the same time, but its impact, however wide among the population, was not as dramatic as that of the other two products during the first decades of the French century. Condensed milk soon became the milk given to Vietnamese infants, instead of or as well as breast milk, but it would not be long before it became an obligatory additive to the next French product that many Vietnamese took to heart: coffee.

COFFEE

The early French colonists brought with them another delightful product that soon became a cult among many Vietnamese, especially young men and, to a much lesser extent, women who had grown up under French rule. Coffee was very expensive and not widely available at first, but it was not long before coffee beans were grown in Vietnam. Generous tax concessions for French enterprises encouraged many French individuals and companies to enter Vietnam and develop their own plantations for growing a variety of crops, and coffee was one of those.

The establishment of French plantations in Vietnam did not happen without causing great resentment and controversy, and it even led to serious uprisings during the early part of the twentieth century. However, the protests were subdued, the plantations remained and the products entered the market. Seeds of non-Vietnamese plants were brought from Europe and adapted to grow in the moderate climate of the central highlands, and their produce was widely available to both French and Vietnamese citizens by the early twentieth century. The introduction of coffee into Vietnam during the French century had a huge and lasting impact on the Vietnamese economy, since it is now one of the country's top exports. Vast plantations created by the French still exist in many parts of the central highlands, making Vietnam one of the most prolific coffee-producing countries in the world.

Many different varieties of coffee were available during the French century, some produced locally and others imported. At the same time, coffee houses, patisseries, bakeries and tea houses were set up on fashionable boulevards, but these were almost exclusively the domain of the French and the rich Vietnamese, owing to their prohibitive prices and the owners' haughty attitude. The coffee-loving members of the Vietnamese middle class were not deterred, however, and set up their own coffee shops, serving lesser brands of coffee at affordable prices. This was where young Vietnamese men converged to talk, to plot revolutions or just to enjoy the taste of the coffee. They drank it in glasses, black or with condensed milk,

Plantation life. Early French settlers in the late 19th and early 20th centuries built their houses on the central highlands in local style, with thatched roofs for coolness.

Vietnamese coffee, a strong brew made by filtering ground coffee through an individual filter to retain its strength and quality. Waiting for the drops to drip into the glass is considered part of the joy of drinking coffee in Vietnam.

either hot or with ice, and so strong that it would make the uninitiated feel faint after a single glass. The ground coffee was passed through a filter that allowed the liquid to drip into a small glass underneath, and indeed the anticipation as the glass filled drop by drop seems to have been part of the fun. So slow was the process, in fact, that the glass might be put in a bowl of hot water to keep the coffee warm. Later, in the late 1940s and early 1950s, Vietnamese coffee houses became the places where young men would sit and contemplate their existence, not always in the political sense but as part of the newly imported existentialism.

Coffee did not just become enormously popular among the upper and middle classes during the French century. As soon as it became available from local plantations, coffee stalls appeared at every street corner in the city and on the main street of each village. This coffee was crudely filtered, not fresh for each cup but in large amounts through a cotton bag, prompting its nickname, 'sock coffee'. This was coffee for the poor, who drank it standing up or sitting on low stools by the stall. Rickshaw drivers, street vendors and market-goers all preferred to have a break at these undemanding coffee places.

At the other end of the spectrum was fox (also known as racoon or weasel) coffee, which many Vietnamese considered to be the mother of all coffees. It was made with special beans partly pre-digested by the animals living around the plantations. These animals ate the best berries, and passed the beans whole through their digestive systems. The planters then collected the beans, washed them and roasted them as usual. Planters usually kept the fox coffee for themselves, or to give to friends; if they did sell it, it would be in small quantities at a high price.

During the French century, some planters attempted to grow cocoa beans along with coffee, but the result was so poor that the land was soon taken over for more coffee instead. Tea plantations were also established in the highlands. The yield was good, but tea export revenues were low compared to the more profitable coffee.

PASTRIES

For many French people, pastries are an essential part of life. They quickly became a part of Vietnamese life, too, after their arrival at the beginning of the French century. The snack-loving Vietnamese welcomed another group of *bánh* to add to their extensive list of rice *bánh*. These *bánh* were made with wheat flour and baked in an oven, instead of being steamed, as their rice counterparts were. Likewise, croissants and brioches became favourite foods for breakfast, next to the traditional glutinous rice, *xôi*. The Vietnamese versions were often made without butter and were known as *bánh sữa* (milk cake) for the brioche and *bánh sừng bò* (cattle-horn cake) for the croissant.

Bánh Patê Sô

Many French *bánh* were Vietnamized during the French century, and each acquired its own Vietnamese pronunciation. For example, choux pastry became *bánh su* and *tarte* became *bánh tộc*, but the favourite was the savoury pie called *pâté chaud* (*bánh patê sô*). This pie is made with puff pastry and filled with minced pork, onion, garlic and a little liver pâté. It became so well-loved by the Vietnamese that it could be found almost everywhere, at every coffee shop, and even in noodle shops, to be dunked in soup.

French gateaux were welcomed with open arms by those who could afford them. For those who could not, Vietnamese versions were created, made with less butter, no butter or margarine. The Vietnamese gateau then was much lighter than its French counterpart, since the eggs were whisked for longer to create more froth at less expense. These cakes were often left undecorated, but were still much appreciated. During the first decades of the twentieth century, when refrigeration became available, Vietnamese cake shops began to offer cream cakes decorated with butter or, more commonly, margarine icing.

Until the late twentieth century, ovens were rare in Vietnamese homes, and existed only in professional bakeries or Chinese roast houses. Early cakes were usually baked in a rudimentary metal box on top of a charcoal stove. Later, street vendors began to use a cast-iron cake-maker, again on a charcoal stove. It was similar to our electric cake-maker today. Cake mixture would be poured into the indented shapes of the cake-maker, eight or ten at a time, and a lid put on; a few minutes later the cakes were ready. The Vietnamese version of Marcel Proust's beloved madeleine was made in this way after it became one of the most popular cakes in Vietnam, thanks to its small size and low price.

By the early twentieth century, cakes and pastries were being offered at patisseries and also at many ice-cream parlours, which had by then become an important feature of Vietnamese social life. Unlike the male-dominated coffee shops, ice-cream parlours were family places, where indulgent parents and their children could enjoy a treat of ice cream and perhaps a pastry or piece of cake, and where friends could meet to gossip or flirt.

CHARCUTERIE

During the French century, ham, pâté and *saucissons* were novelty foods that soon became daily fare for many Vietnamese. The French versions of these products were generally too expensive for the majority of Vietnamese, so they set about making their own imitations. Such endeavours were successful to the extent that locally made charcuterie became an industry catering almost exclusively to the Vietnamese. Vietnamese pâté was cruder than its French version but more flavoursome, being made for immediate consumption, and therefore without preservatives or other additions. It was often steamed rather than baked.

Garlic sausages and the dry *saucisson* were made in Vietnam with lots more pepper, but tasted almost as good as the originals. The reason for the

Poster advertising French charcuterie, possibly early 20th century.

success of the Vietnamized *saucisson* was its method of production. By the end of the nineteenth century the Vietnamese and Chinese in Vietnam had become adept at making Chinese sausages, stuffing chopped meat, fat and spices into lengths of dried pork intestine and drying the sausages in the sun. It was an easy step to adapt this technique to suit the fattier version, the *saucisson*, albeit with different spices.

Ham was another matter. It was not an easy food to re-create locally, because the meat had first to be cured. The Việt invented a similar product, which took off spectacularly and became the dominant feature of all Vietnamese sandwiches: *thịt nguội* (cold meat). A roll of pork shoulder or belly, skin on, was marinated according to the house secret and pan-roasted until the meat was firm but still succulent. Once cooled, the roll of meat would be sliced thinly in the same way as ham and added to a Vietnamese sandwich, along with other ingredients.

VEGETABLES

From very early in the French century, seeds and seedlings of many vegetables were imported into Vietnam, most being grown in the cooler climate of the central highlands but some also planted in the Mekong delta. Carrots, tomatoes, leeks, French beans, artichokes, cauliflower, celery and potatoes had become entrenched in the Vietnamese cuisine and culinary vocabulary by the end of the nineteenth century, each with its own Vietnamese pronunciation: *cà-rốt* for *carotte* (carrot), *cà tô mát* for *tomate* (tomato), *súp lơ* for *chou-fleur* (cauliflower), *đậu ve* for *haricot vert* (green bean), *đậu poa* for *petit pois* (pea) and so on. Those products that already had Vietnamese cousins would be given the word *tây* (Western or French) to differentiate them from the local versions, such as *khoai tây* (potato or French yam), *tỏi tây* (leek) and *mùi tây* (parsley). One was soon elevated to the highest rank of special vegetables in Vietnam: asparagus (*măng tây*), which came at first in a tin. Fresh asparagus did later become available, but for Vietnamese cuisine, only the canned version was the right thing. Incidentally, asparagus was called *măng tây* to differentiate it from its local cousin, the bamboo shoot, which was called simply *măng*. Not only did the Vietnamese give the French vegetables local names, they gave them local partners as well. French vegetables soon found themselves in Vietnamese pots with other Vietnamese ingredients, seasoned with *nước mắm* and Vietnamese herbs. By the beginning of the twentieth century, cauliflower, asparagus or petit pois soups, Vietnamese-style, had joined the list of the required 'four bowls' in a Vietnamese banquet.

For many middle-class Vietnamese, the potato became a magic food to help boys grow into strong men. They believed that Frenchmen were so much bigger than the Việt because they ate potatoes rather than rice, and that their size and strength were the reason for their domination of the Việt. When potatoes became available in Vietnam, parents began to feed them to their boys as a food supplement, between their meals of rice – since no Việt should be deprived of rice. The most popular way of serving potatoes was by mashing them with condensed milk. Needless to say, eating them was an ordeal for many young Vietnamese boys. The fad gradually died down and had disappeared altogether by the end of the French century. The potato, however, remained very popular among the Việt, to add to soup or in the form of French fries. The latter were often served as a starter before a meal with rice.

CONDIMENTS

The Việt have always loved pickled food and eaten a large variety of pickled vegetables, meat and fish. During the French century a new type was added to the Vietnamese larder: the French cornichon, a small pickled cucumber. Cornichons were usually served to complement classic French dishes such as pâté and pork. It is not clear when they were imported into Vietnam, but by the time the French left, these tiny pickled gherkins had become a favourite for the Việt to add to their baguette sandwiches.

Many Vietnamized French dishes were accompanied by a clear brown sauce called Maggi, named after its creator, Julius Maggi of the eponymous Swiss company founded in 1872. Julius Maggi created this protein-rich vegetable-based sauce from vegetable extracts, water, salt, wheat gluten, wheat, wheat bran, sugar, acetic acid, artificial flavourings, disodium inosinate, disodium guanylate, dextrose and caramel colouring. (It originally contained soy extract, but that was later taken out.) The sauce was introduced in Europe in the 1880s as a cheap substitute for meat extract, and became an instant hit in many European countries. Following in the footsteps of French colonists and visitors, it arrived in Vietnam and other parts of East and Southeast Asia at about the same time, and was soon adopted by the middle class as an everyday condiment. Maggi sauce arrived in Vietnam in another iconic and instantly recognizable container that is still used today, a square bottle with a long neck and a yellow, red and brown label. The sauce tasted slightly sweeter than light soy sauce, with a more pronounced caramel flavour, making it enticing to the young and appetizing to older people. In fact, it seemed to go with everything and, consequently, was used with everything imaginable.

After launching Maggi sauce into international markets, the firm created another product, Maggi noodles. These did not take, however, in Asia – Vietnam included – probably because fresh noodles were already readily available there. Maggi stock cubes followed, with some success in Asia and a warm welcome elsewhere. With the popularity of his products assured worldwide, in 1897 Julius Maggi founded a company, Maggi GmbH, in Germany, and the company merged with the dairy giant Nestlé in 1947. Regardless of which company owned Maggi, the sauce remained a favourite condiment for many children and young adults who did not like the stronger taste of fish sauce. It is still found on almost every Vietnamese table in and outside Vietnam, for it has become a 'French' product as coveted as Laughing Cow or Beurre Bretel.

COLONIAL FRENCH CUISINE

The Vietnamization of French food began soon after the French arrival, without waiting for the right ingredients to become available locally. Early French colonists in Vietnam lived in conditions that were difficult for

Corner street market, Hanoi, turn of the 20th century.

Europeans; the climate was hot and humid, and poor housing and general difficulties made life uncomfortable. The thing they complained most about, however, was the lack of good French cooking. At the beginning of the colonization process, many if not all colonists were single men, or family men who did not want to bring their families to a faraway land to live in such harsh conditions. However, they still had to eat, and properly cooked French food was what they hankered after. Most nineteenth-century men did not cook, so they were forced to attempt to re-create the taste of home using local cooks. Since their recollection of their home foods may not have been perfect, and not all the ingredients were available, the result was inevitably that the dishes were similar but different. A new breed of French cuisine, the colonial cookery style, was born, and later, when living conditions had improved enough for the French to bring their families over, local cooks were still employed. The French mistresses might know how to cook or have brought proper recipes with them, but since the Vietnamese did the cooking, they would need to train them or do the work themselves. French cooking then went through another stage of modification to incorporate what the cook had already known and what they now learned. Over time, Vietnamese cooks leaving French families spread their French culinary knowledge far and wide among their friends and relations. In the ordinary Vietnamese kitchen, colonial French cuisine went through yet another stage of transformation to become a hybrid of French and Vietnamese cuisine.

So much for the adoption of French food into the Vietnamese culinary repertoire. Pure French food was another matter. As was the case with Chinese food, authentic French food existed as a different strand of cuisine entirely. It was served in French restaurants reserved for the colonists and some rich Vietnamese, cooked by regional French chefs who had migrated to Vietnam from all parts of France, from Brittany to Marseille to the island of Corsica. The result was that those Vietnamese who could afford it were exposed to the most specialized French regional dishes, including those that were considered to be high culinary art, such as the fish soup bouillabaisse. The abundance of marine products off the coast of Vietnam made it an ideal place for this special dish to thrive and enthral French and Vietnamese alike. Not only that, the cheapness (by French standards) of its ingredients meant that it could be made rich with large clams or huge shrimps that were expensive in Europe. The irony is that once a person has been exposed to the colonial bouillabaisse, its real version in Marseille, however tasty, pales by comparison in terms of the seafood it contains.

During the French century and beyond, French restaurants were extremely popular among those who could afford to visit them. Even after the French departed, in 1954, their restaurants continued to thrive

The Chinese quarter (Chợ Lớn) in Saigon, 1866. The canals were a prominent feature of Saigon during this period as they were a major means of transport.

throughout Vietnam, serving the Vietnamese middle class, Western expats and European visitors. They closed their doors only after the reunification of the country, in 1975, when life became austere for many and visitors to the country few and far between.

The flow of French food into Vietnamese cuisine could not have happened without Vietnamese food also being embraced by French residents. The regular appearance of the Vietnamese spring roll (*chả giò* or *nem rán*) in French patisseries in France itself is evidence of this. However, the two-way flow of culinary delights during the French century did not happen without mishap, at least at first. One of the most celebrated incidents was recorded by a French doctor working in the royal capital, Huế. Dr Auvray wrote in the *Bulletin de la Société de Géographie de Paris*, published in France in 1883, that the emperor often gave the French legation foods they found inedible, such as various birds shot by the emperor himself, or local cakes. What baffled Auvray most, however, was an elephant foot brought back by the emperor's hunters. He did not know what it was for or why it was given to them to eat. Little did he know that it was a gesture of appreciation, for elephant foot was one of the rare foods that the royals loved to have in their banquets – after a lot of cooking, of course.

Crocodile meat was widely available in Cochinchina during the French century, and crocodiles were raised for meat even in the centre of Saigon. The old crocodile-meat market was on one of Saigon's main boulevards. During the first decades of the French century, Saigon was still full of canals, and the main method of transport was the small boat. Crocodiles were raised in one of these canals – subsequently aptly named the Canal of Crocodiles – and were wrestled out of the water and killed for their meat and skin. It is not known how the meat was cooked at the time, but it was apparently popular, for it is mentioned by older Vietnamese citizens as an ordinary meat. It ceased to be available in Saigon only when the canal was filled in and became Boulevard de la Somme; after the French departed the street was given a Vietnamese name, Hàm Nghi Boulevard.

At the end of the nineteenth century, life was still very difficult for many colonists, especially in the remote plantations in the hills of north and central Vietnam. However, one of the rewards they enjoyed was the abundance of wild animals, which they hunted and ate with great relish. Several French texts mention the delight of eating big and small game. Writing in the *Bulletin des amis du vieux Huế* in 1931, the French agricultural commissioner L. Gilbert noted that there were plenty of elephants in the central highlands, and many tigers, panthers, wild boar, deer and rhinoceroses to hunt for their skins and for profit.

When they were not hunting, high-ranking French officials were regularly exposed to ritual food during national ceremonies, such as the Nam Giao in Huế, or at official banquets. Humbler French men and the soldiers stationed in the many garrisons throughout Vietnam were exposed to street food and other Vietnamese delights, such as rice with condiments or even *mắm*.

NATIONAL DISHES

The Vietnamese did not eat a lot of beef before the arrival of the French; the meat was expensive, and many also found the taste too strong. However, after a few decades of French presence, beef became a familiar part of Vietnamese cuisine. The cheaper cuts were preferred, such as stewing steak, oxtail and other parts of the animal that were not considered fit for the colonist's table. Price was one reason, but taste was another. The Vietnamese like to gnaw on their food, and pork spare ribs and oxtail fitted the bill perfectly. The gelatinous texture of the connective tissues once cooked was also much loved by the Việt. French beef stew took off in restaurants and in Vietnamese home cooking, and had become staple fare by the turn of the twentieth century. It was even on offer at food stalls as *bò kho* (stewed beef) or *bò sốt vang* (stewed beef with wine sauce), seasoned with fish sauce and garnished with Vietnamese sweet basil. Other French dishes followed. Something *farci* (stuffed) was the next most popular: crab *farci* and stuffed tomatoes were welcomed into Vietnamese cuisine, again seasoned with fish sauce and garnished with herbs. By the end of the French century, it was normal for the Việt to come to a street stall, sit down and order a plate of *bò kho*, which was served with a length of bread to mop up the sauce.

In 1931, according to French statistics, pork was still the preferred meat for local consumption and for export. Chicken and duck were also favoured locally, and regularly exported to Hong Kong and Singapore. Goat, on the other hand, was much less popular throughout the country. In the south, there were only a few herds totalling about 20,000 head.[1]

As for beef, from being an unpopular meat at first it had become widely used by both French and Vietnamese by the time these statistics were compiled. According to these, the bovine herd in Vietnam had grown so large that a figure of 500,000 head was mentioned as a modest estimate.

Each cow could provide 150–200 kg (330–440 lb) of meat, although the milk was considered poor. The meat was so abundant that it was exported from central Vietnam to both the north and south of Vietnam, and to the Philippines. The annual figures were put at 25,000 head for the north, 4,000 for the south and 1,500 for the Philippines. Buffaloes were not as popular as beef, but the herd of 350,000 head was large enough to supply the whole country, and even to export to Hong Kong.

Phở

The inclusion of beef in Vietnamese cuisine during the French century may have given rise to the most Vietnamese dish of all, and one that – controversially – the French may even have unwittingly given a name to: *phở*. This wholly Vietnamese bowl of flat rice noodle soup has often been called a national dish. There are two main types according to the central ingredient, beef or chicken, of which beef is the more authentic. For beef *phở*, stock is made by boiling beef bones with spices, such as star anise, cinnamon sticks and ginger, and roasted onions. Other ingredients and extra spices may be added according to the house speciality and the region. Rolled brisket or other big chunks of beef, such as shin, are usually boiled with the bones. Often, other parts of the cow, such as stomach, leg tendon, oxtail or anything else that takes the cook's fancy, will be cooked in the stock as well. An extreme version of *phở*, made with stewed bull's genitals cut into bite-sized pieces, is popular with men, who believe it to be beneficial for their sexual prowess, similar to the way they view rhino horn. The beef is served as a topping, for the diners to select for their individual bowls. To assemble a bowl of *phở*, first the flat rice noodles are added to the beef stock, then come the pieces of beef, followed by finely chopped spring onion and coriander. Thin slices of good-quality raw beef may be added to the bowl just before boiling stock is poured on top, cooking the meat to pink.

Chicken *phở* contains stock made by boiling chicken and pork bones, and is served with chopped or shredded chicken, spring onion and coriander. Chicken giblets, such as liver, gizzard or intestine, or even half-formed chicken eggs can be added to the bowl if the diner asks and pays extra for them. The noodles served in chicken *phở* are usually thinner than those used in the beef version.

People from northern Vietnam prefer their noodles wider than do southerners, and might add lime and fresh chilli to their *phở*. Southerners, on the other hand, would expect a side dish of lime, chilli, beansprouts, sweet basil and saw-tooth coriander (*ngò gai*), a herb that looks like blades of grass with jagged edges and tastes slightly sour.

The origin of *phở* is still obscure. Some Vietnamese believe it was invented at the end of the nineteenth century, after the arrival of French settlers, given the Việt's historical dislike of beef. They reason that the popularity of beef among the French eventually rubbed off on the Việt and beef *phở* was born. Others prefer to think that *phở* was created during the 1920s or 1930s in Hanoi or perhaps a nearby town, Nam Định, as a dish served to French soldiers. Both theories presume a French connection, and the name *phở* is offered as evidence of this connection, or cited as a point of contention.

The word *phở* sounds like a Vietnamized version of *feu*, the French word for fire, prompting some Vietnamese to deduce that it is a version of the French dish *pot-au-feu*. However, *phở* is a completely different dish in many ways; for a start, it is a thin soup with noodles, not a casserole. With or without the French connection, one option that has not been considered so far is that the dish may have existed under a different name before it was given the peculiar-sounding *phở*. What that original name was is another matter for debate, of course.

Bowl of *phở* with cooked and raw beef toppings.

Mobile *phở* vendor and his customers, Hanoi, *c.* 1920s.

Beef *phở* was traditionally a street food, sold by a vendor carrying his bits and pieces in two boxes slung at either end of a bamboo pole on his shoulders. One end of the pole supported a wooden box designed as a cage to house a big pot of stock. Under the pot was a wood or charcoal fire to keep the soup hot at all times. Slung over the other end of the bamboo pole was another wooden cage containing shelves to store bowls, noodles, sliced beef, onion, coriander and other condiments. It is a wonder that the heated pot was kept from spilling as the vendor walked through the streets, and, more importantly, that the fire did not set its housing alight. This pot set over a fire was probably how *phở* acquired its name from *feu*.

During the decades straddling the turn of the twentieth century, French soldiers were stationed in Hanoi and many other towns and cities throughout Vietnam, since resistance to the French was strong. These soldiers may have felt peckish in the evenings, and when they went on the look-out for something to eat, a street vendor with light would have been visible from afar in the poorly lit streets. On seeing the fire under the *phở* stockpot, the soldiers perhaps called out to get the vendor to stop. 'Hey, *feu*!' may have been appropriate, the fire being the most visible sign of the food to come. Trade was probably good, especially since evenings in the north of Vietnam are cool, making a bowl of hot soup most welcome. Over time, the vendor may have started calling out '*feu*' in his Vietnamese accent, *phở*, to catch the buyers' attention, and the name stuck. Mobile *phở* was always sold by men, probably because the stockpot was too heavy for a woman to shoulder.

Whatever its origin, *phở* was an overnight success with both the French and the Việt in the north. It was introduced to the south of Vietnam in 1954, when half a million northerners moved south after the Geneva Accord on the partition of Vietnam, and it was an instant success there, too. *Phở* can be found everywhere in Vietnam, in dedicated restaurants, stationary stalls and mobile carts, but lately the image of the man carrying the pot over its fire has vanished, surviving only in drawings by the fascinated, or the writings of the nostalgic. Modern *phở* can include prawns, fish, stewed beef or tofu, and many condiments are available to top it up even further. Even hoisin sauce is occasionally found in Vietnamese *phở* shops, just in case. The most usual condiments are chilli sauce and neat *nước mắm*, as well as the usual plateful of beansprouts, chilli, lime wedges and sweet basil.

The *Bánh Mì* Revolution

While the origin of *phở* is still shrouded in mystery, the parentage of another product born during the French century could not be clearer: the French baguette, first called *bánh tây* (French bread) but later known more commonly as *bánh mì* (wheat bread). It arrived with the early colonists during the first decade of the French century, and stayed to become another Vietnamese national dish. It was a further case of love at first bite for the entire population. Perhaps because of the climate, it was lighter in Vietnam than in France, and mostly came in the shape of a long stick, the baguette. A thicker version was available, but was less popular because it went soft and chewy very swiftly. The baguette tended to harden quickly in the climate of Vietnam, so many shops baked at least twice a day to provide fresh bread all day long.

The baguette first joined other humble Vietnamese foods, such as *xôi* (glutinous rice), for breakfast. A piece of baguette spread thinly with margarine or butter and topped with a sprinkling of sugar was a normal breakfast for southerners. A luxury version would have a layer of jam, without the butter or margarine. However, at some point near the beginning of the twentieth century, the baguette staged a revolution that is still spreading far and wide. It began to be filled with Vietnamese ingredients to become a convenient sandwich that could be eaten at any time of day.

It is not known exactly who first thought of turning the baguette into a filled sandwich, Vietnamese-style, but it seemed that *bánh mì* stalls appeared almost overnight everywhere in south Vietnam. A limited number of fillings were offered at first, such as Vietnamese-style ham, cold meat (pork), pâté or *saucisson*, and condiments such as pickled radish and carrot or cucumber to make the bread less dry. (Dry food is something the Việt hate, so they would do anything to make the bread more moist.) Over time, the *bánh mì* sandwich became more complicated, with more fillings, more condiments and more combinations. With the change in fillings, the shape of the *bánh mì* changed as well. By the time the French left Vietnam, two distinct kinds of *bánh mì* were available, the posh and the stall types. Posh *bánh mì* were sold in shops as small oval rolls filled with mayonnaise, roast chicken or French ham, a lettuce leaf, slices of tomato and a piece of spring onion. Another version was made with sliced garlic sausage and/or *saucisson* with a layer of pâté, also with lettuce, tomato and spring onion. These rolls were wrapped in greaseproof paper clearly printed with the name of the shop. Needless to say, this version of posh *bánh mì* was more expensive, and a status symbol for many Vietnamese. The mayonnaise – Vietnam-style, slightly eggy and without vinegar or anything else sour, but with pepper and garlic – was what made this type of *bánh mì* popular, since it moistened the bread considerably. Mayonnaise and Vietnamese liver pâté were later incorporated into stall *bánh mì* to compete with the posh version.

For the less well-off, the stall *bánh mì* was good enough, or perhaps even better, for it was more versatile, with more combinations. No fancy rolls were needed; instead a long stick of bread was cut into lengths of about 20 cm (8 in.) and split open. Butter, mayonnaise or pâté (or all three) were spread inside, before the main ingredients were added. These could be slices of Vietnamese cold meat, *giò* or *chả* (Vietnamese garlic sausages or patties), or all together. Next came shredded pickled radish and carrot, a slice of cucumber, a sprig of coriander and whole or sliced red chilli. Last to be added were a few drops of the magical Maggi sauce, or light soy sauce. The finished *bánh mì* was then put on a charcoal stove underneath the stall to heat up and to restore its crunchiness, before being half-wrapped in a piece of newspaper and secured with an elastic band.

Many types of filling and many combinations were on offer at these stalls, according to how much the buyer wanted to spend and what they preferred to eat. It would be a surprise for the uninitiated to be asked at a stall, 'How much for your *bánh mì*?', but the answer would determine

Bánh mì filled with cold meat and condiments.

the number and combination of fillings. Later on, a new filling was added to those already on offer: meatballs in tomato sauce, which proved very popular among southerners. Another popular filling was tinned sardines in tomato sauce. *Bánh mì* with Laughing Cow cheese was also on offer at such stalls, but was not as popular, perhaps because it is difficult to combine that type of cheese with pickled vegetables.

A new *bánh mì* appeared on the stalls in 1954, but it took a long time to be accepted by the Vietnamese: one filled with Cheddar, called *bánh mì phô mai* (from *fromage*). Laughing Cow cheese had by then been beloved for almost a century, so the Vietnamese were not unfamiliar with the concept of cheese, but they were highly suspicious of Cheddar. The reason Cheddar made an appearance in Vietnam then was that it came as food aid, after the partition of the country. To feed half a million displaced people in southern Vietnam, Western food aid arrived by the boatload. Powdered milk, tinned meat and red or orange Cheddar were distributed to refugees from the north, many of them from remote villages. Unfortunately, the oblong blocks of food-aid Cheddar were about 35–40 cm (14–16 in.) long, exactly comparable in shape and size with the blocks of soap these villagers used to wash their laundry. For the bewildered refugees, the chunks of soap-like cheese were too suspicious to eat. For the southerners, who were used to more sophisticated cheeses after a century of French rule, Cheddar was a poor addition to what they already knew. The rejected food-aid Cheddar was resold cheaply or given away to the *bánh mì* stalls, whose enterprising owners incorporated it into their fillings, to be sold at a low price. It took several months for the *bánh mì phô mai* to become popular, and, like the Laughing Cow, it still cannot compete with the more interesting meat or fish combinations.

Much-loved though it is, the filled *bánh mì* remains a breakfast and snack food because it cannot replace a hot meal with rice for lunch or dinner in the eyes of the Việt. During the late 1960s and early 1970s, when Vietnamese offices in the south no longer allowed their workers to have a long lunch break of two-and-a-half hours, as had been the case under the French, many workers stayed at work over lunch. At first they scoured the food stalls for something to eat, but later they began to bring with them tins and boxes of rice and meat, fish or vegetables. The rice might have been cold by lunchtime, but it was still better than anything available near the offices, mainly *bánh mì*. For those who did not have time to prepare a rice lunch in the morning, it was a great hardship to eat a length of *bánh*

Mobile *bánh mì* stall and customers.

mì for lunch because, they said, it was so dry. And how could it be called a meal without rice? The shortened lunch hour later gave rise to a new industry: mobile rice lunches. Instead of offering snacks, which the Việt usually liked but for some reason rejected for lunch, the street vendors now offered hot rice with cooked foods, all served on one plate, earning this type of lunch the name 'plate rice'. It was a great success until even more enterprising business people opened little shops near the offices to offer a full lunch of rice, soup and meat, fish or vegetables at a reasonable price. This is what we find today throughout Vietnam under the name *cơm văn phòng* (office rice).

THE ROLE OF RICE DURING THE FRENCH CENTURY

For most of the French century, rice was Vietnam's top export and produced the main income of the new colony, estimated to be 68 per cent of the French total income by 1926. In the north of Vietnam, rice was harvested twice a year, while in the south it came from the Mekong Delta, and might be harvested once or twice a year depending on the variety. The Mekong Delta rice was later joined by rice from Cambodia to be processed in both Saigon and its sister town, Chợ Lớn (Chinatown), before being exported to Southeast Asia, Europe and even America. Rice exported from south Vietnam at the turn of the twentieth century was ranked second in the world in terms of quantity, but was considered inferior to Thai and Burmese rice in quality.

Under the rule of consecutive French governors from the 1860s until 1930, parcels of land were sold to the highest bidder, or given away at nominal prices to Vietnamese collaborators and French speculators. This policy created a new class of landlords whose landless tenants worked the fields for rents of up to 60 per cent of the crop. The landlord then sold his share at the Saigon export market. The export income was high not just because the area of rice cultivation was enlarged, but because of the exploitation of the peasantry.[2]

According to *Encyclopaedia Britannica*, from 1900 onwards the thriving rice industry benefited only the French, the Chinese wholesale merchants and a minority of Vietnamese, while the Vietnamese people at large became impoverished. In the Mekong Delta, the area of land devoted to rice cultivation quadrupled between 1880 and 1930, but during the same period the typical individual peasant's consumption of rice decreased, and without the substitution of other foods.[3]

Logo of the French brewery in Hanoi.

The first rice mill was established in 1869 in Chợ Lớn. By 1885 rice mills had become an important feature along the main canals of Saigon and Chợ Lớn, and the largest ones, such as the Rizerie à vapeur and the Rizerie Saigonaise, were owned by French companies such as Denis Frères. Smaller mills belonged to the Chinese and the Việt. This picture changed rapidly as the local Chinese were joined by their clan people from Hong Kong, Singapore and southern China. The Chinese soon took over from the French to become the top rice merchants in southern Vietnam.

Rice, however, was not the only product from which the French profited in Vietnam. Under the governorship of Paul Doumer (1897–1902), Paul Beau (1902–7), Albert Sarraut (1911–14 and 1917–19) and Alexandre Varenne (1925–8), large plantations were set up to grow other agricultural products, such as sugar cane and mulberry leaves (for silkworms), and industrial products for export, such as rubber (the biggest plantations of which belonged to the Michelin company). At the same time, many French monopolies were also set up, aiming at the local market, such as the alcohol producer Fontaine.[4] Such alcohol factories produced rice wine for the locals, while the French government issued a decree stipulating that each village would have to meet a quota of consumption. Beer manufacturers soon set up in Vietnam, and names such as Larue and 33 became familiar to the Việt throughout the French century and beyond.

OPIUM

As well as alcohol, the Vietnamese were also encouraged to consume more and more of another agricultural product that was imported into Vietnam and manufactured into a deadly, addictive drug controlled by the French authorities. During the French century, opium was a state-sponsored product that was grown and processed on an industrial scale. Those who could afford it could buy their own opium-smoking set, comprising a pipe, a knife with which to scrape the substance off its container to form a tiny pea, a spirit lamp and needles to cook the opium pea over the lamp and to insert the smoking pea into the pipe. These opium sets gradually became more elaborate, with intricate designs, and later became prized possessions for many French and Vietnamese collectors.

Those who could not afford a set, or who wished to hide their addiction from their families, went to opium dens. In these large rooms set up like dormitories with bare wooden beds and attendants, the smoker lay down and was served a pipe or two by an attendant. He or she then fell into a short sleep and woke up feeling calm and contented, without any side effects such as a hangover.[5] This may be why opium became addictive so quickly and so easily. Eventually, as with all addictive drugs, the addicts lost interest in everything except the drug, and financial ruin was inevitable, not to mention other high costs.

In the early nineteenth century, before it became a state-sponsored drug in Vietnam, opium was the cause of a bitter war between the British and the Chinese, which China lost. From Vietnam, the Nguyễn emperors viewed the situation with alarm and officially banned opium. However, during the early years of the French century, opium was introduced into Vietnam by the Chinese and sold privately in opium dens under licence. The Chinese were at first given licences to farm poppies for opium extraction, but in 1881 the French governor Charles Le Myre de Villers decided to place opium under direct governmental control, making it a French monopoly, as alcohol was. The reason for this, he said, was that he believed the farms owned by the Chinese could become a threat to the security of the territory and a challenge to French interests. A manufacturing plant was established in Saigon that year, accompanied by many distributors. The opium business grew enormously at the beginning of the twentieth century when the five current opium agencies of Indochina were grouped into a monopoly under Doumer. Official opium was still available in large quantities in Saigon even after the signing of the Convention of La Haye in January 1912, which made opium trafficking illegal, except for medicinal purposes. For most of the French century, opium was an important source of income for the colonial authorities, and the cause of misery among many generations of Vietnamese. Following the departure of the French from Vietnam in 1954, campaigns to eradicate the opium poppy were launched in earnest, opium dens and manufacturers were closed, opium smokers were driven underground and the habit eventually petered out.

SEVEN

Food at War

Throughout the history of the world, food has often been a deciding factor in the outcome of battles or even wars, and Vietnam is no exception. The lack of food during the three Mongol invasions in the late thirteenth century is one example. Not finding enough supplies for their army in the small state of Đại Việt, in today's northern Vietnam, the Mongols sent for food from Yuan China. When two consecutive fleets carrying their supplies were sunk in Hạ Long Bay, the Mongols were forced to withdraw. The founder of the Nguyễn dynasty (1802–1945), Nguyễn Ánh (Emperor Gia-Long), and his army suffered similar periods of extreme hunger during the late eighteenth century, while fighting their rivals. Later, after establishing military plantations in the Mekong Delta to grow enough rice to eat, they were able to gain military victory.

Just as the lack of food seriously affects the well-being of an army, so plentiful food boosts morale. For example, in 1788, in the middle of a war against an invading army from Qing China, the then king of northern Vietnam, Quang Trung Nguyễn Huệ, ordered his troops to celebrate the feast of Lunar New Year (Tết) in advance, so that they could launch an attack on the Qing forces during their own Chinese New Year celebrations. With the feast satisfactorily out of the way, the Việt troops proceeded with their attack and won the war, chasing the Qing army out of the country.

More recently, the ripple effect of the Second World War devastated food supplies in Vietnam between 1940 and 1945, causing at least a million people to die of starvation in northern Vietnam. The famine was called the Great Famine of 1945, but its root causes began years before, and not even in Vietnam.

THE GREAT FAMINE OF 1945

During the years immediately before the Second World War, the world was struggling with the effects of the Great Depression. Most Western countries were obliged to modify their economic policies to cope with the harsh new reality. France chose to change its policy in colonial Indochina by switching from growing rice and other food crops to producing more profitable industrial cash plants such as cotton, jute, hemp and vegetable oil, leaving less rice for the population to eat. At the same time, natural disasters struck, with drought and flood bringing more misery to many parts of the country, particularly the north. By the time the war reached Vietnam, with the arrival of Japanese troops in 1940, France had been greatly weakened by its defeat in Europe. The administration of Vietnam and Indochina was passed on to a Vichy-controlled local government led by Admiral Jean Decoux. It would not be long before Decoux effectively ceded control of Vietnam to Japan, under an agreement for cooperation against China. One part of this agreement was that the French would supply Japan with rice, rubber and other materials. To fulfil this promise, the French authorities imposed a policy of enforced buying of rice from the farmers.

Vietnam was now squeezed by two authorities, both of which wanted to exploit the land for themselves. According to official statistics for 1940–45 published by the French Ministry for the Economy, production of rice in north Vietnam decreased steadily during this period, from 190 kg (419 lb) per head in 1941–2 to 184 kg (406 lb) in 1943 and 175 kg (386 lb) the following year.[1] The more industrial crops were grown, the less food acreage was left for the Việt people, resulting in a severe shortage of rice in northern Vietnam. Even then, farmers still had to fulfil their quota of selling part of the rice they grew to the authorities at a low price.

In northern Vietnam, where food was already scarce, peasants were required to supply 130,305 tonnes to the state in 1943, and 186,130 tonnes in 1944. Bad weather hit the north of the country in 1944 and destroyed the harvest. The Allies, meanwhile, constantly bombed Japanese positions in Vietnam. Bridges were destroyed and civilian transport became a low priority compared to military use. It was impossible to transport rice and other foodstuffs from the more fertile Mekong Delta into the north. For a people who ate rice as their main food for every meal, rice became a rare commodity and the cost soared to impossible levels. The inevitable result was widespread hunger for northerners and, to a lesser extent, people from

'The Admiral says France is committed to peace, just like the peasants being committed
to their fields.' French propaganda during the Japanese occupation, 1942.

central Vietnam. Going to market became an ordeal, a race past hordes of
hungry people waiting in ambush at every corner. Even when they were
armed with stout sticks, market-goers often succumbed to the raw force
of desperately hungry people.

One of the factors cited in official records is that only the poor suffered
because of the way Vietnamese society was constructed, and the rich

survived because they could afford to buy rice. The fact is, however, that for most of the famine, even wealthy families resorted to having one meal of rice gruel a day; the rest of the time they either went without or substituted root vegetables or corn for rice.[2] To make the famine even worse, the winter of 1944–5 was bitterly cold in northern Vietnam. In some villages, up to 40 per cent of the people died from the combination of hunger and wintry weather. In Hanoi, hundreds of thousands of malnourished and poorly clad people fell and died on the streets, and every morning student volunteers went around collecting bodies by the cartload. It was the worst famine in Vietnamese memory. The number of people who starved to death in 1944–5 has been recorded as two million, although the figure has been questioned and is generally considered to be an exaggeration. Whether the number of deaths was in the hundreds of thousands or the millions, there is no doubt that a huge number of Vietnamese people died as a direct result of being without food during the war in the Pacific.

After the defeat of the Japanese in August 1945, the famine in Vietnam continued, made worse by typhoons and floods in the same month. Another harvest was destroyed, and more starvation followed. The arrival of 152,000 Nationalist Chinese troops in northern Vietnam to disarm the Japanese made the matter worse, since it meant more mouths to feed in an already desperate situation. Matters improved only when rice was allowed

Vō An Ninh, photograph of a group of people breaking into a Japanese rice depot in 1945 during the worst famine in Vietnamese living memory.

to be transported from the south of Vietnam to the north and centre. Relief efforts that began during the peak of the famine, March–April 1945, now began to bear fruit. Junks carrying much-needed rice began to arrive from the south, and the worst of the crisis was over.

Many analysts believe that the aftermath of the famine helped to increase the popularity of the Việt-Minh, the alliance created between Nationalists and Communists under the leadership of Ho Chi Minh to fight colonial rule. The alliance took power when Japan's surrender left a political vacuum and it was the only political and military force strong enough to do so at that time. Along with a shattered infrastructure, they inherited the aftermath of the Great Famine of 1945. The Việt-Minh government immediately launched the Campaign Against Famine, and made that central to all its post-war activities. With rice from the south and also that seized from French and Japanese rice depots in the north, the famine was gradually reduced to just malnutrition and then 'insufficient food', which lingered as an endemic feature of the following years and, intermittently, decades.

Japanese prisoners of war growing vegetables at their camp in Vũng Tàu, south Vietnam, 1945.

Vietnam's post-war independence was short-lived, since it was not recognized by the Allies. When the British 20th Indian Division under General Douglas Gracey arrived in Vietnam in September 1945, their mission was to protect the population, both local and colonial, and to restore the 'ruling rights' of the pre-Japanese period, namely the French government in Vietnam.[3] Confusion, chaos and violence ensued as all parties fought for control of the country. By the time order was restored, the French had returned and the Việt-Minh retreated to rural areas to continue its anti-colonial activities for another seven years, until the French were defeated at the battle of Điện Biên Phủ and the war ended temporarily with the Geneva Accord of 1954. By then the French occupation of Vietnam had lasted close to a hundred years.

The seven years of renewed anti-colonial war, from the end of 1946, were particularly hard for northerners, who had just emerged from the worst famine in modern Vietnamese history. Tens of thousands of city-dwellers left for rural areas to continue their struggle against the colonists and to avoid the fighting in urban areas. In the liberated zones, soldiers and civilians shared a makeshift existence in utter poverty. Despite the efforts of local leaders, life was desperately hard for both evacuees and villagers, who had to share their homes and meagre rations with the newcomers. Rice, or the lack of it, was once again a serious problem. Older people were weakened by hunger and babies were short of nourishment and medicines. As the conflict over food increased in intensity, city people began to return to their homes.

MORE LAND FOR RICE

Whether the departure of the city-dwellers reduced the demand for rice in the countryside or not, the pace of the anti-colonial war had increased by the early 1950s. All this happened against the background of a return to a land-reform programme initiated in rural areas of northern Vietnam by the Việt-Minh decades earlier, whereby rents were reduced for landless peasants and land was seized from landowners (both colonial and Vietnamese collaborators) and distributed to the peasants to encourage the production of rice. The programme proved popular among the peasants, who enthusiastically threw their support behind the resisters, but was disastrous for wealthier landowners.

From its moderate start in the late 1940s, the land-reform programme in the north accelerated in 1952. It subsequently became an ideological

Refugees boarding USS *Montague* at Hải Phòng to move south, post-Geneva Accord, 1954.

class struggle that resulted in the deaths of tens of thousands of people who were denounced as 'wicked landlords' regardless of their political affiliation. They were either executed after being swiftly tried in a village court, or killed by lynch mob. Ruthless as it was, though, the programme mobilized the peasants to such an extent that they themselves made a serious contribution to the outcome of Điện Biên Phủ, the endgame of the anti-French war in 1954. Without the food and other supplies carried by the peasants to the battlefields, the soldiers would not have had enough to eat to continue fighting.

Rice, as ever, remained the central problem for the Việt following the Great Famine of 1945, not just in terms of quantity or quality, but also the method of cooking it while at war. During the French century, despite the calm and prosperous appearance of the cities, Vietnam was constantly at war in the countryside. Resistance groups were formed as soon as the French military took over in the south of the country in 1859, and they continued to operate in large and small pockets of land all over Vietnam until partition in 1954. These forces of resistance were a thorn in the side of the French authorities, who in retaliation launched constant raids deep into rural areas and highland jungles to try to eliminate these groups. Such raids were often successful because, knowing that the Việt preferred to eat warm rice for their meals, the French military looked out

The Smokeless Cooking System

The system started with a rectangular hole measuring roughly 1.5 × 1.2 m (5 × 4 ft) dug nearly 1 m (3 ft) into the ground, or into the side of a hill. The cook would squat in a hole opposite, facing a stove fuelled by charcoal or wood. A simple roof of bamboo or banana leaves covered the holes to keep out the rain. From the cooking hole, two tunnels branched out to lead the smoke away from the stove, to gather in large underground chambers some distance away. From each of these chambers, two trenches led the smoke further away. The trenches were covered by tree branches and a thin layer of soil. The soil was kept moist to help the smoke to turn into steam and evaporate just above ground level, leaving no trace in the air.

This original design worked to some extent, but the resisters would still be detected and raided occasionally. A system of deeper holes and tunnels was soon developed that resembled the shape of a cuttlefish with a fat body and many tentacles. The system was now up to 1.8 m (6 ft) deep, nearly twice the depth of the original design. It was later enlarged to incorporate areas for storing food and fuel, helping to keep the wood dry and therefore causing it to give out less smoke when lit. This system became the model for the much more elaborate networks of tunnels that were used during Điện Biên Phủ and subsequent battles.

for the tell-tale sign of cooking smoke rising into the air to pinpoint the location of the resisters. Soldiers in aircraft could detect the smoke easily; they then bombed their targets or alerted the ground forces to come and attack. The Vietnamese resistance suffered heavy casualties as a result.

The situation was very difficult to rectify, mainly because of the inability or unwillingness of the Việt to eat cold food. Over the centuries, if not millennia, it had become ingrained in the Vietnamese psyche that no matter what, a meal must be hot and served with rice to be healthy and fulfilling. Without such meals the morale of the troops would soon collapse and their fighting spirit would be eroded. The problem was exacerbated in the north of Vietnam and high in the mountains as the weather became cold in winter, making hot water and hot food necessary for survival. After several incidents of being caught out while cooking, and many periods of going without hot meals, the resisters tried cooking by night to avoid detection. The fire could still be seen, but sometimes it worked – however, the rice would still be cold for the daytime meals.

In 1951 the head cook of a unit operating in Hòa Bình in northern Vietnam invented an elaborate system of trenches, dugouts and tunnels by which the cooking smoke was led away from the stoves and released far away. For the first time it was possible to cook hot food during the day without detection. The so-called Hoàng Cầm cooking system (named after its inventor) became so successful that it played an important part in the decisive battle of Điện Biên Phủ in 1954, after which the French military surrendered.

FOOD PROBLEMS AFTER 1954

Following the French defeat at Điện Biên Phủ, an agreement was signed at Geneva, under international supervision, to end the war officially and set out terms for the political future of Vietnam. The Geneva Accord of 1954 split Vietnam into two parts at the seventeenth parallel: the pro-Chinese communist north and the pro-American south. Given a choice of political systems, as many as a million Việt people moved south or north to start new lives, with the greater number heading south. The displacement of such a large number of people placed a strain on the resources of both regions, and necessitated drastic measures to keep the population fed.

In the north of the country, the land-reform programme continued to become a 'core objective in the efforts to consolidate peace for the

Dam construction work in north Vietnam, 1950s–'60s.

north'.[4] In addition, a system of state monopoly was applied to all basic food supplies, beginning in the late 1950s. Rice and all other types of food would be sold through the state Agricultural Co-operative system. This did not go down well with the farmers, and it became a cause of resentment in the years to come. Traditionally, the Red River delta has been prone to bad weather and adequate harvests have never been guaranteed. In bad years, the policy of state collectivization put greater strain on the peasants and, in some cases, caused acts of civil disobedience. Even so, by 1965 about 90 per cent of peasant households had been organized into the co-op system.

S-2-63

IRS/AF
Memorandum
February 18, 1963

North Viet-Nam's Agricultural Failures Create Serious Food Problem

North Viet-Nam's failure to achieve any significant advances in agricultural production over the past three years -- in the face of its rapidly expanding population -- has created serious food problems which Hanoi obviously views with concern. Figures released by the DRV in late December and early January indicated clearly that the DRV's agriculture fell behind both planned norms and the population growth in North Viet-Nam. While the DRV claimed that the gross value of agricultural production in 1962 increased 4.3 percent (as against 8.9 percent in 1961), the increase in the amount of food available to the population was considerably less.

The Viet-Nam News Agency (VNA), for example, reported that the total production of paddy rice for 1962 was 5,600,000 metric tons; only 70,000 more than last year, a percentage increase of about 1.2 percent. This increase is slight compared to the DRV's population growth of 2-3 percent a year.

Recent Hanoi birth control pleas through the media have reflected the DRV food problem. On January 10, 1963, the daily Thoi Moi called for greater efforts in birth control during 1963, and made it clear that some efforts had already been exerted in this direction. The article referred to talks by medical cadres on methods for preventing conception, "experimental units" where birth control has been carried out, and courses conducted by labor unions. It then argued against the largeness of the family by stressing the plight of young widows with several children, numerous work hours lost because of children's illnesses or confinements, and the general burden of maintaining a large family. It failed, naturally, to mention the primary reason for the increased interest in birth control -- the disproportionate increase of population over agricultural production.

In the same vein, the Communist party organ Nhan Dan admitted a year ago that even if the rice target of the five year plan were met, the DRV could not produce enough rice to meet the needs of its rising population. Then, on January 21, 1963, this same paper again stressed DRV concern over the expanding population and revealed that measures taken to date were inadequate. It noted:

> In five years of agricultural development, 1961-1965, the North will, it is planned, clear 550,000 additional hectares of land. Because of our rapid increase in population -- it is estimated that the northern population will reach 19 million persons by the end of 1965 -- we will be able to maintain the 1961 average per capita acreage only if we achieve the above norm of land clearance.

1.

A page of the U.S. assessment of north Vietnamese agricultural problems in 1963.

A multi-tier food-stamp system was also established. Each productive worker on a farm or in light industry would be allowed to buy from the state store 13.5 kg (30 lb) of rice per month. Secondary individuals, those who worked in very light jobs, would be allowed 12 kg (26½ lb) per month. The elderly and those aged under fifteen would have a stamp worth 9 kg (20 lb) per month. Harder jobs qualified for an increased ration, with the highest awarded to mine workers at 18 kg (40 lb) and soldiers at 21 kg (46 lb) per month. Meat and fish rations were on average 200 g (½ lb) per person per month. Party and state officials, on the other hand, were exempt from the rationing system altogether. The shortage of food became serious in 1961 after a bad harvest caused by poor weather. Citizens of the north were again on the edge of famine, but somehow the country pulled through after the next year brought a better harvest.

Land reform was also a problem after 1954 in the south, where officials settled northerners carelessly among southerners, who resented having to share their land and resources with the newcomers. After a century of being kept separated under the French administrative system, northerners and southerners saw each other as aliens, as not of the same Việt race. By 1959 the land-reform programme had come to a standstill in the Mekong Delta and the central highlands of southern Vietnam. However, the problem of food was eased for southerners by the Western food aid that poured into the region in 1954–6.

The Crucial Role of MSG

In the north of Vietnam, the meagre rations made it necessary for the population to do everything they could to stretch their food further and make it palatable. For this they resorted to the chemical flavour enhancer monosodium glutamate (MSG), which became a sought-after commodity.

Simply speaking, MSG comes in the form of a white powder or tiny crystal-like flakes and contains glutamic acid, a natural chemical extract that can intensify a savoury flavour and add sweetness to a dish. It was invented by a Japanese biochemist, Professor Kidunae Ikeda, in Tokyo during the first decade of the twentieth century. By solidifying the juice of the Japanese seaweed *kombu* and stabilizing it with salt, fermented molasses or wheat, he produced a substance similar to salt or refined sugar that could be added in tiny quantity to any savoury food to obtain instant tastiness. A pinch of this powder can transform a plain bowl of broth into a wonderfully rich-tasting soup.

It is not known exactly when MSG was imported into Vietnam, or by whom (French, Chinese or Japanese merchants), but that must have happened soon after it became widely available, at the beginning of the twentieth century. It was first known as Vetsin after its Chinese trade name, and was welcomed into the cuisine, quickly becoming a required additive for all Vietnamese savoury dishes, from broth to vegetables to mixed *nước mắm*.

Over the years MSG has become crucial to Vietnamese food, being added to every pot whether it needs it or not. For the poor, it was a magic potion to add to poor food at a fraction of the cost of meat or fish. In many cases, MSG became a substitute for a meat or fish stock; for example, a bowl of water that had been used to boil vegetables could be made into a tasty soup by being seasoned with MSG and fish sauce. During the war years in north Vietnam, from being a flavour enhancer, MSG became a flavour replacement for the non-existent meat or fish. Over time it was elevated to the rank of luxury commodity, and its price soared. Even then, the price of a spoonful of MSG was still lower than that of a portion of meat or fish, and it was more readily available. The dependence on MSG is a defining feature of northern cuisine throughout the wars of 1945–75 and beyond.

Southerners also liked to add MSG to their food during this period, but they did not depend on it so much, perhaps because in the fertile Mekong Delta there was no problem with food supplies until war broke out again in 1959. Rice and other food then became difficult to transport through battle zones, but the average rice intake in the south was still around 20 kg (44 lb) per person per month, and plenty of fish and agricultural products were available all year around.

THE AMERICAN DECADES IN SOUTHERN VIETNAM (1954–75)

Paradoxically, while northerners grappled with the scarcity of food, southerners were exposed to food problems of a completely different kind. During the period immediately after the Geneva Accord, those living in south Vietnam were introduced to new types of food from abroad: American-style canned meat and fish, cheese in slabs and American long-grain rice, all of which they greeted with disdain.

Having been used to French cooking and French tinned products for a century, the southern Việt could not get used to the taste of American food, however cheap and readily available it was. For those who would accept the new food, a new type of home cooking was developed to modify the taste of the alien tinned products. For example, American canned roast chicken would be doused in *nước mắm* and dry-fried to become Vietnamese-style chicken floss, eaten with rice. While the old French cans of beef bourguignon, cassoulet or even plain cannellini beans had been treasured as a treat for all, the new tins of baked beans and frankfurters were viewed with horror by adults but welcomed by children, who liked the sweet taste of the beans particularly. Cheese in big slabs was a no-no, and peanut butter was a baffling idea. Coca-Cola and chocolate, on the other hand, were instant successes.

From 1963, as the United States became more involved in the war in Vietnam, American food of all descriptions flooded the markets of south Vietnam, through imports, food aid and a black-market system that brought American goods out of their Post Exchanges (PXS) and into Vietnamese hands. The vast system of American PXs consisted of a string of warehouse supermarkets that sold everything an American might need, more cheaply than in the United States itself. They were set up in cities and larger American bases for the exclusive convenience of Americans abroad. The currency used in the PXs in Vietnam was not the local Vietnamese dong nor the American dollar, but a set of notes called Military Payment Certificates, designed to stamp out black-market abuse. However, through

$1 worth of MPCs, 1960s.

Street scene, Saigon, 1966.

Vietnamese–American friendship or shady commercial arrangements, PX goods – from stereo sets to cans of meat, fruit, biscuits, Coca-Cola and alcoholic drinks – were regularly brought out to be resold in Vietnamese street markets.

SOUTHERN FOOD SUBSIDY

In the cities of south Vietnam, following the example of these PX warehouses, the Vietnamese government initiated a subsidized food system for government officials, soldiers and their families, whereby staple foods such as rice, sugar and condensed milk were sold at lower prices than on the open market. It worked for the most part, but once in a while the system suffered surprise hiccups, such as in the late 1960s when frozen meat was introduced into the subsidized stock.

Traditionally, the Việt bought their fresh meat in small quantities, perhaps 100–200-g (3–7-oz) portions, to use immediately. Now, at the state supply stores, massive slabs of frozen pork and whole frozen chickens became available at low prices. The idea was welcomed by all, but the reality was mind-boggling for many cooks, who had never seen such huge rock-hard pieces of meat and did not know what to do with them. Some tried to chop and crack them into smaller pieces, the way they would crack ice, but a few trial sessions later, the brave cooks were defeated. The dishes they cooked turned out to be a disaster because the meat was not defrosted properly and tasted awful. Later on, even after the majority of housewives had learned to thaw the meat properly first, the taste of the imported chicken was considered bland or fishy because the birds would have been fed with industrial feed, much of which contained fishmeal. These chickens were a far cry from the free-range hens with which most Vietnamese had been familiar. Similarly, cheap powdered egg was ignored by most.

In general, except for drinks, sweets, biscuits and chocolate, southerners did not welcome American food or find it as acceptable as their French counterparts – which were still available (though expensive) at French stores – even at giveaway prices. American national foods such as the hamburger and the hot dog never took off there, and instant coffee was viewed with curiosity but used only as a fashion statement among the young, similar to Lipton tea bags. The soft white sliced bread for making Western-style sandwiches was tolerated as modern and fashionable; it was available at expensive patisseries and sandwich shops for a small clientele, but did not become widely popular the way the crunchy French baguettes had. Meanwhile, Laughing Cow, Gruyère, mocha coffee beans and Beurre Bretel continued to be the preferred products for the Vietnamese middle class, while Vietnamese fresh food, however meagre, was favoured in both the city and the countryside.

French food, drink and restaurants in the south of Vietnam, on the other hand, took off spectacularly during the American decade, when the region was flooded with U.S. military and civilian personnel, international diplomats, aid workers and thousands upon thousands of international journalists, who flocked to the country to cover the war. They could not believe their luck at finding French beer, wine, cheese and, above all, hundreds of good French restaurants on their doorstep, all at relatively low prices thanks to the preferential exchange rates and the thriving black market in dollars.

CIVILIAN FOOD PROBLEMS, 1959–75

After only five years of relative calm while the north and south of Vietnam wrestled with their respective troubles, from political problems to security and economic concerns, in 1959 the prospect of war loomed large, following the decision of the Communist Party in north Vietnam to 'carry out the revolution by violence, combining the political struggle with an armed struggle to overthrow the Southern administration'.[5] The decision was said to be a response to the failure to hold a referendum planned for 1956 in the Geneva Accord to determine the political future of Vietnam, and to an increased American presence in the south. A guerrilla war ensued in the south of the country, and gradually turned into a full-scale war that drew in the United States, its allies, the Soviet Union and China. The conflict came to a conclusion only in April 1975, when north Vietnam took over the south. The country was officially reunified the following year.

During the renewed war years, food was again a thorny problem for northerners, who were already subject to rationing. The centralized economy, in place since 1955, restricted both the production of food and consumers' preferences. The co-op system took away the incentive for farmers to work harder, and as a result food production decreased while the rural areas remained poor. The low rate of food production, in turn, caused a generally low standard of living, and food became the main preoccupation of the population at large, whatever the quality of the food available.

The heavy bombing and blockades of northern Vietnamese ports in the late 1960s and early 1970s did not help. Food was severely curtailed throughout the north, where queues to buy rations formed in the early morning and ran around the block, sometimes for the food-stamp holder to buy just a marrow or a few kilograms of rice.[6] Even rice rations for prisoners of war were resented by the population at large, and the amount granted was eventually reduced to appease both the military and the people. By the end of the war, according to Vietnamese statistics, the bombing of northern Vietnam had destroyed 10 million ha (25 million acres) of farmland and 5 million ha (12.5 million acres) of forest, and had killed 1.5 million cattle.

For the southerners, food was at first not so hard to find, particularly in the cities and towns. As the war progressed, however, food production was severely disrupted in the countryside, where – typically of guerrilla warfare – there were no clear front lines. Crops could be damaged or destroyed at any time, anywhere throughout the Mekong Delta and the highlands. However, in a region known for its abundance, food might have been a serious problem for many but starvation was unheard of. Continued fighting in the countryside later turned the south of Vietnam, once a fertile region with surplus rice for export, into a rice importer. Other foodstuffs were also imported at preferential exchange rates. The cities were better off than the countryside, with plenty of subsidized foods, as well as supplies from the countryside whenever possible and the ever-present black market, which was often saturated with illegal PX goods ignored by the authorities.

MILITARY RATIONS

The picture was very different for the fighting forces of both Vietnamese sides. For these traditional rice-eaters, no matter how heavy it was to carry around and how hard to cook in combat, rice continued to be the central part of the diet on the battlefields. When going out to fight, Vietnamese soldiers of all sides carried several kilograms of rice grains or dried cooked rice as part of their military kits, which they supplemented with tinned or dried rations or whatever they could obtain locally, such as meat, vegetables and fish.

According to a memoir by a member of the National Liberation Front, the ration for each communist soldier was 20 kg (44 lb) of rice per month, a chunk of salt, a portion of MSG and perhaps a piece of dried fish or meat.[7] Although fresh fruit and vegetables were abundant in the Vietnamese countryside, it was much more difficult to find them in bombed-out areas, abandoned orchards and fields, especially along the Ho Chi Minh Trail, the north Vietnamese military's main supply route, which ran through mountains and jungles in the west of the country and over the border in Laos and Cambodia. Sesame seeds and salt with rice seemed to be a regular meal for the north Vietnamese soldier on the move. A fish caught along the way would be heavily salted to last longer, and much treasured.[8] North Vietnamese soldiers were well-known for being able to live off the land. Wild vegetables played an important part in their diet throughout the war, with the versatile and ubiquitous bamboo shoot being valued most highly.

Rice was also the main staple carried by the southern Army of the Republic of Vietnam (ARVN) in the field. In general, the daily ration for each ARVN soldier was 800 g (1¾ lb) of dehydrated rice, a can of meat or fish, and a package containing salt, pepper and sweets. However, red tape and logistical problems often prevented the rations from reaching the soldiers. Poor nutrition for ARVN soldiers in the field was a serious problem, according to a report by the Military Assistance Command in Vietnam (MACV), the American control centre for war activities in the 1960s and early 1970s.[9]

Even when the distribution machinery was running well, the system was inefficient, making it impossible to supply all units in the field evenly. Rations that were inadequate both in terms of quality and quantity forced the ARVN soldiers to search for food. According to a report of December 1967 by the MACV, many ARVN soldiers supplemented their Vietnamese rations with U.S. rations, not by official policy, of course, but in the field as need dictated. That helped to bond Vietnamese and U.S. combat units, and made it unnecessary for the ARVN to venture into local markets to seek food, therefore denying the opposition intelligence about their movements, strength and so on.[10] What was considered tasty and nourishing for an American soldier, however, was not necessarily suitable for the Vietnamese, for the same reason that Vietnamese civilians shunned American food. For many Vietnamese, even a bowl of thin vegetable soup, Vietnamese-style, would have been preferred to a nourishing can of meat of alien taste. For example, on a Vietnamese combat ship, a bowl of thin vegetable soup, a few pieces of meat and vegetables were often served at the captain's table. It was a meagre meal by any definition, and yet it was what the Vietnamese soldiers could afford and would prefer to eat. For the same reason, ARVN soldiers in the field often sought out the local fresh produce bought by their supply officer to supplement or replace their rations. The USA-made tinned food in the Vietnamese ration was often considered a last resort, since, to the Vietnamese, the food was neither fresh nor freshly cooked, and had unfamiliar flavours. Not only that, the cost of their tasteless canned food ration was deducted from their meagre pay, so if they

American C-rations for an airman in combat, 1966–7. Every U.S. serviceman in Vietnam was issued with one of 12 prepared menus per meal. The food was designed to provide them with 1,200 calories per meal. Each C-ration has one can of meat, one can of bread or crackers with cheese or peanut butter, one can of dessert of fruit or cake, cigarettes, matches, a can opener, coffee and creamer, and a few sheets of toilet paper.

also bought fresh produce in the field, they would have paid twice for their food.

As the third combat party of the Vietnam war, the American force, which at its peak amounted to over half a million men, did not have the same problems with food as the Vietnamese of either side. In the field, American soldiers were issued with their own rations. Official documents describe three different types of ration, and twelve menus. Each menu comprised a can of meat, a can of fruit, bread or dessert or crackers and cheese/peanut butter, a packet of cigarettes, matches, chewing gum, toilet paper, coffee, dehydrated cream, sugar, salt and pepper. The rations were designed to provide 1,200 calories per meal, the total planned calories being 3,600 per person per day.

The problem worsened in the late 1960s, when the fish sauce in the military ration for south Vietnamese soldiers was replaced with soy sauce. This calamitous decision, made by a U.S. officer who believed fish sauce would spoil easily in the field, was a disaster for Vietnamese morale. The canned food made in the USA was alien enough for many south Vietnamese soldiers, but the replacement of the much-loved, traditional *nước mắm* with soy sauce was the last straw.

Whatever individual problems they had with their food rations, during most of the USA–Vietnam war the need to eat hot rice was common to the Vietnamese opposing forces, and a difficult one to resolve. Vietnamese communist soldiers operating in the south again applied the smokeless cooking method that had been so successful during the anti-colonial war. It was a great help in moving troops and supplies along the Ho Chi Minh Trail during the 1960s and early 1970s. Although the trail was subjected to heavy bombing by B-52 planes, the movement of troops continued until the end of the war. The experience was repeated throughout the south of Vietnam with the much larger Cu Chi tunnel system, the best-known today.

FOOD AT PEACE, 1975–PRESENT

The rapid victory of the Democratic Republic of Vietnam in the south in 1975 turned into an economic nightmare for all Vietnamese. As the government tried to integrate the two completely different economic systems of north and south Vietnam, in its own assessment the country entered a decade of economic stagnation.[11] By 1975 more than 96 per cent of north Vietnamese peasant households belonged to the co-op system, and the model was soon applied to the south. In mid-1977 a voluntary collectivizing programme for the southern farmers met with strong resistance. It was changed to a brief period of forced collectivized agriculture by harsh measures, which turned out to be highly counterproductive. Agricultural production decreased sharply, and security became a problem in the countryside. Vietnam was quickly plunged into a severe economic crisis, and food shortages became a fact of life for most people for more than a decade.

Southern Vietnamese households now joined those in the north in following a food-rationing system, according to which each household was allowed to buy a small amount of low-quality rice, supplemented by corn, barley or oats, wheat flour and noodles, root vegetables, tofu and sugar. A meal with pure rice, without corn or barley or cassava mixed in, became a luxury for most.[12] Even then, queues for the essential items sold in the state-run shops were long. The low-grade wheat flour and noodles were not welcomed by rice-eating Việt families, until the Vietnamese and Chinese in the south found a way of dealing with their rations by exchanging the wheat products for rice. By the end of the 1970s a black market for rice and other products thrived in both north and south, and inflation continued to soar.

The causes of these food shortages were manifold. The post-war efforts at economic integration combined with poor food distribution, the abolition of private enterprise, bad management and severe weather made the decade 1975–85 a particularly hard time for all in Vietnam. Food production was low, and inflation went through the roof. Nevertheless, agricultural and other types of produce were still sold to state co-operatives at low prices, before being exported or resold at higher prices. The incentive to increase productivity was lost because of this. In 1985 the Vietnamese per capita income was U.S.$239 per year, making Vietnam the fifteenth poorest country in the world.[13] All but one (Bangladesh) of those below Vietnam were in Africa. In the same year, according to government records, a wage and allowance system was put into effect for state employees and the military, but that too failed to have an effect. By this time, although no one was starving, the average diet for the Việt was seriously deficient in protein and barely reached 1,940 calories per person per day, compared to the UN's recommended figure of 2,300. Some 25 per cent of all children suffered from malnutrition, according to analysis by the Vietnamese Institute of Nutrition. In 1986 the rationing system was reinstated, after having been stopped for only a few months, to control staples such as rice, sugar and meat. According to Vietnamese media, 80 per cent of a worker's monthly wage had to be spent on food, and even then the food went only as far a feeding their family for part of the month. By 1986, after two disastrous five-year plans, there was not enough rice to feed the people. The constant lack of food over the previous ten years was officially described as 'chronic hunger' among the population.[14]

The New Economic Zones

As part of its post-war plan, the Vietnamese government initiated a system of new economic zones for the south of the country. These were meant to encourage displaced people, the urban unemployed and so-called non-productive people (those who were not allowed to work or to enter higher education because of their connections with the former government of south Vietnam) to move to rural areas and cultivate the land. According to the plan, four million people were targeted for the move between 1976 to 1980, but by the end of the period only 1.5 million had moved to the new zones. New plans were formed to send up to ten million people out to the new economic zones by 1999, but in the end only a total of three million were resettled there. Conditions were harsh, and much of the land was infested with a host of tropical diseases. Many people died from hardship or disease, and others found their way back to the city.

For southerners, the economic zones became a dreaded punishment for those who did not conform. The harsh conditions, chronic hunger and threat of being sent to these zones gave rise to a new type of refugee in the late 1970s and 1980s. These so-called boat people fled both north and south Vietnam in flimsy vessels to reach neighbouring countries, in the hope of settling elsewhere or of joining their relatives who had fled to the West at the end of the war, in 1975. Some 204,600 Vietnamese boat people arrived in other Southeast Asian countries in 1979 alone, but their true numbers will never be known, for many perished on the way.[15]

The Soviet Union Decades, 1975–89

As post-war Vietnam became an economic nightmare for all, its former military ally, the Soviet Union, entered its culinary scene. As the Americans had a decade earlier in southern Vietnam, but in smaller numbers, officials, business people and visitors from the Soviet Union came to Vietnam during the late 1970s and the 1980s, bringing with them Russian bread, sour cream and other hitherto unfamiliar foods. Vietnamese food markets and restaurants began to cater for their culinary tastes. Russian black bread became available in the markets, while the crunchy baguette became scarce and was now made with low-quality flour, to the dismay of ordinary people. However, the lack or shortage of good baguettes was just part of the harsh new reality of austerity and chronic hunger. In the end Russian food was too expensive for most, and its texture too dense for the tropics, so despite being available it never took off among the general public.

In 1987 the new Vietnamese leadership announced a plan that would give greater incentive to the private sector. It turned out to be the miracle drug for the ailing Vietnamese economy, since it finally offered an opportunity for farmers to reap the benefit of their labour for themselves, not the hateful co-ops. The existing black market was legalized. Food production increased dramatically almost overnight, and by the early 1990s Vietnam was well on the way to food sufficiency. The new economic policy was launched just in time for the collapse of the Soviet Union in 1989. Facing open competition in the free world market was a new experience for both, as the rouble floundered. As the international socialist umbrella folded, personnel and visitors from the Soviet Union began to leave Vietnam, taking with them their demand for Russian food, and the Vietnamese market quickly forgot its decade of Soviet cuisine. Only a few tiny corner shops specializing in Russian food survived to cater to a very small clientele.

FOOD TODAY

Strolling through the markets or visiting the paddy fields and orchards of Vietnam today, it is hard to imagine that this country was once fifteenth poorest in the world, that its people hovered on the edge of starvation and endured chronic hunger for decades on end. There is food and eating everywhere, at any time of day, in the markets, on the streets, at the roadside. Next to Vietnamese traditional food, new products from abroad are now on display in abundance. Restaurants and market stalls vie with one another to promote their specialities of *bún chả Hanoi* next to *bún bò Huế*, *hủ tíu Saigon*, won-ton soup, Japanese sushi or Thai steamboat. Starbucks, Kentucky Fried Chicken and Baskin-Robbins ice cream sit comfortably side by side on the city streets. Crunchy French baguettes are once more for sale everywhere. Even Russian food is available, if only in a few specialized shops catering for the diplomatic corps and for nostalgic Vietnamese who once studied in the Soviet Union.

Fried cake stall in Hanoi.

A new shopping phenomenon is beginning to take shape in towns and cities: the supermarket, where all kinds of product are grouped in one place for the convenience of shoppers. However, their products, whether imported or locally made, are more expensive and the food is less fresh than that of the traditional markets, so they cater only for a small minority of better-off city-dwellers.

Stationary *bánh mì* stall.

Chicken restaurant, Hanoi.

After centuries of fluctuation and divergence, the food of war and the food of peace have now converged to become Vietnamese modern food, appreciated not just by the Việt but also by many visitors to the country. This appreciation has led to some Vietnamese dishes, such as *phở*, being brought out of Vietnam and contributing to the culinary diversity of the world's most cosmopolitan cities. Among the Vietnamese foods popular in the West, filled *bánh mì* seem to be favoured the most, to the extent that *bánh mì* takeaway shops have become a familiar feature of some high streets among the earlier arrivals, the Chinese, the Japanese, the Thai and, most recently, the Korean.

EIGHT

From Traditional to Modern Vietnamese Food

It is impossible to pinpoint a date of origin for many of the Vietnamese dishes we know today. With some exceptions, such as *bánh chưng* and *bánh dầy*, there are hardly any Vietnamese documents or any other type of record of the dishes. General illiteracy among the population until the early twentieth century made it difficult for cooks to write down their recipes, while the literati believed that writing about food was beneath them. Family recollection could refer only to 'some time ago', or say that a particular dish had 'been in the family for generations'.

Another reason for this vagueness is that food preparation was traditionally a family secret, taught by a mother to her daughters or by a mother-in-law to her son's new bride. Each family had a different way of preparing certain dishes, and that was a secret to be guarded. Restaurant or street food secrets were guarded even more closely. What the Vietnamese call 'traditional food' are the dishes that have been around for several generations and are still popular. The most traditional dishes are probably those eaten by a family for their daily meals.

A Family Meal

The key to Vietnamese food is freshness, to the extent that chicken was traditionally bought or caught live only minutes, or a couple of hours at most, before it was to be cooked. Prawns or fish would be sold swimming or jumping in their vats. In a hot and humid country like Vietnam, food goes off easily, and before the arrival of the refrigerator the only way to keep things fresh was to keep them alive. Until recently, the sight of someone chasing a squawking hen in the back garden was a familiar scene of Vietnamese life. 'Not being able to catch a hen' was even used as an excuse

Symbol of prosperity, Vietnamese traditional woodblock print.

to mask the host's poverty when a friend came to visit and was not invited to stay and eat.

Freshness does not apply just to chicken and seafood. One of the earliest recipe book, Van Dai's *Good Cook*, of the twentieth century even went so far as to advise the cook to 'go to the abattoir first thing in the morning to buy a piece of freshly killed pork for this dish.' The exception is when dried fish is used as a main ingredient in its own right. Even then, other fresh ingredients are added, for fresh vegetables and herbs are always on offer at the table for the diners to add to their bowls. For this reason, some Vietnamese dishes do not work with frozen ingredients, and cannot be cooked ahead of time. Every dish must be freshly cooked and put on the table straight away, except for braised dishes, dried pork floss or specialized *Banh Chung*. Some are even cooked at the table, despite the fact that cooking with live fire makes the meal a sweat-drenching experience. The requirement for freshness makes Vietnamese cuisine labour-intensive and hard on the cook, considering the Việt eat two hot meals a day.

The dishes vary from meal to meal and from region to region, but the format is the same: at every meal plain boiled rice, a bowl of stock with vegetables, a plate of something salty such as meat, fish or tofu, and a plate of vegetables are served. Condiments such as *nước mắm*, lime wedges, chopped chilli or fresh herbs are always present. A meal for richer families consists of many dishes, whereas for poorer families the dish of meat or fish may be

Live chickens for sale at Vũng Tàu market.

replaced by a bowl of *mắm* (fermented shrimp or fish paste) of some sort, and the stock might be the water used for boiling the vegetables. A small dish of pickled vegetables or fruit might be included with the meal as well.

The dishes are arranged on a large round tray, made from aluminium or bamboo for the poor and copper or silver for the rich. The pot or serving bowl of freshly cooked rice is put on one side, and one person is in charge of being 'mother'. The family sits around the tray and eats the meal quickly. It is very rare that any food is left, since it will only go off. In fact, there are leftovers only when the food is poorly cooked, and this is a calamity for the cook, since wasted food is frowned on in Vietnam.

Most Việt do not drink anything before or with their meals, since they say they cannot eat much rice with a bellyful of liquid, and will be hungry soon afterwards. Beverages such as hot tea are offered to the adults after a meal, with fruit as a dessert, while the children may have cold water with their fruit.

TABLE MANNERS

Whether at home or out, the way to eat Vietnamese food has not changed over the centuries. It is always with a pair of chopsticks and a spoon. Since Vietnamese food is cut into bite-sized pieces, the diner can use his or her own chopsticks to pick pieces of food from the communal plates. Serving spoons are available for the communal rice and soup, and smaller spoons are used for the communal bowl of *nước mắm* or for scooping up sauce. It is bad manners to put your chopsticks into the communal bowl of soup to pick out vegetables or pieces of meat or fish. It is normal for the diner to hold up their rice bowl and use their chopsticks to push rice into their mouths, but soup should be eaten with a spoon, not held up to the mouth and drunk (although that is perfectly acceptable in some other cultures). To eat a bowl of noodle soup, one hand holds the chopsticks and the other the spoon. The strands of noodles are picked up with the chopsticks and deposited on the spoon before being eaten with some soup. Biting on the pieces of food that are too large to eat in one go is also acceptable, as is gnawing on bones, such as spare ribs or chicken wings. It is all right in many families to put the bones on the table in front of you, although plates or bowls for bones may be provided in restaurants.

Except for very rich families who can afford help, the family cook is a designated female of the household, such as a wife, mother, daughter or, most likely, daughter-in-law. She goes to the market twice a day to buy fresh ingredients. Before kerosene and gas bottles became available, she would also have had to build a fire of wood or charcoal two or three times a day. It is no wonder that most Vietnamese dishes are cooked quickly, to save fuel and time, otherwise the family cook would spend the whole day in the kitchen, with no spare time for other household chores or to look after children or ageing parents.

The Việt do not usually cook or prepare breakfast at home, preferring to buy it at the morning market or by hailing a mobile vendor. A traditional and favourite breakfast is *xôi*, a glutinous rice sometimes cooked on its own and with other cooked ingredients added afterwards, such as Chinese sausage, chicken and Chinese mushrooms, or plain fried spring onion with dried shrimps. Most commonly, the rice is cooked with mung beans, soy, black or red beans, fresh peanuts or sweetcorn, and served with ground sesame seeds and salt, or sugar. In the south, coconut milk or coconut cream is added to the cooking process to give the *xôi* a richer flavour. Sometimes a sprinkling of shredded coconut is added to make it even richer. Breakfast *xôi* is sold by the street vendors in lumps the size of a fist, on a piece of banana leaf. It is cheap but filling enough to sustain the diner until lunch. Following the arrival of French bread, a length of baguette became equally popular, with or without fillings. Plain baguette can be dipped into a saucer of condensed milk, flavoured with a few drops of Maggi sauce or, more often, spread with a thin layer of butter. *Phở* and other types of noodle dish are also available, but are eaten for breakfast only on special occasions.

Breakfast foods are usually bought as a treat when the family cook goes to market to shop for the family lunch, a trip that can be made as early as 6 am in order to get the best ingredients available. To make the cook's life a little easier in her twice-daily search for fresh ingredients, street vendors, usually people from faraway farms or market gardens, bring their products to a street corner to form a mini pop-up market that lasts perhaps a couple of hours before everybody returns to where they came from. These mini twice-daily markets have been a feature of life in the ancient capital Thăng-Long (present-day Hanoi) since the eleventh century, and they have carried on through the centuries to become a fact of life all over Vietnam.

Every town or city has always had a number of pop-up markets all over town, to complement the main markets, where more products are available all day and all year around. Even today, in Hanoi, there are still many pop-up mini-markets in and near the centre. These markets appear first thing in the morning, along with breakfast vendors, and vanish at about 10 am, to reappear at about 4 pm for the afternoon shift. No matter how hard the authorities try to clear them up for reasons of hygiene and general order, they are always around. Ironically, many set up on a street corner where there is a sign saying 'no gathering for market', because it is hard to find and announce a new location. That brings about the rather comical situation whereby the whole mini-market vanishes instantly at the sight of a police officer, leaving the surprised shoppers holding bundles of vegetables or a flapping fish that they are in the middle of bargaining

Corner market, Hanoi, early 1960s.

Vietnamese pancake stall in Hanoi.

over. However, just as quickly as it vanishes, the market reappears once the police officer has turned their back, and trading activities happily resume.

Where there is food, there is eating, and this can be a bone of contention between the female head of the family and the designated shopper. Any market, be it a grand one or a mini street-corner one, has always attracted a number of sellers offering cheap and enticing snacks such as bowls of noodles, rolls of something delicious or pieces of cake. Market-going was therefore traditionally a great opportunity for the shopper to eat something nice by herself, away from the scrutiny of the female head of the household, who held the purse strings. It made a tiny dent in the family's daily food budget, but was a delightful guilty secret for the shopper, despite the fact that it would cause a big family row if it was found out.

The picture is different now. The consecutive wars of the twentieth century did not just affect Vietnamese food supplies and eating habits, but subverted the family hierarchy. New generations of Vietnamese women still assume the duty of cooking for the family, but when going to the market they no longer have to hide their guilty secret of snacking on the job. As in Europe and America during and after the Second World War, the war effort in both north and south Vietnam gave younger Việt women significant economic independence, away from the traditionally tight grip of the female head of the household, and they were subsequently able to have a say in the family budget, the household expenditure and, naturally, the snacking.

RICE COOKING

Rice, as ever, occupies a central position in Vietnamese cuisine. It is eaten at both lunch and dinner and plays a large part in the well-being of society. In the mid-nineteenth century its importance was immortalized on a giant bronze urn dedicated to the founder of the Nguyễn dynasty, Emperor Gia-Long. Plain boiled rice acts as a base for prepared dishes of meat, fish or vegetables, and as a measurement of a person's eating capacity. For example, a person who can eat three bowls of rice in a single meal is looked at with awe. Rice is also used to signify the quality of the meal. Sayings such as 'the food was so good, so-and-so ate an extra bowl of rice' are seen as a great compliment to the cook. Being the most important element of a traditional Vietnamese meal, rice must be cooked to perfection. The art of cooking rice was spelled out clearly in one of the first Vietnamese cookbooks, which was published in 1915 entirely in verse (see page 205).

Until the mid-twentieth century, cooking rice was an art that all female Vietnamese were obliged to master. The rice must be fluffy, and sometimes, if preferred, with a crust on the bottom. It sounds easier than it is, even with strict measuring, since each rice crop is different from the next, and the grains require more or less water according to the quality of the season. The traditional rice pot was usually made of cast iron, with a flat lid for even distribution of heat, but a clay pot was preferred in some

Rice stalks engraved on the royal symbolic urn of Emperor Gia-Long, imperial citadel, Huế.

> ### How to Cook Rice
>
> In ancient times we only had straw and grass.
> Now that we have rice, we must take care to cook
>   a good pot.
> First, wash the rice till it becomes opaque.
> Then, scrub the pot till it gleams white.
> Two fingers of water is sufficient, don't overdo it!
> Keep the fire up, don't let it go low.
> When the pot boils dry, turn it around for even
>   heat, keep lid on.
> Put pieces of charcoal on the lid, the rice will be
>   perfect when scooped out.
>
> Lady Trương Đăng Thị Bích,
> *Thực Phổ Bách Thiên* (*One Hundred Good Dishes*, 1915)

households for better flavour and consistency. The pot of rice would be cooked directly over the fire until all the water had been absorbed. At this stage, pieces of red-hot charcoal would be put on the flat lid, if the pot was a cast-iron one, to dry the rice all over. Rice that was too soft or too hard would earn the cook a black mark and shame that would endure for weeks. A good cook should be able to time the cooking so that all the other dishes are ready to serve at the same time as the rice. For royalty and the rich, rice was cooked in individual clay pots, but this type of preparation was a luxury that only the elite could afford.

Leftover rice is rare in the warm south, but in the north, where it is cooler or even cold in the winter, cooked rice from the evening before can make a good breakfast for farmers before they go out to work in the fields. They say it sits well in the stomach, unlike the much cheaper sweet potato, cassava and yam that are common for breakfast. Leftover boiled rice from lunch is sometimes fried with other ingredients, such as onion, garlic or egg, for a snack or meal. It is very rare for the Việt to eat other foods with fried rice, since the flavours clash.

Plain boiled rice is essential for every Vietnamese meal, but boiling is not the only way to cook rice. It can be made into porridge for the sick, the old and babies, or for anyone as an occasional change from the usual solid rice. For example, plain porridge can be eaten with pickled vegetables, dried fish, tofu or anything salty to give it flavour. The luxury version – served with chicken, duck, any kind of minced meat or offal – can be eaten for breakfast, or as an occasional meal in itself.

Cooked rice is sometimes made into a roll for sandwiches, usually for easy carrying on trips. It is not dainty, like a sushi roll, but a hefty sausage 6–10 cm (2–4 in.) in diameter. To make it, freshly boiled rice is tipped on to a piece of fabric, such as a tea towel, and rolled tightly into a large sausage. The rice must still be hot, otherwise the roll will fall apart. When cool, the rice roll can be cut into rounds about 2 cm (1 in.) thick. Slices of cold meat, such as pork or beef sausages, dried prawn or pork floss are put between the rice pieces to make a convenient sandwich. Since the rice is packed tightly, the slices keep their shape. The thick slices of packed rice may also be cut into cubes and dipped into something salty. The rice sausage does not go off as quickly as ordinary boiled rice, making it safe to take on a day trip. During and after the French century, baguette sticks could do the same job, but, as we have learned, for the Vietnamese a meal must include rice. Farmers like to carry smaller versions of this rice sausage filled with something salty, such as *mắm* or dried fish, for their midday meals, if the fields are too far away for them to return home for a hot lunch.

Sausage

One way for the Việt to preserve meat is to make it into sausages. Traditionally, pork was used for this, and beef from the mid-nineteenth century onwards, but today chicken and vegetarian versions also exist, although they are not as popular. Whatever the ingredients, there are two types of sausage: the boiled version, *giò*, and the fried version, *chả. Giò* tends to be sausage-shaped and wrapped in banana leaves, while *chả* is more often cooked as a patty the size of a saucer.

The method of production is the same for both types. Fresh meat is minced to a smooth, thick paste. Fish sauce, cornflour, pepper and a raising agent such as baking powder are added, and the paste is left to prove for several hours. For *giò*, the paste is remixed, similar to kneading a loose bread dough, then rolled into a large sausage and wrapped in banana leaves. If beef has been used, finely chopped fresh dill, garlic and more pepper are added before the wrapping stage. The rolls are cooked until firm in a large pot of boiling water. *Chả* is spread into a thick, round shape and shallow-fried, or pasted around a metal tube to be grilled until its skin turns golden. Spices such as cinnamon are sometimes rubbed into the skin to give it a distinctive

A roll of *giò* wrapped in banana leaves.

taste, or young green rice may be added to the paste itself. Both *giò* and *chả* are very popular throughout the country, since they can be kept for a day or so in a cool place and eaten without further cooking.

A FAMILY BANQUET

Traditionally, the Việt people do not give dinner parties for friends, as people do in the West, but they treat family gatherings seriously. They are usually held to celebrate a particular occasion, such as the birthday of an elderly family member, Lunar New Year, a wedding or funeral, or the anniversary of an ancestor's death. Wedding feasts in the cities tend to be held at Chinese

Offering to the celestial power during the Lunar New Year celebrations.

Vietnamese engagement feast.

Gấc fruit.

restaurants, but in villages and small towns they are held at home. A family feast, especially on the occasion of a death anniversary, may well be offered to friends as well, since there will be surplus food.

Before anybody can sit down to enjoy their meal, small portions of each dish are put on the altar as offerings to the ancestors. A traditional family feast requires at least eight dishes, since – as we have seen – that number is considered propitious. Four of the dishes are served on plates and four in bowls. A few plates of *xôi* (glutinous rice) are usually served as well. Unlike the *xôi* that is bought in for breakfast, ritual *xôi* is made at home, in a larger quantity, and offered to the family and guests as a starter with cold meat or as an accompaniment to the main meal. For weddings, *xôi* is dyed with the sweet, bright-red pulp of a vine fruit called *gấc*, which is the size of a melon and has a texture similar to the marrow, but softer. For a family gathering to commemorate the death of an ancestor, the *xôi* is usually served with mung beans.

The four plates vary from family to family, but they often contain cold meats such as *giò* and *chả*, cooked slices of *lap cheong*, bought roast meats (perhaps crispy pork or *char siu*), boiled chicken or duck and salted or century eggs. One of these dishes might be swapped for a house speciality more suitable for the men to eat with their aperitif of rice wine. Plates of salad or pickles are also offered. The four bowls contain substantial soups and braised dishes. They can be luxury food, such as shark's fin or abalone, braised stuffed pigeons, or braised pork leg with bamboo shoots, or, in the south, a curry. Boiled rice is a must, but does not count as a dish. A family feast can last for hours and is a noisy affair, in contrast with a normal family meal, when diners are expected not to speak with their mouths full. Family members sit with those of the same generation and share their own dishes, which are sometimes slightly different from those at the top table (which is reserved for the highest-ranking member of a family, a grandfather, grand-uncle or head of the family, such as the eldest man or boy who will carry the family name forward to future generations). It is important for the lady of the house to organize the seating carefully, for putting a senior member with a junior group can provoke a huge family row.

FOOD FOR THE DEAD

Feeding the soul of the departed is one of the most important rituals in Vietnam. A hungry soul is a restless soul and will unsettle the lives of the living, so the anniversaries of death are observed strictly by all families.

Wandering Souls' Day

A special day has been chosen to commemorate unclaimed souls with no known death dates or families to honour them – those who die in war, for example, or without relatives. It is one of the most important days of the year, and falls on the fifth day of the seventh moon. The Việt believe that unclaimed souls are perpetually hungry and wander in search of food, having no home altar and no family to offer them sustenance. These unfortunate souls may become angry and disturb the living to demand their attention. To appease them, the festival of Wandering Souls is observed strictly by all in order to keep the peace on earth for the living. A meal is prepared and left on a table outside the house; it may consist of just fruit or a few vegetarian dishes, or be a lavish banquet, depending on the wealth of the family. In reality, this is a day when beggars can feast royally without the homeowner complaining.

After the storming of Huế by the French army in 1885, an event that resulted in thousands of deaths and the end of Vietnamese independence, Wandering Souls' Day became an occasion for the whole city to mourn. From morning until late afternoon, every household in the city offers food on tables set up in front of their houses, each bearing a lit oil lamp and incense sticks. The lamp is to help the lost souls find their way to the feasts. It is a serious food custom that is still strictly observed today.

One of the most important occasions in the Nguyễn royal calendar of rituals was the Nam Giao offering, when the Nguyễn emperors communicated with their ancestors and the celestial beings who had empowered them. The solemn ceremony, which required months of preparation, took place at 2 am on a high platform on the south bank of the Hương (Perfume) River in the royal capital, Huế. During the ceremony, the emperor reported to his ancestors what he had been doing and then offered them freshly killed meats, such as cow, buffalo, goat or chicken. The meat was cooked on a huge fire built at one corner of the platform, so that its

Preparations for a Le king's funeral, 17th century (Lê dynasty), from Jean-Baptiste
Tavernier's *Relation nouvelle et singuliere du Royaume de Tunquin* (1692).

Buffalo waiting to be slaughtered for Nam Giao ceremony, *c.* 19th century.

essence would rise up high to be accepted by the souls of the ancestors and the celestial beings above.

A Royal Meal

Just as their citizens did, the royal family ate three times a day, although their breakfast would be prepared by the royal cooks rather than bought in from outside. Apart from the official banquets presided over by the emperors, regular meals of the last royal family of Vietnam, the Nguyễn, contained dishes found in the poorest Vietnamese households. This reflects the humble early life of the first emperor, Gia-Long (*r.* 1802–20), who spent decades in the Mekong Delta fighting his rivals for the throne. He was often forced to hide among farmers and fishermen, and sometimes even went hungry. He was a simple eater in general, and not a drinker; it has been said that *mắm rươi*, a dish of fermented worms (see page 202), was one of his favourites, along with braised fish.

Other humble dishes were introduced to the court by the common women who were brought to Huế as concubines for the emperors. Some of these women later became favourites, and even queens or queen mothers, such as Lady Từ Dũ, Emperor Tự Đức's mother, who came from the Mekong Delta, or Lady Từ Cung, mother of the last emperor, Bảo Đại, and previously a street vendor on the outskirts of Huế. Another influential source for the royal cuisine was the regional products sent to Huế as tribute, such as wild meat from the highlands or special rice from a particular field. Most of the time the royals ate what was available locally, such as cockles from the Hương River, which runs past the imperial citadel. *Cơm hến*, a speciality of Huế and a favourite of the royals, is a complicated dish made with cold rice, topped with the stir-fried meat of tiny cockles from this river, chopped banana flowers, herbs and roasted peanuts, and doused in a fiery *nước chấm*, the mixed and diluted version of neat *nước mắm* Huế-style. It assaults the palate before leaving its chilli burn mark around the mouth.

The second emperor, Minh Mạng (*r.* 1820–40), introduced a book of rules concerning royal cuisine, in which he set out the number of dishes to be served for each meal, along with the time and how they were to be served. He did not forget to make clear the punishment that would be meted out to those who violated the rules. Any chef who served the emperor a type of food that he was not supposed to have, for example, would be caned a hundred times; if the food was not clean enough, the chef would be caned eighty times; if a wrong ingredient appeared in a dish, the chef would be caned sixty times; and if the chef did not taste the dish before offering it to the emperor, to ensure that it was not poisoned, he would be caned fifty times.

The emperor ate alone. Each meal consisted of fifty dishes prepared by fifty chefs who were strictly forbidden to engage in impure activities, whatever those might be. Each chef was solely responsible for his dish, and his well-being, even his life, depended on it. When the dishes were ready, they were put in ornate boxes with the names of the dishes pasted on the lids. Eunuchs carried the boxes from the kitchen and handed them to five royal maids, who would feed the emperor.

A royal meal usually contained meat, fish, vegetables, fruit, cakes and sweets, all of which were presented one by one on special blue-and-white china after maids took them out of the boxes and arranged them artistically on plates. The emperor would pick at the food with his special pair of chopsticks, made of fine young bamboo, which would be destroyed after each meal. Emperor Đồng Khánh (*r.* 1885–9), however, preferred a different type of chopstick, made from a special wood that changed colour if the food contained poison. The last emperor, Bảo Đại (*r.* 1926–45), who

Carrot dragon: royal-style decoration.

had been educated in France from the age of nine, ate with his wife, Queen Nam Phương, and their children *en famille*. By then, the number of dishes required for each royal meal had been reduced to 35.

The Nguyễn royal cuisine began in the field and garden, where special plants, fruits and herbs were bred specially for the delicate royal palate. The royal banana – *chuối ngự* – is a good example of this fine culinary tradition. It grew only to a tiny size, to fit dainty royal hands. *Chuối ngự* is now a common sight at markets in Asia, and is even exported to Europe, but it was once reserved exclusively for the court of Huế.

All royal dishes, whether humble or not, would be presented exquisitely. They were served in or next to intricately carved vegetables and fruit which followed the general royal designs of dragon, phoenix, flowers and fabled animals, although the quantity of each dish and the morsels were tiny. Rice was also the main staple food for the royals. The rice the emperor ate would be checked grain by grain and cooked in a tiny clay pot.

According to the royal cookbook *Thực Phổ Bách Thiên*, the Nguyễn royal family ate river fish, shellfish and seafood with their rice; next came vegetables, and meat occupied only third place. Fermented fish and prawns and pickled vegetables were also very popular. Surprisingly, luxury foods such as game, shark's fin, abalone and bird's nest were used only sparingly. Desserts were often shaped into little birds or tiny flowers. Fruit was offered in season and came from all over the country.

Throughout the Nguyễn dynasty, the production and preparation of royal food were supervised by a special department related to the Medical Institute of the Interior Ministry. This department was responsible for each royal meal from beginning to end, from the selection of ingredients to the provision of toothpicks.

A Typical Kitchen

Unlike Western kitchens, until recently Vietnamese kitchens had only three burners and no oven. One burner was for rice, the other two for soup and salty dishes. Although the burners might simply be tripods of clay or cast iron, they were cherished by the cook and revered by the family as their kitchen gods, that must be pampered and bribed to work properly. Similar to the Chinese, the Việt believed that the kitchen gods were an ill-fated trio of two husbands and a wife who were appointed by the Jade Emperor to watch over the family. They are said to fly off to heaven a week before the end of the Lunar Year to report on the state

The Legend of the Kitchen Gods

Once upon a time, there were a couple of peasants who had been married for a long time without having children. It was a cause of shame for the husband and of great sorrow for the wife, and it made the two fight constantly. One day, during one of these fights, the man struck his wife, and she left. She wandered to a faraway village, where she met a good man and married him. Her old husband felt very bad about what he had done, so he too left home to look for his wife. He looked and looked until he ran out of money and became a beggar. One day, he begged at a house and found his old wife as its mistress. She recognized the beggar as her former husband, and invited him in for a good meal. Halfway through the meal, her new husband came home. Afraid that he would find out about her ex-husband, she hid him in a haystack behind the house. Unaware of this, the new husband set fire to the haystack to clear up the yard. His wife jumped into the burning haystack to save her old husband. Not knowing why his wife had jumped into the fire, the new husband jumped in to save her, and all three burned to death. Their souls floated up to heaven and met the Jade Emperor, who allowed all three to stay married and sent them down to earth to be kitchen supervisors, each one in the form of a burner. They live in the kitchen to keep an eye on the food preparation and the cooking.

of affairs in the family for which they are responsible. To ensure a good report, most families bribe their kitchen gods heavily before they depart, by giving them a farewell feast and a carp to ride on. The gods are usually depicted wearing mandarin robes and hats but without trousers, since those would have been burned in the fire of the haystack in which they died. All three share a ride on a fish. A less derogatory version shows the three surrounded by cattle, pigs, dogs and chickens, all the meats a family would cook in their kitchen.

FOOD AND PRIDE

As we saw earlier with the case of the wooden fish, for the majority of Vietnamese, not being able to afford food means loss of face and a shame that they must do everything in their power to hide. It is quite normal for families to use their meagre savings, kill their only chicken or borrow money to give their visitors a decent meal, so that the guests won't know that they cannot normally afford such luxury. One nineteenth-century host, so poor that he could not hide his poverty, turned to humour to explain why his visitor was not invited to stay for a meal. In a perfect Tang-style poem, the poor scholar lamented:

> It's been a long time since you've paid me a visit.
> The youngsters are away, the market far.
> My pond is deep, the water choppy, difficult to net a fish.
> The garden is large, its fence far apart, difficult to catch a hen.
> The vegetables are young, aubergines just sprout buds.
> The marrows are minute, the gourds still in flower.
> A betel quid for you to chew, I have not.
> Well, here we are, just you and me.[1]

SNACKS AND ALTERNATIVE FOODS

Since Vietnamese meals are low in calories and rice is easy to digest, many Vietnamese become peckish at about 3 or 4 pm, and go in search of a snack to tide them over until dinner. Evening snacks are also popular, and can easily be had by hailing a mobile vendor passing the door, if you can afford it. *Phở* and won-ton soup are the most popular dishes for moments like this. In some towns and cities, the musical click-clack of the won-ton boy is a familiar evening sound. The snack industry in Vietnam is huge, and provides a steady income for many families. It is a delight for visitors to the country, but unfortunately also a source of concern for many in terms of healthiness. Most snack vendors don't have access to running water in which to wash their noodle-bowls between clients, for example. A quick wipe with an unclean cloth that has been used for dozens of wipes can be a health hazard. Food exposed for hours in the heat is another health concern, not to mention the fact that vegetables at snack stalls or sold by vendors are not usually washed in antibacterial solution. Some snacks are outright unhygienic, such as the blood dish (see below). With snacks

Mobile street
vendor.

or street food becoming more and more popular among visitors to the
country, the hygiene situation has improved but there is no guarantee that
the eater will be trouble-free. Of course if you accept that a tummy ache
or worse is part of the fun in a tropical country then it is not a problem to
eat such foods.

There are hundreds of snack dishes, some of which may be eaten in
double portions as main meals. Some are substantial, such as *phở* or bowls
of rice noodles called *bún*; others are less so, and are offered in the shape of
a bun or cake, made of either rice, glutinous rice, bread or anything that can
be made into finger foods. All *bún* are by-products of rice, but are cooked
in various ways, so all are completely different.

Rice Noodles and Rolls

Despite being an import from southern China during the Chinese millennium, *bún* is now so Vietnamized that its origin has been forgotten
and it is seen as a versatile Vietnamese food that comes in all shapes and
sizes. Of the round types, the thinnest are the southern *bánh hỏi*, which
come in fine strands, like sewing thread, woven into an intricate net. These
delicious noodles make a light base for all kinds of meat and fish, such as
roast pork or grilled prawns.

Other round types are called *bún* in general, no matter what the size, and can be eaten in hot soup or cold with fish sauce, salad, herbs and meat, fish or tofu. There are many sizes of *bún*, the largest being the size of a fat string. It is used only in a spicy beef and pork soup that originated in ancient Huế. Each of the other sizes of *bún* is used in a different type of soup or cold dish.

Traditionally, *bún* is made fresh to be sold at markets, but today all shapes and sizes of *bún* are sold dried, to be boiled until soft, just as dried spaghetti and linguini are used in the West. In Vietnam, since fresh *bún* is always available in the morning, the dried version is not used until later. Once bought, even fresh *bún* must be scalded or rinsed in hot or boiling water before it can be eaten. *Bún*-making is a cottage industry that is dying out, now that even fresh *bún* can be made with machinery. It traditionally brought a decent income to a family or whole village, being such a popular product for breakfast, snacks or occasional alternative meals.

As it soaks, the rice ferments a little, making fresh *bún* slightly sour. This sour taste can be rinsed off with boiling water, but it makes the noodles go off easily in the humid climate of Vietnam. For this reason, fresh *bún* is available at the market for only a short time, usually first thing in the morning, and is rarely eaten in the evening, because the Việt believe it can upset the stomach.

Bánh hỏi and roast pork.

Bún

Bún is not made at home, since the process is long and complicated. The noodles are made by soaking rice grains in water overnight, then grinding and kneading the mixture into a loose paste. Other flours, such as tapioca, may be added to improve the consistency and texture. The paste is next pushed through a large tube with a perforated bottom; the size of the holes determines the type of *bún*. When the paste is pressed down through the tube, strands of noodles pass through the holes and drop into a pot of boiling water underneath for the first cooking. The blanched *bún* strands are scooped out of the pot and left to drain in a bamboo basket. When cool, the soft strands can be twisted together to form bundles like balls of wool, or left loose in a mound over a banana leaf to keep fresh.

Popular hot *bún* soups are *bún thang* (mixed topped noodles), *bún ốc* (snail noodles) and *bún riêu* (paddy crab noodle soup), to name but a few, while among the popular cold *bún* dishes are *bún chả* (grilled pork noodles), *bún chả cá* (grilled or fried fish noodles), *bún thịt nướng* (the southern version of grilled pork noodles), *bún đậu mắm tôm* (fried tofu and shrimp-paste noodles) and *bún bò Huế* (beef noodles Huế-style). Each *bún* dish is totally different from the next, because of what is added to the noodles. In common with rice, *bún* does not have a strong flavour itself, so it can be used with almost anything, whether soup or dry ingredients.

The Vietnamese are keen snackers, so a stall selling any kind of snack can do brisk business at any time of day, and people do not hesitate to travel across town to their favourite stall or restaurant for a bowl of *bún* of some sort. It is hard to say which *bún* dish is preferred among the Việt, though. *Bún thang, bún ốc* and *bún chả* were traditionally northern dishes, but they are now popular throughout Vietnam. By the same token, *bún bò Huế* is no longer a regional dish of central Vietnam but one consumed with gusto by all Việt from north to south.

Of all *bún* dishes, *bún thang* is the most delicate and difficult to prepare. The first step is to make a good chicken stock, usually by boiling a whole chicken. Dried shrimps or dried squid are added, along with a piece of pork, to give a deeper flavour. The stock must be clear and well-seasoned,

Bún thang, a delicate noodle soup from north Vietnam.

and the amount of dried shrimp or squid must be just right to stop it from becoming too fishy. For the topping, the boiled chicken breast is shredded into fine strands, the pork chopped into small cubes and the brown chicken meat also chopped. The meat is fried quickly with the cooked shrimp or squid and finely chopped onion. Next, a very thin omelette, like a crêpe, is cut into fine strips. The last ingredient is very thin strips of pork sausage.

All the above must be as fine or as small as possible, without being actually minced. To assemble the dish, the bought *bún* is rinsed quickly in boiling water with a piece of fresh ginger to kill off the sour taste, if any. The strands are left to drain in a colander for a few minutes before being put into bowls. The toppings are arranged in an artistic pattern, yellow egg, brown pork and shrimps, pink pork sausage and white strands of chicken breast. A little finely chopped hot mint is added in the middle of the toppings and then boiling stock is poured on top until the bowl is full. Slices of fresh chilli may be added by the diner, and some like to eat the dish with shrimp paste (*mắm tôm*), although how the dish can retain its delicate quality with this pungent addition is a mystery. Sometimes chopped Chinese mushrooms are added to the fried mixture, or the mixture is left out altogether to make the *bún thang* even more delicate. This elaborate dish is served at home on the third day of the Lunar New Year to send off the souls of ancestors who came to celebrate the occasion with the family, or on special occasions instead of lunch. In some families, all the ingredients are served separately on the table for diners to prepare their own bowls. These days, *bún thang* is available in restaurants throughout the country.

Another *bún* dish from the north of Vietnam harks back to prehistoric times by using the snail as the central ingredient. The Việt have never lost their taste for molluscs. Cockles, snails, clams and all kinds of shellfish are still very popular with meals or as a snack such as *bún ốc*. The snail in this dish is called *ốc bươu* in Vietnamese and the paddy mollusc in English (*Pila polita*). This freshwater mollusc, which can be harvested from ponds, lakes or, more conveniently, paddy fields, looks like an apple snail but is smaller, the size of a ping-pong ball. Living as they do in muddy waters, the snails must be cleaned thoroughly before they can be eaten. The most usual way is to soak them overnight, or for several days and nights, in water that has been used to wash rice. The snails are washed again in fresh water and then boiled. The meat is teased out of the shells and lightly fried with chopped onion and fresh ginger.

Bún ốc is a soup dish, so the quality of the stock is as important as that of the snails. The stock is made by boiling pork bones with a tomato sauce seasoned with ginger, chilli and tamarind juice or vinegar to create a slightly sweet but mainly sour flavour. The dish is served with *bún* in a bowl, topped with the prepared snails, a touch of fresh minced ginger and the boiling

Paddy snails stuffed with minced pork and ginger.

tomato stock. (It is not known what was used instead of the tomato before this fruit was introduced into Vietnam. However, the soup has been around since the Viet began to farm wet-rice.) A side dish of shredded salad, usually the fine, curly strands of morning glory (*rau muống*) and/or finely sliced banana heart, herbs, lime and fresh chilli, always accompanies the bowl of noodles. There are other versions of *bún ốc*: one is made with thicker stock into which small bundles of *bún* are dipped to scoop up the snails; another is made by adding the snails to another dish of paddy crabs, *bún riêu*.

Bún chả Hanoi is a rice noodle dish of cold *bún* and freshly grilled pork. This street food, for which Hanoi is famous, is also available in restaurants everywhere in Vietnam. It is one of the simplest *bún* dishes, but is widely loved for its unique flavour. There are two kinds of *chả* for this dish. One is sliced fatty pork, such as belly or shoulder, marinated in caramel

---

Bún Chả Hanoi

500 g (1 lb 2 oz.) pork belly or loin, thinly sliced
half a bundle of spring onions, finely chopped
2 tbsp sugar or 1 tbsp honey
1 tsp light soy sauce
1 packet rice vermicelli, medium size, round strands
1 round lettuce
a few sprigs Thai basil and coriander
a few sprigs Vietnamese red perilla (*tía tô*) and a handful of shredded morning glory stalks (if available)
1 lime
1 or 2 fresh chillies
mixed *nước mắm* (recipe p. 195)
1 tbsp sugar
a little light olive oil or sunflower oil
a handful of shredded pickled radish and carrot
4 tbsp crushed unsalted roasted peanuts (optional)
100 g (3½ oz.) raw beansprouts (optional)
salt and freshly ground black pepper

Marinade the pork in a bowl with the spring onion, sugar or honey, soy sauce, ½ tsp salt and a pinch of black pepper for half an hour, or longer if preferred.

Cook the vermicelli in a large pot of boiling water until soft but still springy, or according to the directions on the packet, usually 3–5 minutes. Do not let them go mushy. Rinse the noodles immediately in a colander under a cold tap, and leave to drain for 20 minutes.

Arrange the lettuce and herbs on a plate. Quarter the lime, chop the chillies into fine pieces or thin slices, and put both in a small dish.

Prepare the mixed *nước mắm*. Add 1 tbsp water and 1 tsp sugar to the mixture, and put it in a large serving bowl.

Thread the pork on to 12 bamboo skewers and brush with the oil. Grill, on a charcoal barbecue if possible, until the fat sizzles and turns crispy. Strip the pork off the skewers, put into the bowl of prepared *nước mắm* and serve immediately. For a luxury version, add small patties of hamburger-like minced pork, seasoned and cooked in the same way as the sliced meat.

Each diner assembles their bowl by taking a bundle of noodles, some lettuce, herbs and pickled radish, a spoon-ful of pork and mixed *nước mắm*, and a sprinkling of crushed peanuts and/or beansprouts. Mix everything together, and adjust with lime juice and chilli to taste.

sauce, spring onion, salt and pepper; the fat is important, for to give the dish its full flavour the meat is grilled over charcoal until the fat sizzles and turns brown and crispy. The second type of *chả* is patties of minced pork, chopped spring onion, salt, pepper and caramel sauce. These patties are also grilled over charcoal. Once grilled, either or both types of hot *chả* are put into a bowl of mixed fish sauce and served with cold *bún* and a side dish of shredded morning glory, lime, chilli and herbs. Traditionally, *bún chả* is served on a round, flat tray of woven bamboo, in small dishes, one containing mixed fish sauce and pork pieces, one the cold *bún* and one vegetables. These days, *bún chả* is offered in this simple yet elegant way only in the most traditional restaurants or by the most traditional vendors; otherwise, the ingredients are mixed up in one bowl.

The *bún chả* street vendor is usually a woman, who carries her food in two bamboo baskets slung at either end of a bamboo pole. One basket is for a bowl of hot charcoal, the other contains all the necessary ingredients. The vendor will set up at a particular street corner or market, and barbecue the marinated *chả* to perfection while you wait. As with all barbecued meat, the smell of grilled pork is irresistible and makes certain street corners in Hanoi extremely enticing.

In the south of Vietnam, this dish is called *bún thịt nướng* and is served slightly differently. It does not contain the patties, and chopped roasted peanuts are added along with pickled strands of carrot or white radish, and beansprouts instead of shredded morning glory. Everything is put in one bowl with mixed fish sauce.

Bún bò Huế is a culinary phenomenon, combining several ingredients that do not usually go together: pork (pig's trotters), beef (shin) and fermented shrimp paste. Without even one of these three ingredients, *bún bò Huế* is not considered authentic. The stock for this soup dish is made by boiling a chunk of shin of beef or any other stewing cut with pig's trotters, or a piece of pork shoulder or leg, along with beef and pork bones, a few sticks of fresh lemongrass and a whole onion. When the meat is cooked, it is scooped out to cool, and the stock is seasoned with the fermented shrimp paste *mắm ruốc*. As we have seen, *mắm ruốc* was incorporated into Vietnamese cuisine during the Nguyễn's movement south, and it is what

Portion of *bún chả Hàng Mành* (meaning Curtain or Blind Street), Hanoi. This restaurant is famous in Hanoi for its signature dish.

Bowl of *bún bò Huế*, an iconic rice noodle soup of the old royal capital, served with thick strands of noodles and lots of hot chilli.

makes the dish, since it is made in a different way from other fermented fish or shrimps elsewhere. It gives the stock a pungent flavour and a sweet taste. Another traditional ingredient for this dish is fried chilli powder, sometimes with onion or garlic, for *bún bò Huế* is famous for its spicy heat.

The *bún* used here is the large type, similar to spaghetti. The bowl is first filled with noodles, which are then topped with slices of cooked beef, pieces of pork or chunks of cooked pig's trotters, and sometimes with slices of a typical Huế pork sausage, which is sweeter than those found elsewhere. Sliced onion and chopped hot mint are also added to give the bowl the proper flavour. Boiling stock is poured over everything and a spoonful of fried chilli powder is added. More *mắm ruốc* may be added to the individual bowl. This is not a dainty dish nor food for the squeamish or faint-hearted, for it is bold, brassy and spicy without mercy. Not only do diners expect to gnaw on the pieces of trotter, they are often left with a ring of redness and puffiness around their mouths, from the fierce heat of the chilli. It is also common for diners to shed tears as they eat because of the chilli bite in the soup. These days, *bún bò Huế* is served as a tamed version of its original self in restaurants all over Vietnam.

Bánh cuốn, another food made from rice flour, is derived from the Chinese *cheong fun* but has a much thinner skin and a different filling, or

Rice paper wraps drying in the sun.

no filling at all. Unlike *bún*, *bánh cuốn* is made as a thin sheet of steamed rice paste, before being rolled with fillings or by itself. The sheet is made by spreading a thin mixture of rice flour and water on to a sheet of muslin fixed tightly over a pot of boiling water. It is similar to the way crêpes are made in the West, but over steam instead of by contact with a hot surface. The sheet of *bánh cuốn* cooks very quickly and is lifted from the muslin with a stick on to a flat surface before being rolled. The northern version is served with a filling of fried minced pork, Chinese mushroom and onion, and dipped into a bowl of mixed *nước mắm*. Shrimp floss is often sprinkled on top, and a few slices of *giò* sausage are served on the side or in the bowl of *nước mắm*. The southern version has no filling; the rolls are cut up, served on a bed of blanched beansprouts, sweet basil, coriander leaves, crispy fried onion and slices of pork sausage and doused in mixed *nước mắm*.

All the rice-based foods used in these Vietnamese dishes were adopted or modified from the time of the Chinese millennium, but there is a uniquely Vietnamese rice product that cannot be found anywhere else: the *bánh tráng* or *bánh đa nem* (rice-paper wrapper). No rice product is more Vietnamese than this versatile dried rice sheet, so thin that it is almost transparent, imprinted with a basket-weave pattern. It is made from rice flour and water, and small amounts of other flours that make it slightly less likely to tear when wet. *Bánh tráng* is made by spreading the mixture on to a piece of muslin over steam, similar to the way *bánh cuốn* is made

Chả Giò or *Nem Rán* (Spring Rolls)

50 g (1¾ oz.) dried Chinese black fungus
50 g(1¾ oz.) glass or transparent noodles
300 g (10½ oz.) lean minced pork or chicken
100 g (3½ oz.) grated carrot or finely chopped raw
beansprouts
50 g (1¾ oz.) finely chopped water chestnuts (optional)
1 egg
200 g (7 oz.) raw prawns and/or 100 g (3½ oz.) white
crab meat
100 g (3½ oz.) finely chopped shallot or onion
a pinch of sugar
20–30 Vietnamese rice-paper wrappers or Chinese *popiah*
wrappers
sunflower or vegetable oil, for deep-frying
salt and freshly ground black pepper
lettuce, mint, Thai basil and coriander, and a bowl
of mixed *nước mắm*, around 4 tbsp per bowl, to serve

Soak the black fungus and the noodles in a bowl of warm
water for 20 minutes, or until soft but not mushy. Chop
both finely, put in a bowl with the pork or chicken, grated
carrot, water chestnuts, egg, ½ tsp salt and a pinch of pepper,
and mix thoroughly. Add the prawns and/or crab, onion or
shallot and sugar and mix gently. (For vegetarians, substitute
chopped fried tofu and shredded bamboo shoots for the meat
and fish.)

To wrap the rolls, spread a rice-paper wrapper on a flat
surface and wipe it with a wet cloth to moisten. Spoon the
mixture on to the sheet, fold the two short sides in and roll
into a cigar shape. Deep-fry the rolls over a medium–high
heat until golden. Serve as a starter with the lettuce and
herbs, to be dipped into the mixed *nước mắm*. Smaller rice-
paper wrappers will result in tiny rolls that can be served on
their own as a canapé.

but with a much thinner paste. The rice-paper wrapper acquires the round shape of the pot and is lifted on to a bamboo mat to be dried in the sun, half a dozen to a mat. The patterns we see on the sheet are the imprint of the woven bamboo of the drying mat.

Of the large variety of *bánh tráng*, the thinnest is used for summer rolls. By being wetted with a damp cloth, the dried sheet becomes soft enough to wrap around other ingredients as a neat roll. The filling for summer rolls consists of *bún*, lettuce, herbs, cooked prawns, slices of pork, a thin strip of omelette and a stick of garlic chive. The almost transparent wrapper shows off the ingredients inside enticingly, and many snackers have succumbed at the sight. The rolls are eaten without further cooking, dipped into mixed *nước mắm* or another dipping sauce, such as fermented yellow bean sauce. This type of roll is very popular as a starter or snack.

Another type of roll is equally popular, called *chả giò* in the south and *nem rán* in the north. It is a Vietnamese national dish and can be found everywhere in the country, and even in the finest patisseries in Paris, where it is displayed next to a host of French cakes and pastries. *Chả giò* can be big and long, like an uncut roll of sushi; *nem rán* are smaller, the size of a short cigar. Both types are deep-fried until golden. The northern type is then cut up into sushi-like pieces to be served with lettuce, coriander,

Summer rolls, made with lettuce, herbs, cooked rice noodles, pork and prawns wrapped in rice-paper wraps. These rolls are a favourite dish for their fresh taste.

Chả giò and its accompaniments. Another version of food wrapped in rice-paper wraps. The rolls are deep-fried and served with fresh herbs and lettuce.

mint or other fresh herbs; the southern type is presented as a pile of mini logs on a bed of lettuce and herbs, with the addition of fish herb (*rau rắp cá*), which – as its name suggests – tastes exactly like fish. Pieces of *chả giò* may also be served in a bowl of cold *bún*, to make *bún chả giò*, or added to *bún thịt nướng*, to make *bún thịt nướng chả giò*, a favourite of southerners.

While the use of *bánh tráng* is essential for fresh rolls, it is not very popular these days for *chả giò*, since it is more difficult and time-consuming to work with. The rice-paper wrapper must be wetted first, and is easily torn, so it has gradually been replaced by the more resilient Chinese *popiah* wrapper, made with wheat flour, which does not need to be wetted. Having said that, truly authentic *chả giò* must be made with the Vietnamese rice-paper wrapper, however troublesome for the cook.

Many other types of dried rice-paper sheet exist, both sweet and salty, to be eaten on their own as snacks, including a type embedded with sesame seeds. Snack rice paper is thicker and is cooked from dry by grilling above an open fire until little bubbles form all over it and the sheet becomes golden and crunchy.

Mixed *Nước Mắm*

All cold noodles and rolls require a vital ingredient to make them palatable: mixed *nước mắm*, called *nước chấm*. Neat *nước mắm* is used to season most dishes during cooking, and is also served as a condiment at the table. In the north of Vietnam, *nước mắm* is offered neat in a little bowl at every meal, whereas in the centre and south of the country, it is served mixed. A well-mixed bowl of *nước chấm* can transform the most humble vegetable into something delicious. It also makes or breaks a bowl of cold *bún*.

Nước chấm is always made from the same ingredients – neat *nước mắm*, water, sugar, vinegar, lime juice, garlic and fresh chilli – but each region, or indeed each household, uses them in slightly different proportion. The result is sweet, sour, chilli-hot and not too salty. Northerners make a thinner version, with more vinegar, and add a little lime juice and chilli. One can tell a bowl of northern *nước chấm* easily from its appearance, which is the colour of weak tea with a few floating pieces of garlic and chilli. Because of this apparent blandness, northern mixed *nước mắm* goes well with dishes like *bún chả Hanoi*, since it serves as a quiet background to the main ingredient, grilled pork, without competing with it for centre stage.

Southern *nước chấm* is very different, rich and colourful in appearance, its surface often completely covered with finely chopped red chilli, white garlic and green lime pulp. The taste is much stronger: sugar, lime juice,

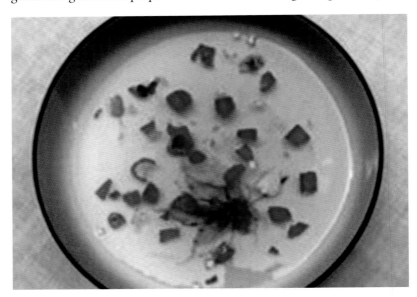

Basic *nước chấm*.

Basic Mixed Nước Mắm

2 tbsp fish sauce
juice of 1 lime or ½ tbsp vinegar
4 tbsp sugar
6–8 tbsp water
1 small clove of garlic, crushed
a pinch of finely chopped fresh chilli

Mix all the ingredients together in a bowl or jar until the sugar has dissolved. Scrape out the pulp of the used lime (if using) and add to the mixture. Taste and adjust, since the saltiness of the fish sauce varies from brand to brand and some limes are sourer than others. The sauce can be kept in the fridge for a couple of weeks (although it is better fresh) and used as a base for many dishes.

chilli, garlic and fish sauce all make themselves known, but without overwhelming one another. Southern mixed *nước mắm* often forgoes vinegar in favour of lime juice. Not only is the lime juice used in the mixture, its pulp is scraped out and added to the sauce as well for extra flavour. Because of its stronger taste, southern mixed *nước mắm* does not go well with *bún chả Hanoi*, but it is perfect with the southern version of that dish, *bún thịt nướng*, which is mixed even further with other strong ingredients, such as roasted peanuts.

A good bowl of *nước chấm* is a symphony of taste, pleasant to eat but with a little bite of chilli. Southerners like to have a bowl with every meal, in which to dip herbs and lettuce. The central Vietnamese version of *nước chấm* is sweeter and much hotter, with double the amount of minced chilli. Mixed *nước mắm* is used in every version of cold *bún* and a large number of savoury steamed *bánh*. The proportion of the ingredients may vary according to the dish it accompanies. A little more water, a little less lime juice or sugar can change the taste remarkably. *Nước chấm* should be made fresh for every use, and should contain only a hint of garlic so as not to leave an unpleasant taste in the mouth. Old *nước chấm* has a stronger taste of garlic that stays around for a long time.

Mixed *nước mắm* is also used throughout Vietnam as a salad dressing, without oil. Vietnamese salad is an unconventional dish that can be made with lettuce, cabbage or any type of green fruit. Each ingredient requires a different herb as companion.

FRUIT, HERBS AND SPICES

In Vietnam, fruit of all descriptions is used both as a sweet dessert and as a savoury ingredient, often before the flowers turn into fully formed fruit. Gourd flowers, for example, can be used in stir-fries or soup. The banana flower, a big bundle of layered purple petals like a pointed cabbage, protects the newly formed bunches of bananas between its thick petals. The whole bundle is treated as a vegetable and much-loved by many Vietnamese. It can be sliced thinly and made into a salad mixed with *nước chấm*, or served on its own to accompany many *bún* dishes, such as *bún ốc*. Green bananas can also be eaten raw as part of a salad, or cooked in a braised dish.

Similar to the banana, the giant papaya is a humble fruit and a familiar sight in rural Vietnam. When ripe it makes a delicious dessert or breakfast fruit, but when it is still green and firm, it can be made into a salad. All Southeast Asian countries have their own versions of green papaya salad, depending on the additional herbs and ingredients. In Vietnam, the fresh, green meat of the fruit is cut into long, thin strips and mixed with *nước chấm*, and sometimes pieces of boiled pork, chicken or prawns, to make a delicious and refreshing salad. It is also popular as a street snack called *bò*

Fruits of Vietnam at Bến Thành central market, Saigon.

Vegetable and fruit seller at Cần Thơ floating market, Mekong Delta.

khô, after the main ingredient added to it, beef jerky. This is a simple dish made with a few leaves of sweet basil and doused in a weak, sweet *nước chấm*.

Sweet mango is another delicious fruit, but its green form also makes a delightful salad or sour soup. Mangoes are much more expensive than papaya, so green mango salad is usually offered only in restaurants, or occasionally at home as a treat. Shredded green mango is sometimes added to a bowl of *nước chấm* to give the mixture another dimension, usually when it is served with fried fish.

Pomelo salad originated on the royal table of the Nguyễn emperors. The membrane is peeled from the segments and the inside is teased out into a bowl, to be mixed with thinly filleted boiled prawns, chopped boiled pork and coriander leaves or other herbs, before mixed *nước mắm* is added. It is a rather unusual dish, but very popular for its refreshing quality.

Herb Pairings

Vietnamese folk songs and folk tales are full of reminders about which spices and herbs go with what meat or fish. For example, one of the most popular songs, and one that every Vietnamese knows by heart, is this quartet:

The hen squawks for her lime leaves
The pig oinks: buy me some onion
The dog weeps bitterly:
O mistress! I must have a cent worth of galangal.

Many other green fruits are used in this way, before they are fully ripe, making a Vietnamese meal a colourful, fresh and tasty but low-calorie experience. Pomelo can be used green or ripe; the green version is more difficult to handle but gives out a fresher flavour and more sour taste. Ripe pomelo may be considered too sweet by some.

Vietnamese cuisine relies on herbs to enhance the freshness of the main ingredients, and for their distinctive flavour. Herbs are usually offered fresh at the table, whereas spices are mixed with the meat or fish before cooking. Each herb or spice is strictly intended for a particular dish, for example, boiled chicken, a favourite of northerners, is always accompanied by shredded lime leaves. Snail dishes should always include ginger, perhaps galangal according to taste, garlic and the purple leaves *tia to*, equivalent to the Japanese shiso leaves served with sashimi. *Bún bo Huế* needs some chopped hot mint to complete it. Diners can choose to add whatever herbs they like to other dishes such as *Cha' Gio*, including the fish herb, which is too fishy for some. Sometimes a dish requires more than one herb or vegetable to be complete. Hanoi grilled fish, for example, requires both fresh dill and spring onions in large quantities to make the dish, which is eaten with lettuce and more secondary herbs, among other things.

THE HUNDRED RICE *BÁNH*

Flours made from both ordinary rice and glutinous rice are used to make a variety of sweet and savoury steamed or boiled 'cakes'. *Bánh giò, bánh nếp, bánh bèo* and *bánh xu xê* are just a few examples of the hundreds of products.

Bánh xu xê.

Bánh giò, which originated in the north of Vietnam, is a popular snack or breakfast food made with rice flour. The flour is poured into a pot of boiling stock, such as pork or chicken, stirred vigorously so that it forms a loose paste without lumps, and left to cool slightly. The filling is made with stir-fried minced pork, onion and black fungus. When cool enough to handle, the rice paste is put into a banana-leaf cone with the filling and wrapped into a pyramid-like dumpling, which is tied with string to keep its shape and then boiled for 20–30 minutes. *Bánh nếp* is made in a similar way, but with glutinous rice flour, making a slightly chewy and more filling dumpling.

An interesting-looking dish made with rice flour is *bánh bèo*, a product of central and southern Vietnam. It is made with a loose paste of rice flour and water in tiny ceramic saucers, and steamed until the flour turns opaque with a dimple in the middle. Mashed mung beans, pieces of pork scratching, minced dried prawns and spring onion are placed in the dimple and seasoned with mixed *nước mắm*. Each portion consists of ten or twelve of these tiny saucers served on a bamboo tray; the entire saucer can be eaten in a single slurp, or with a spoon.

Variety of rice *bánh*.

Bánh xu xê, also known as *bánh phu thê* (husband-and-wife cake), is a sweet, soft dumpling made with glutinous flour and filled with sweetened ground mung beans and shredded coconut. It is a pale yellow, transparent dumpling housed in a small, square container of woven coconut leaves. It is generally believed that this dumpling originated in the eleventh century, under the Lý dynasty, when a loving wife made it to send to her husband who was away fighting a battle for the Lý emperor. For some reason, the emperor tasted the dumpling, liked it very much and called it *bánh phu thê* to celebrate the love between a wife and husband. These dumplings are often served at engagement ceremonies, as part of a ritual that includes betel and areca nuts.

FERMENTED FOOD

The more extreme version of fish sauce is *mắm*, a salted, fermented paste made from many kinds of tiny fish and shrimp that are too small to cook with, or any creatures the poor can scavenge in small streams, from the sea or in paddy fields. All *mắm* have a pungent smell, but each type is pungent in a different way, which can be heaven or hell depending on the preference of the diner (in the same way that the taste of ripened Camembert and blue cheese is wonderful for some people and hellish for others).

Mắm varies according to region, but in general it is made by adding salt and other ingredients, such as ginger, chilli or galangal, to tiny shrimps or any fish that are too tiny to eat otherwise. The mixture is left to ferment in earthen jars for weeks or months until the fish disintegrate into a flavoursome paste with a highly pungent aroma. For peasants who eat rice as their main food, and often for breakfast as well, it can be made tastier by adding a spoonful of *mắm*. A roll of rice sausage with a touch of *mắm* in the centre can make a tasty lunch for farmers working in faraway fields.

Mắm Street (Fermented Food Street), Hanoi, early 20th century.

Women fishing in Hai Phong, *c.* 1900.

Mắm tôm is a product of northern Vietnam, made with ground shrimps and salt and fermented until it becomes a greyish-purple paste. It is used as a condiment for seasoning soup, or eaten on its own with rice or meat, tofu and vegetables. It can also be diluted and mixed with lime juice, sugar and chilli to make a dipping sauce. It is a popular ingredient for a northern version of cold *bún*, in which the *bún* is served with fried tofu and herbs and doused in a mixed *mắm tôm* dipping sauce.

Some regions of Vietnam are known for their *mắm* alone, such as Trà Vinh (in the Mekong Delta), famous for *mắm rươi*, a normal, everyday food for many Vietnamese but not recommended for the squeamish. It is made with a type of sand worm, *rươi*, that lives underground at river estuaries and can tolerate brackish water. The worms surface en masse at high tide in October to January, when salt water floods their tunnels, suffocating them. They usually come up at dawn, as large or small writhing bundles, and can be collected easily using sieve-ladles or bamboo baskets. These worms are considered extremely delicious and are valued by rural people as 'earth dragons'. So far there is no known equivalent of this species anywhere else.

In the south of Vietnam, the sauce is made by putting the *rươi* into an earthen jar with salt and water, covering the jar with a piece of muslin and leaving it in the sun to ferment for two or three weeks. The impurities that float to the surface are skimmed off, leaving a two-part product. The clear liquid part of the mixture, a deep honey colour, is siphoned off to become a highly valued seasoning liquid like fish sauce, called *nước mắm rươi*. The remaining paste becomes *mắm rươi*, which will keep in a cool place for a long time.

Fermented Prawns

Wash the prawns, pinch off heads and tails,
Make them sour to accompany wine and ale.
Clear wine must be added drop by drop,
Then white-flesh galangal as it's just sprouting.
A little of sugar and pepper will sharpen the taste.
Salt and garlic would turn the prawns crimson red.
Add some hot chilli to kill off harmful pests.
Lipstick red prawns, oh so deliciously tasty!

Lady Trương Đăng Thị Bích,
Thực Phổ Bách Thiên (One Hundred Good Dishes, 1915)

Dried shimps, fish and *mắm* outside the Lady's Temple, Chau Doc, Mekong Delta.

In the north of Vietnam, the fermentation process is much longer. The worms are mashed to a paste before being put into a jar with salt. Wine is added after three or four weeks, then roasted glutinous flour, ground ginger and dried orange powder are added at intervals of two weeks until the mixture has been fermenting for three months. This type of *mắm rươi* is a paste.

Mắm rươi is eaten with rice, either simply, with just a few drops of lime juice, or further prepared by adding all kinds of ingredients. The paste is sometimes mixed with other foods to make a dipping sauce. As unusual as it may sound for many in the West, of all typical Vietnamese products this one ranks high in the list of delicacies from north to south. The worms are also used fresh in other dishes, such as omelettes or *chả rươi*, a favourite dish in the north, in which patties of whole worms mixed with minced pork, onion and other ingredients are deep-fried until golden.

Mắm tôm chua is a unique central Vietnamese product, completely different from other types of *mắm*. It is made with whole medium-sized marine prawns, *nước mắm*, rice wine, galangal and ginger and left to ferment for about three weeks, until the prawns turn pink. Roasted ground rice, shredded green papaya and chilli powder are added to the mixture and it is allowed to ferment for several more weeks. The end product is a delicious dish of whole prawns soaked in a sweet-and-sour liquid; it is served with slices of boiled pork, ginger, sweet basil, green fruits such as star fruit and green banana, and any other herbs preferred by the diner. Each mouthful is a combination of all the ingredients. It is known to have been a royal favourite, and was included in the royal cookbook *Thực Phổ Bách Thiên* (*One Hundred Good Dishes*).

Nem chua is a national Vietnamese product that varies from region to region. It is made with finely minced pork, garlic, sugar, salt, roasted ground rice and fine shreds of cooked pork skin. The mixture is wrapped in banana or other fruit leaves, such as guava or *tầm ruộc*, to make small balls or rolls and left to ferment, usually for two or three weeks, until the raw meat is sour. Traditionally, *nem chua* is eaten on its own as a snack or put in a summer roll with lettuce and herbs; it may also be served fried or grilled. The taste varies according to the region: northern *nem chua* is just plain sour; that from the centre is the sweetest, and is sometimes made into a different fermented product, *tré*, using galangal, sesame seeds, chopped pork and pork skin instead.

Traditionally, most Vietnamese people do not drink alcohol regularly, but there is an unusual use of glutinous rice wine that is worth mentioning. It is to celebrate the special occasion of the fifth day of the fifth moon (Tết

Nem chua, fermented raw pork, a Vietnamese delicacy.

Đoan Ngọ). This festival dates back to prehistoric times, when the people commemorated the mother of all Việt, Âu Cơ (see Chapter One). One of the main activities of the day was eating alcoholic glutinous rice called *rượu nếp* for breakfast. *Rượu nếp* is cooked unpolished rice fermented in a clay pot with yeast until the grains plump up, and become soaked in a sweet, alcoholic liquid. The grains are eaten on their own, and the liquid is drunk as rice wine. The southern version is called *cơm rượu*, since the fermented rice is made into balls soaked in its alcoholic wine. On this day everybody in the household, including women and young children, is given a bowl of *rượu nếp* to eat, the idea being that the alcohol will cleanse their systems of harmful parasites. It is the only day of the year when it is acceptable for Vietnamese women and children to stagger about under the influence of alcohol.

INTO MODERNITY: THE BIRTH OF THE COOKBOOK

> Meat and fish are there for rice and vegetables.
> It is how you cook them – grill, boil or fry – that makes them
>   palatable.
> Birds' nests would not be precious if badly prepared;
> Swamp vegetables could be delicious if done well.
> Good food brings harmony, high and low.
> Good eating means good feelings for all in the home.
> To know how to sew and embroider is not good enough –
> To gain the top position, one has to be a good cook![2]

One of the most modern aspects of Vietnamese cuisine is the cookbook. It was not until 1915 that a Vietnamese cookbook was published, by a royal member of the Nguyễn court, Lady Trương Đăng Thị Bích. Written entirely in verse and intended for the royal kitchen, *Thực Phổ Bách Thiên* (*One Hundred Good Dishes*) is rather vague. The quantities, cooking times and order of adding ingredients are not mentioned, making the recipes either highly individual for the experienced cook or very risky for the novice:

> Fatty pork is needed for this dish.
> Cut the meat into cubes for easy cooking.
> Add salt, honey and *nước mắm*.
> Braise the meat till succulent, just salty and perfectly tasty.

In the early 1950s, one of the first printed cookbooks in Romanized Vietnamese was published. The simply named *Làm bếp giỏi* (Good Cook) was written by a French-educated lady, Ms Vân Đài, a high-born poet, writer and active anti-colonial fighter during the late 1930s and '40s. She arranged her recipes in two main sections, one for traditional Vietnamese dishes and the other for their French counterparts. The colonial French foods were presented with Vietnamese hybrid dishes in between. Each section, whether Vietnamese or French, was accompanied by a set of suggested menus for different seasons or occasions, from daily meals to dinner parties to family feasts. The menus reflected the traditional meals of both cultures, with new elements added. The ordinary Vietnamese meal started with appetizers and then soup, meat or fish, vegetables and/or salad, and rice – all served at the same time – followed by fruit, sweets and tea. French menus consisted of the usual soup, fish, meat, vegetables or salad, potatoes, desserts and coffee or tea. Since the Vietnamese had been exposed to many

Caramelized pork and a boiled egg, southern style.

Daily Vietnamese Menus of the 1950s, from *Good Cook*

Breakfast
Pâté foie
Bánh mì
Coffee, black or with milk

or

Beef phở
Bánh mì
Soft-boiled eggs
Coffee

Lunch
Stir-fried kidney with carrot
Fried eggs with bulb vegetable
Braised caramelized pork
Pickled vegetables
Soup of prawns and celery

or

Stir-fried cauliflower with prawns
Pork sausage
Steamed minced pork with Chinese pickled vegetables
Soup of celery and dried prawns

Dinner
Fried fish in tomato sauce
Stir-fried leek and celery with beef
Steamed tofu
Braised pork hock with radish

or

Braised pigeon with green rice
Stir-fried French beans
Roast chicken
Braised fish
Bird wings with spring onion

French regional dishes, some of them highly intricate, during the French century, each French menu included at least one of these dishes for either lunch or dinner, making the meal a feast by modern standards, and taxing for the cook. Such dishes as *daube délicieuse* (delicious stew), *civet de lapin* (rabbit), *poulet à la marengo* (chicken with crayfish) or even the fish soup *bouillabaisse* were common features of these menus.

Each of the menus casually included French vegetables such as cauliflower, celery, carrots and leeks, which by then were taken for granted in Vietnamese cooking. For breakfast, needless to say, *bánh mì* had become the norm.

According to this cookbook, some modified French dishes were by then being included in Vietnamese family feasts, such as the ancestors' anniversaries of death. For example, one menu suggested braised chicken with French mushrooms; another stipulated French asparagus and crab-meat soup. Roast chicken seemed to be the most popular dish for these occasions. Some of the special menus included all three types of food that constituted modern Vietnamese cuisine: Chinese, Vietnamese and French.

The most remarkable thing about *Good Cook* is that the author lists clearly the measurements and the methods of preparation for each dish. She even adds a glossary of ingredients with their Vietnamese regional names to help the cooks find the right things in their local markets. The reason for this glossary was that the different political status of the three regions of Vietnam during the French century changed much of the Vietnamese vocabulary, making certain ingredients incomprehensible to people outside the region in which they were known. For example, many ingredients in Cochinchina were called by their Vietnamized French names, making them difficult for northerners to understand. At the same time, in northern Vietnam –a region most influenced by the Chinese – many herbs and spices were still called by their Vietnamese–Chinese names, making them unfamiliar to the people of the Mekong Delta, who had until the seventeenth century been subject to different cultural influences, from Cambodia, the Hindu faith and the Islamic world. Regional food names from the central region were yet another minefield for the outside cook to negotiate. Without translations, misunderstanding was a risk, spelling disaster for the pot and unbearable shame for the cook.

As well as its usefulness in setting out the measurements and methods of cooking for the first time in the Vietnamese cooking tradition, the publication of this cookbook also signalled the maturity of French cuisine in Vietnam and a complete acceptance of French food in Vietnamese daily life. *Good Cook* was an instant success. At least thirty editions have appeared since, and it is still cherished in many Vietnamese kitchens today.

THE ARRIVAL OF THE RICE COOKER

Rice continues to be the central element of any Vietnamese meal. The method of cooking it, however, changed dramatically in the 1960s in the south of Vietnam with the invention of the electric rice cooker.

The idea was considered as early as the 1910s and '20s in Japan, but the first model was not available to the public until 1955, when the company Toshiba managed to create a machine that cooked rice perfectly. It was an instant success, since it freed the cook from the most difficult task in the kitchen: how to cook perfect rice every time. Other manufacturers joined in, and in the 1960s the rice cooker was modified to become a steamer as well. Other modified models followed, until the electric rice cooker

Rice cooker and measuring cup.

became the versatile, chip-controlled cooking device we know today. It can now cook other food, such as bread, cakes, dumplings and braised dishes. The cooking time and temperature can be controlled by buttons on the lid. However, models like this are not available worldwide, being too versatile for most people and too expensive. For the world outside Japan, a simple electric rice cooker was developed in the late 1960s by Toshiba and Matsushita simply to cook the rice and keep it warm. Millions of these cookers have been sold, not only in the markets of Southeast Asia but elsewhere in the world as well. It has now become such an essential gadget in Asian kitchens that Asian students cannot do without it, even in their dormitories. They happily take their rice cookers with them to university, along with their computers and smartphones.

The electric rice cooker entered Vietnam in the late 1960s and took off in the early 1970s in urban areas of the south. The north was by then beset by austerity measures, since both north and south were going through the last stages of the war, so electrical gadgets might have been beyond most people's budget in northern Vietnam – not to mention rendered almost useless by the scarcity of the electricity supply.

The arrival of the rice cooker heralded a new era of food preparation for many Vietnamese cooks, for it took away the need to keep a close eye on the rice pot while cooking other dishes. By putting a measure of rice and one-and-a-half measures of water into the cooker and pressing a button, the cook could now relax and experiment with other dishes. Cookery classes became more popular, and daily dishes became more refined or adventurous as the cook had more time to make an effort. The only problem with the electric rice cooker is that it cooks rice almost too perfectly, without any variation, such as the crunchy crust on the bottom that some people consider so delicious. That is, however, a tiny problem that many are willing to put aside for the benefit of having a perfect pot of rice every time.

WEIRD AND WONDERFUL FOODS

Amid the culinary upheavals during the French century and the war that followed, life went on for many Việt. Next to the new foods that many liked and embraced, they still had a large repertoire of Vietnamese food that they carried on eating. Snacking was and still is a dominant Vietnamese eating habit, and some of the snacks are challenging for those who are not familiar with the taste or the concept.

Molluscs

The Vietnamese have never given up their taste for molluscs, in many forms and under many guises, which they call by the generic names *ốc* for the round ones and *nghêu* or *hến* for the bivalves. Over the centuries, if not millennia, *ốc*, *nghêu* and *hến* have featured largely in Vietnamese life, from the highest to the lowest table. Two of the 100 dishes given in the royal cookbook *Thực Phổ Bách Thiên* involve preparing and cooking molluscs, such as clam patties, and instructions are given on how to deal with snails and cockles in general:

> To get cockles one has to dive down into the mud.
> They cling on to tree roots, posts and pillions, unlike clams.
> White cockle meat should be picked out with a lemon thorn;
> Black cockle shells should be cracked open on a chopping board;
> Rice cockle is small and round, its flesh is bound to be tiny;
> Paddy snail is hugely fat, its flesh is ample.
> Do not boil cockles when the moon is waning.
> A cockle puzzle: crawling by mouth but not a cow's mouth?[3]

Snack cockles and snails were and still are big business in Vietnam, offering a large variety that can be cooked in many ways. Sometimes a whole street is devoted to selling many types of mollusc for snacks. Alternatively,

Blood clams, a favourite of the Vietnamese.

mobile vendors carrying basketfuls of cooked cockles can be seen walking the streets at any time of day, but more often in the evening. One can hail a vendor, then squat down to enjoy a plateful of cockles cooked in coconut milk and garnished with sweet basil, picking out the soft but chewy flesh with a sharp pin. Traditionally, the tool was a lemon or lime thorn, which lent its delicate citrus scent to the mollusc flesh, but modern convenience has taken over and the steel pin is now the main tool for picking out cockle flesh. Sometimes the snails or cockles are so small that the flesh is little bigger than a pinhead, but presumably the fun is in the picking and the taste is in the cooking liquor. Other snails are so big that the flesh can be a gob-stopping chewy mass. The mollusc flesh can be eaten as it is, in its own cooking liquor, or dipped into a fish sauce laced with chopped ginger and chilli. Bivalves are often dipped in a mixture of salt, pepper and lime juice. For the connoisseur, mountain snails are the best, since they come from clear streams untainted by pollutants or other human intervention. They are greatly valued and often sold at high prices.

Most often, instead of walking around, mobile vendors choose to sit at markets to offer their cockle specialities, next to many other snacks that market-goers find hard to resist. In the evenings, snail-, cockle- or clam-eating places can be fashionable meeting points for friends and lovers, who sit down to share a bowl of their preferred molluscs, washed down with beer or rice wine. In Hanoi today, a whole area bordering the main West Lake is devoted to snail shops, which offer paddy snails harvested from the muddy shore or rice fields near by. The large snails on offer, the size of an English garden snail, are cooked in spices or a mixture of medicinal ingredients. Here, every evening, under the cover of a tarpaulin strung between trees to keep out the rain or dew, courting couples or groups of friends pick, chew, exchange endearments or catch up on their daily lives.

Apart from being cooked whole in a variety of ways, *ốc* can be chopped finely and mixed with a minced pork paste, chopped shiitake mushrooms and ginger, then stuffed back into the shells before being steamed. To ease the mixture out of the shell, the diner pulls at a ginger leaf lining the shell, underneath the mixture. This leaf provides a fresh ginger taste that counters the earthy flavour of the mollusc itself. When ginger leaves are not available, a blade of bamboo leaf can be used as a replacement. This is one of Hanoi's famous traditional dishes, and is still served at many restaurants in the city.

Large marine conches are plentiful off the coast of Vietnam, from Hạ Long Bay to Phan Thiết and Mũi Né in the centre. The flesh can be cut into thin slivers and then either boiled or fried with a variety of sauces to replace a much more expensive ingredient that the Việt often use in banquet dishes, the abalone. The texture of the meat is so similar that it is difficult to tell which is which. Also, like all elaborate banquet dishes, the abalone dish depends on other ingredients for its tastiness, such as bamboo shoots, vegetables and mushrooms. It is hard to tell if it is conch meat or abalone in such a complex mixture.

Snake and Eel

While the sight of either of these creatures on a plate can be alarming for some, for many Vietnamese, eel is a coveted delicacy, similar to the way the Japanese value their equivalent, *unagi*. In Vietnam, eel is most often served with transparent vermicelli, but it can be cooked in many other ways to eat with rice.

One of the tales that visitors to Vietnam love to tell is how the Việt drink the blood of a live cobra and then eat its beating heart. The drinking of cobra blood in Vietnam is traditionally a dare among young men from certain backgrounds, a pledge of allegiance among members of a gang, or a desperate act by someone who hopes to enhance his sexual prowess.

Royal Eel

Scrub the eel with ashes and rice husks till it's squeaky clean.

Slice it lengthways to take out the guts.

Boil the meat till it's just cooked and yellow.

Vermicelli should be soaked till the strands are white.

Stir-fry the eel pieces with lard, don't let them fall apart.

Quickly season with sugar and pepper, avoid breaking up the vermicelli.

Add a few teaspoons of fish sauce.

Garnish with coriander leaves and chopped chives, then serve.

Lady Trương Đăng Thị Bích,
Thực Phổ Bách Thiên (One Hundred Good Dishes, 1915)

Snake wine, a strong tonic believed to warm the body due to its *yang* quality.

It has never been standard among the population at large, or appeared regularly in restaurants. However, the long reach of Hollywood changed all that. After watching scenes of cobra-blood drinking in films about the USA–Vietnam war, many viewers had the impression that it was the norm and a thrill they would like to experience in Vietnam.

Following the open-door policy of the late 1980s, many visitors came to Vietnam, mostly backpacking youngsters or pioneering businessmen. With this preconception in mind, they began to ask for this thrilling experience. At US$50–100 per snake, it was cheap enough for the daring visitor and a fortune for the Vietnamese, who happily complied. It did not help that television programmes subsequently promoted the activity as part of the travelling experience in Vietnam, a sensational glimpse into the life of the barbaric Other. Over time, cobra blood gained such notoriety that it became a dark but thriving industry. Because it was not a normal activity for the Vietnamese, these thrill-seekers would have to look beyond the norm, making the experience even more exciting for them. The Vietnamese cobra providers, who knew how to exploit that, would entice the visitors into a poorly lit room down an obscure alley, and offer them the wriggling cobra at a table. When the price had been agreed, the cobra was killed on the spot and its blood caught in a glass of strong spirit for the visitor to drink in one gulp. Sometimes, for extra effect, the heart of the cobra was ripped out and placed in the glass of blood while still beating. Although cobra blood is not banned in Vietnam and there is nothing illegal about the activity, the trek into the dark alley, the thrill of watching a killing and the taste of blood made it a memorable experience for those who went in search of it.

Ironically, the high price the visitors paid and the popularity of the experience fostered a misconception among ordinary Vietnamese that all foreign visitors liked drinking cobra blood, and that it was what they would do normally in a social situation. Today, the drinking of cobra blood has blossomed into a thriving industry, with the Vietnamese and the foreign visitors both believing that the other is the barbarian who perpetuates the fad.

Snake wine or spirit is another matter. Many Vietnamese and Chinese believe that drinking wine or spirits with one or more snakes soaked in it can cure many ailments, strengthen bones and ligaments, and keep arthritis at bay. Snake meat is also highly valued as a medicinal food. It belongs to the *yang* category, and its 'warm' quality is believed to make it a cure for aches and pains. It is meaty and tasty enough to be cooked in a variety of ways. Those in the know, both French and Vietnamese, say that snake meat tastes like chicken.

Insects

Although the concept is off-putting for many, insects are routinely digested by two billion people in the world today.[4] Some of us have

Silkworm cocoons. The silk strands are harvested from these cocoons, leaving the pupae exposed.

been unknowingly eating them for years. The American Food and Drug Administration handbook on the level of defects in food states that it is acceptable for every 10 g (⅓ oz.) of hops to contain some aphids, every 250 ml (8½ fl. oz.) of tinned fruit juice to contain one maggot, and every 25 g (⅞ oz.) of curry powder to contain up to a hundred insect fragments.[5] Most people, though, eat insects by choice, in 36 African countries, 29 in Asia, 23 in the Americas and 11 in Europe.

According to the Food and Agriculture Organization (FAO) of the United Nations, there are 1,900 edible species of insect, the most common being crickets, beetles, caterpillars, bees and ants. The FAO also says that since insects are high in protein – even higher than meat in some cases – we should try to eat more of them in the future, in order to consume enough protein for a healthy life. In a report issued in 2013, the UN said that by 2050 the population of the world would reach nine billion, and there would not be enough agricultural land to feed so many mouths.[6] Insects, on the other hand, occupy very little space, and emit less methane than cattle while providing a high level of protein and minerals, so it is only logical to start farming them for everyday food. Insect farming is quick, since insects have a shorter lifespan than conventional livestock, and it also creates jobs for many people living in poor areas. The individual taste of the various insects is generally not bad, according to those in the know; for example, African termites taste minty, stinkbugs taste like apple and coconut worms taste like . . . coconut. It is easier said than done, however, and the idea of eating a scorpion or a cricket is still unacceptable to many people, even in South America, Africa and Asia, where more people eat insects by choice than in the Western world.

The Việt eat a wide variety of insects and worms as part of a meal or as snacks, from locusts to earthworms. Some are normal everyday food, others special delicacies. The general poverty in rural areas even makes it necessary for people to eat whatever they can find to sustain themselves.

One of the unusual foods, but one that is popular among the northern Việt, is the silkworm pupa, *nhộng*. This is alarming for those unfamiliar with the appearance of the silkworm pupa, and it may even be scarier for those who have tasted them, for the texture is incomparable to anything else edible. A bite through the crispy outer body reveals a soft ooze that can be either revolting or delicious, depending on how adventurous the diner is. As for looks, on close inspection the back of the pupa looks like a normal hairless worm, but its underside resembles a miniature Egyptian mummy. Each pupa is only about the same size as a wingless wasp, yet its dark golden-brown colour, the folded legs on its chest and its fully formed head with bulging closed eyes present a mystical and horrifying image that makes eating it a tough challenge. Many Vietnamese have no such qualms, however; for them, the insect is full of goodness, tasty and cheap.

As the name implies, silkworm pupae are what is left of the domesticated insects that produce silk, once their silken cocoons have been stripped off. One legacy of the Chinese millennium is the silk industry of northern Vietnam. The raising of silkworms continued to be encouraged even after Vietnam gained its independence from the Chinese in the tenth century, and royal concubines were often assigned the duty of raising silkworms when they were not serving the emperors.

The main silk-producing area of north Vietnam is Hà Đông, formerly a village near Hanoi but now a suburb of the city. The silk produced there is famous for its quality, and has been lauded in Vietnamese poetry and songs. Over the centuries the village has been devoted to raising silkworms and weaving the silk they produce. The problem is that to make 1 sq. m (nearly 11 sq. ft) of silk takes hundreds if not thousands of silkworms, each of which must be allowed to mature enough to use its saliva to spin silk strands around its body to form a protective cocoon, inside which it will metamorphose into a moth. The silk is harvested by boiling the cocoon and the worm inside, since the silk strands are easier to pull out when boiled.

Once the silk has been harvested, the villagers are left with the boiled pupae, thousands and thousands of them. Waste not want not, as they say, and their simple solution was to eat them. The eating of silkworm pupae probably began centuries ago, and continues to this day. From the silk village, the worms were brought into Hanoi and other towns and cities in the north to become an everyday dish on the Vietnamese family table. Northern Vietnamese people do not think twice about eating them, but it is still an alien concept for many central and southern Vietnamese, despite now being available throughout the country. The silkworm pupae are usually sold by vendors who carry them through the streets or to the markets in bamboo baskets and sell them by the cupful. In Vietnam, they are eaten fresh, but in some other Asian countries they are available tinned for human consumption, or as fish food.

They can be cooked in several ways, but the most popular is fried with chopped onion, fish sauce and pepper. Prepared this way, the body of the worm is crunchy on the outside but juicy inside. It is said that the protein content of the insect is as high as or even higher than meat. *Nhộng* can

Silkworm pupa (*nhộng*).

also be cooked in an omelette, served with a sauce or just boiled plain to eat with rice.

A less controversial worm is a delicacy of the Mekong Delta and much appreciated by many Vietnamese: the coconut worm. As its name implies, this is the larva of a beetle that lays her eggs inside the body of a coconut tree. Any palm tree will do the job for her, but it seems coconut is the favourite. The larvae are nourished by the coconut's soft core until they grow wings and burst out of the tree, leaving it dead. The larvae are usually harvested before they become fully grown. The locals chop down the tree and empty out the hollow trunk to get at them. Being fed entirely on coconut, the worms are fat (the size of a thumb) and milky white and take on a delicate coconut flavour. Coconut trees grow in abundance around the Mekong Delta, so coconut worms are available all year round; they are quite expensive compared to other food, however, because each tree can accommodate only a limited number of worms, so they are usually served as a delicacy, either at home or in restaurants.

Coconut worms can be cooked in many ways, but they are most commonly deep-fried in batter or stir-fried with butter to eat with wine or beer or as part of a luxury meal. This combination of worms and butter is an eloquent example of how thoroughly and casually a French product has been absorbed into village life in the Mekong Delta. In certain areas in the delta, coconut worms are eaten raw after being soaked in a strong spirit. Of those who have tasted this worm and written about it – both Vietnamese and foreign visitors – some may have had their reservations at first, but eventually all say that the taste is pleasantly coconutty and the texture like that of soft cheese.

Another insect eaten by the Việt is highly valued, not for its flesh but for the sacs of pungent juice that the male produces to attract the female. Called *cà cuống* (*Lethocerus indicus*), only the male of this species is caught for eating or, more accurately, for seasoning. This flying insect, which lives in grassy areas by ponds and lakes or paddy fields, looks like a giant dark cockroach and can grow to a length of 10–12 cm (4–5 in.). It is attracted to light no matter what the source – whether street light, house light or any other kind – perhaps in the mistaken hope that it is moonlight, for its mating time is at the full moon. Each male has two sacs of clear liquid

Cà cuống, a large edible insect. The males are caught for their special sacs of cinnamon-tasting liquid, which is much coveted by the people of north Vietnam and some other Southeast Asian countries.

attached to its body, each sac about 2 cm (¾ in.) long. In these sacs is an oily liquid or essence with a peculiar smell that is valued highly by northerners – who say it smells of cinnamon – but considered a stink by others. Since the bugs are attracted to light, it is easy to catch them hanging on to lamp posts or tree trunks during the rainy season. Once they are caught, the oily essence is extracted, a few drops from each insect. It is therefore very expensive, and is considered a delicacy to add to a bowl of mixed *nước mắm* for *bún chả* or *bánh cuốn*, or to the noodle soup *bún thang*. It is sold in tiny vials for taking home, or by the drop in restaurants. One or two drops can go a long way.

With their sacs gone, *cà cuống* are usually chopped and fried with onion and pepper to eat with rice, or to flavour other dishes. According to folklore, *cà cuống* was first discovered as a condiment in the second century BCE by the southern Chinese emperor Zhao To, who came to rule over the north of Vietnam at the beginning of the Chinese millennium, before losing the territory to the Han. He liked the taste so much that he sent the insect to the Han emperor in Xian, whose appreciative exclamation included something like '*cà cuống!*', and so the name stuck. However, as with all myths and legends, the story is impossible to verify.

These days the essence is reproduced in a laboratory and can be bought cheaply all over Asia. The Vietnamese call it Thai chemical *cà cuống*; it is acceptable, but not valued as highly as the real thing.

Other Weird and Wonderful Foods

So much has been written about the practice of eating dog, cat and other Western taboo foods in Asia – Vietnam included – that writing further about them is futile. All eating habits, however, must be put into a cultural context and considered along with the economic circumstances of the country concerned. In Vietnam, the eating of insects, worms, frogs and mice has revolted many, but it is a necessary way of providing the poor with enough protein to sustain themselves. Cobra meat, on the other hand, is a rare and quirky luxury that fulfils male wishes for enhanced virility. There is no excuse for eating dogs and cats for pleasure, from any perspective – Eastern, Western or otherwise. One food, though, is baffling for those who cannot contemplate touching it: raw blood, *tiết canh*.

Animal blood has been used widely from East to West for centuries, as in the British black pudding or the French *boudin*, both of which are delicacies and are commonly consumed as normal everyday food. In

Vietnam, the boiled blood of pig, duck, goat, rabbit and chicken is normal as an addition to soup and cold dishes. Next to the cooked version, raw blood is also a preferred dish for many. Whether it is thanks to the chopped gizzard, liver and herbs added to it or to the taste of the blood itself, this is a delicious dish that wine and beer drinkers love to have with their drinks.

To make the dish, raw blood is mixed with a small amount of stock, seasoned and poured over chopped gizzards in a shallow dish. The mixture is left to congeal, which usually happens very quickly. Before it is eaten, the dish is garnished with chopped peanuts and sweet basil. Concerns over this dish's food safety and unhealthiness have often been voiced by the media and medical authorities, but it is as popular now as ever.

Although not as popular as it is in the Philippines, where it is called *balut*, the fertilized duck egg is another weird and wonderful food of Vietnam, where it is called *trứng vịt lộn* ('duck turn-over egg'). It is collected when the fertilized egg is about two weeks old, and the embryo is fully formed as a duck but not quite ready to break out of the shell. At this stage, its bones are still soft and it has very few feathers. Its nourishing yolk is still present, along with some egg white. From this time until the egg has matured into a fully grown duck, the eater can boil it and eat it whole with salt, pepper and hot mint. It is a valued snack in the south of Vietnam, but northerners have also acquired a taste for it over time. *Trứng vịt lộn* is usually sold by street vendors in the evening, when it is a popular snack. They walk the streets carrying the boiled eggs in bamboo baskets, wrapped with layers of cloth to keep them warm. There is nothing wrong with eating this type of egg, but the sight of the young duck inside, complete with feathers, can be off-putting for many, especially when the egg has been allowed to mature for longer than two weeks.

Regional Favourites

Every region of Vietnam has its own favourite food. Central Vietnam has several well-known and much-loved dishes, such as *bún bò Huế*, *cơm hến* and dainty steamed rice cakes. Hanoi and Saigon, meanwhile, have two types of unique food: *chả cá* (grilled fish) in Hanoi and *bò bảy món* (beef in seven courses) in Saigon. *Chả cá Hanoi* is so famous that it has given its name to a street in the city. It is a must-eat for all visitors to Hanoi, and a memorable dish for many. The dish seems difficult and mysterious to the non-Vietnamese since it contains many flavours, but it is delicious. In Hanoi restaurants, the fish is cooked in a small frying pan at the table with

Chả cá Hanoi

500 g (1 lb 2 oz.) piece firm white fish, such as cod,
monkfish or halibut

half a bundle of spring onions, cut into 2-cm (1-in.)
lengths

the top of half a bundle of fresh dill, also cut into 2-cm
(1-in.) lengths

2 tsp turmeric

salt and freshly ground black pepper

light olive oil, peanut oil or sunflower oil

1 large onion, finely sliced

1 packet rice vermicelli, medium-sized strands (cooked
according to instructions on packet)

handful of roasted unsalted peanuts, crushed

1 round lettuce, shredded

1 packet ready-to-eat prawn crackers (optional)

handful of pickled radish or fennel

1 small bowl mixed *nước mắm* (for recipe, see page 195)

lime quarters and chopped fresh chilli, to serve

A steaming serving of *chả cá Hanoi*.

Place the fish in a large dish. Mix together half the spring onion, half the dill, the turmeric and a pinch each of salt and pepper and scatter over the fish. Cover the dish with cling film and marinate in the fridge overnight or for at least an hour.

Brush the fish with a little oil and cook over charcoal for best effect, or under the grill or in a hot oven (at least 220°C/425°F). It should take 10–15 minutes. Put the remaining spring onion and dill on a serving plate, reserving a few sprigs for the garnish, then put the cooked fish on top and sprinkle the garnish over the fish while it is still sizzling. Heat 1 tsp oil in a small pan and cook the sliced onion until it is golden but not crispy. Pour both oil and onion over the fish.

Cut the fish into bite-sized pieces to serve, or cut it up at the table. To assemble the dish, put the noodles in a bowl, add some pieces of fish with spring onion and dill, peanuts, lettuce, crumbled pieces of prawn crackers, a few strands of pickles and a spoonful of mixed *nước mắm*. Adjust to individual taste with lime juice and chillies. In Hanoi, the dish is often served with mixed shrimp paste (*mắm tôm*) instead of mixed *nước mắm*.

fresh dill and spring onion, but the dish can be made in a slightly different way so as to reduce the amount of oil it contains.

The habit of eating beef was brought to Vietnam by the French colonists during the nineteenth century, and had become normal by the beginning of the twentieth century, when the dish *bò bảy món* was born. This feast of one meat cooked seven ways is usually served in medium-class restaurants – neither too fancy nor too shabby – so that groups of friends or families can relax and eat with gusto. The dishes are offered in generous portions, making the dining experience a plentiful exercise in good eating.

The courses offered vary from restaurant to restaurant, but in general there are set dishes that every diner would expect. One of these is slices of beef dipped in a communal hotpot called 'steamboat', containing a hot mixture of vinegar, fresh lemongrass, onion and stock to cook, and wrapped in sheets of rice paper, salad, pickles and herbs before being

Shaking Beef

lettuce, rocket, lamb's lettuce or watercress
1 beef tomato, cut into thin wedges, or several cherry
tomatoes, cut in half
2–3 tbsp mixed *nước mắm*
1 lime
light olive oil, for frying
2 rib-eye steaks, about 230–50 g (8–9 oz.) each,
cut into 2-cm (1-in.) cubes
1 onion, cut in half and then into wedges about
1 cm (½ in.) thick
1 clove of garlic, crushed
slices of fresh chilli
rock salt and freshly ground black pepper

Make a salad by mixing the vegetables and tomato pieces
with the mixed *nước mắm*. Add a few drops of lime juice and
a pinch of ground black pepper, and arrange the salad on
a serving plate, leaving a space in the centre.

Heat the oil and fry the steak and onion on a high heat
until the meat is cooked as you prefer (medium-rare or
medium is traditional and gives the best result). Add the
crushed garlic at the last minute and stir it around or shake
the pan vigorously. Tip the meat mixture into the hole in
the middle of the salad and serve with a sprinkling of salt
and black pepper. Scatter the chilli on top to complete
the picture.

dipped in a variety of sauces. This is usually the starter, and is followed by
hamburger-style patties. Next come minced beef wrapped in lard, minced
beef wrapped in *chapru* leaves, beef satay on sticks, and steak or cubes of
beef fried quickly by shaking the pan vigorously. This last dish, *bò lúc lắc*, is
better known among visitors as 'shaking beef' (although a more appropriate translation would be 'shaken'). Rice porridge with minced beef forms
the last course. Each of the first six courses is served with salad and herbs,
rice wrappers and rice noodles, making them very filling, but – although
every meal must contain rice – the porridge at the end is offered as a light

substitute. *Bò lúc lắc* is the favourite of all the courses, and has become a dish on its own terms, served with rice or French bread.

It is not known how the seven-course beef feast came about, but it makes an exotic change for a people who eat mainly pork, chicken or fish. Beef restaurants serving *bò lúc lắc* can be found everywhere in the south of Vietnam, and are as popular as ever.

Flavour Enhancers and Modern Food

Vietnamese cuisine relies on the freshness of the ingredients, and also on herbs and other seasonings. Stock is at the centre of many noodle dishes, from the large variety of *bún* to the national dish *phở*, and so how to make that stock tasty is the most important element of Vietnamese cooking. Traditionally, a rich stock is achieved by boiling bones, dried shrimp or sweet root vegetables for hours. In modern times, a quicker and cheaper route is open to many cooks: adding the wonder product monosodium glutamate (MSG).

For decades after MSG was launched into the culinary world, it was used extensively in almost all food products, from the humble bowl of noodles to snacks and baby food to a huge variety of products churned out by global processed-food companies. For many in Asia and elsewhere, the Japanese trade name Ajinomoto became a synonym for MSG, just as many in Europe call the vacuum cleaner after its trade name, Hoover. Many other trade names followed and, as the product gained popularity, MSG began to be sold in bags containing a kilogram (2¼ lb) or more. Its essence, however, remains unchanged, whatever the name. It is the main flavour enhancer on which vegetarian dishes rely to replace the naturally deep taste of meat and bone stock. For most of the twentieth century, MSG has been used so extensively and regularly in Asia that it is quite normal to see a diner adding a tiny spoonful of the powder to a bowl of noodles or *phở* in a restaurant or at home.

These days, more than a century from its launch in 1909, the world population consumes 1.5 million tonnes of MSG every year, despite a huge scare that started in 1968, when it was blamed for many ailments, such as headaches, hot flushes and numbness that lasted up to two hours. The complaints usually occurred after the diner had eaten a Chinese meal, which would inevitably contain MSG. Many people followed suit and a long list of side effects grew, referred to colloquially as Chinese restaurant syndrome (CRS) in the United States and, later, elsewhere. Media hype did not help, and tales of permanent brain damage among the young, cancer or memory loss circulated around the world. By the 1990s MSG had been branded a silent killer in the kitchen. The scare was so widespread that the product was scientifically investigated in many laboratories throughout the world. The verdict was that MSG was safe as an additive, according to the food regulators of many regions including the United States and the European Union, but it must now be listed among the ingredients of processed food. With or without this verdict, though, it is unthinkable for many home and restaurant cooks to leave this magic powder out of their food – they would be branded bad cooks – and so MSG lives on in many dishes, from East to West.

In Vietnam, after the intense MSG scare of the 1980s and '90s, it became a virtue for many middle-class Vietnamese to forgo MSG, a great sacrifice considering it has been in many, if not all, Vietnamese dishes for almost a century, and everybody expected that delicious deep taste in whatever they ate. Restaurants began to display signs saying 'no MSG', and home cooks began to find ways around the need to use MSG. However, most people still look to this additive as an aid to their cooking skills, no matter what the scientists or other consumers say. The camps for and against MSG, meanwhile, carry on with their respective arguments, with no clear-cut winner at this stage.

BOOMERANG FOOD

During the last days of the war in Vietnam, in April 1975, hundreds of thousands of south Vietnamese left the country to resettle in the West and, to a lesser extent, in neighbouring countries and Australia. They brought with them their tastes of home and, once settled, tried to re-create those tastes wherever they found themselves. In the United States, where most Vietnamese evacuees made their new homes, the yearning for their own food turned an entire generation of men and women into cooks, something that would not have happened back in Vietnam, for Vietnamese food had always been available everywhere. Many Vietnamese home cooks now learned to make their own versions of their favourite dishes, aided by an abundance of good ingredients and labour-saving technology. When typical Vietnamese herbs were not available in the shops, the growing of such herbs from seed became a gardening hobby for many. It was not long before former food-sellers or restaurant owners began to set up shop in areas with large Vietnamese communities and sell the food they had previously sold in Vietnam. A cottage industry was soon set up to manu-facture the necessary ingredients and the dishes of home: Vietnamese sausages, spring rolls, the hundreds of *bánh* and, inevitably, the Vietnamese baguette, which is lighter than the Western one.

By the end of the 1970s, shops selling familiar Vietnamese foods, from the most sophisticated to the humble filled *bánh mì*, were established in many Vietnamese communities in the West and Australia. Some types of food now became house specialities for certain restaurants, with spe-cialist *phở* restaurants being the most popular. Market snacks and street food reappeared, alongside a large variety of *bánh*, from Vietnamese rice varieties to French gateaux. The old *bánh mì* stalls of home were replaced by *bánh mì* shops selling thousands of portions a day. Vietnamese coffee shops once more became the place for young men to sit and gossip while waiting for the drips to drop into their coffee glasses. By the 1980s, wher-ever they were, the Vietnamese in exile had reinvented a rich and extensive repertoire of Vietnamese food.

In a short space of only twenty years, the exiled Vietnamese managed to re-create an imagined home through taste. In doing so, they inadver-tently preserved several traditional and favourite Vietnamese dishes. At the same time, as with any language in exile, if it had a voice Vietnamese food

A modern version of *chả giò* made with lacy rice-paper wraps and mayonnaise added to the filling.

227

in the West would speak with a different accent and many borrowed words, for it has evolved, branched out or modified to suit local conditions. Some dishes have been modified to comply with local food regulations, such as those governing pickled and fermented foods. *Nem chua* is a good example of this. Fermented raw pork is not allowed in many Western countries for reasons of health and safety, so the exiled Việt decided to make it with cooked ham instead. The much-loved fourteen-day-old fertilized eggs were banned in many countries, but, undaunted, many Vietnamese cottage farms secretly produced the eggs themselves, away from official detection. Congealed duck blood became a guilty secret at gatherings of friends and family. Similar to the Prohibition era in the United States, a whisper among friends could reveal the location of certain places selling banned Vietnamese products. Rice wine was made at home and shared among friends, even if doing so occasionally landed the makers in jail.

In the post-war decade of 1975–85, while Vietnamese food in exile was being greatly enriched by an abundance of good ingredients, at home it went through a dramatic transformation as the country suffered a severe shortage of food and hunger became chronic for the whole population. As food became scarce, vital ingredients in many traditional dishes were substituted with cheaper ones or discarded altogether, rendering these dishes unrecognizable to culinary traditionalists. For example, a bowl of *phở* in Vietnam during this period did not contain meat, and the stock was made by boiling bones and MSG; *bánh mì* was made with low-grade wheat flour, and often contained weevils; and MSG now reigned supreme throughout the country as the magic substitute for meat and fish. Sales of MSG went through the roof, at an even higher price than before.

It was not until the end of the 1980s, when the Vietnamese policy of renovation was implemented, that the country began to emerge from its food shortages. The legalization of private enterprise acted as a tonic for the ailing agricultural system, and farmers began to grow more food for their own profit, rather than that of the co-ops. Along with several economic measures, the official open-door policy enticed many foreign businesses to set up shop in Vietnam. In the early 1990s many exiled Vietnamese were granted visas to come home as tourists.

It is difficult to describe the joy of those who decided to take the first steps home, even just for a brief visit. One of the things to which they looked forward was the taste of home, which, in their memories, had been magnified into something close to a culinary paradise. Unfortunately, the reality they found was that their beloved traditional dishes had changed, and even the national bowl of *phở* had become a pale version of its former self. With more overseas Vietnamese returning to visit, however, and an increased demand for better-quality foods, as well as the improved economic situation, the old and new tastes were soon reconciled. The Vietnamese economy grew stronger in leaps and bounds, and it was not long before more meat, fish and other foodstuffs became available in the markets under the new socialist market economy. Slices of meat and many other toppings returned to the bowl of *phở*, although the MSG stayed as a flavour enhancer for the time being. The markets were once again full of snack stalls, and more. Since the turn of the millennium, the food of Vietnam has been joined by many other cuisines: Chinese food never left, but now it competes with Thai, Japanese, Singaporean, Korean and other newly imported cuisines for the preference of the Vietnamese. None reigns supreme for now. At the same time, Western fast food and coffee culture have arrived and become popular among the young, who were born in an austere post-war economy but grew up in a boom time of good food and fast living.

Over two millennia, Vietnamese traditional food has come a long way to become the version we know today. What is most remarkable, though, is that it is fast becoming a much-liked cuisine outside Vietnam. It is a favourite for its lightness and freshness, as well as its taste. In many world cities, *bánh mì* or *phở* shops have come to stay, and some are coming out of their ethnic enclaves to be warmly welcomed on high streets. In London, for example, when the first *bánh mì* sandwich shop opened in the city centre, the queue was around the block. Many other shops followed. The once humble filled lengths of French baguette, Vietnamese-style, are now in serious competition with the traditional Western sandwiches. *Phở* is once again hailed in a Western accent, not by hungry soldiers in a faraway barrack but by the most sophisticated people in the most cosmopolitan cities of the world.

Timeline

21,000–9000 BCE	Sơn Vì culture. The proto-Việt people lived in groups sharing a communal hearth placed in the centre of a cave on high ground. They hunted a variety of animals, including deer, elephant, wild boar, wild cats, monkeys and foxes, and gathered crustaceans and molluscs along the coast, or from the streams and rivers near where they lived
c. 8000 BCE	Archaeological evidence of rice cultivation in the south of the Chinese Yangtze River. This region may include present-day northern Vietnam
7000 BCE	Hòa Bình culture. People began to venture down on to the plain and started hunting more for animals. They made more sophisticated stone tools to hunt, chop, crack and mash their food. Archaeological evidence shows that they grew plants and tamed animals such as dogs during this period. They may have used bamboo tubes for cooking over or in the fire
c. 3000 BCE	The first domesticated variety of chicken appeared in Southeast Asia, as shown by Swedish DNA research in 2008
c. 2000 BCE	Recorded wet-rice cultivation in northern Vietnam. The people also lived by fishing with nets, and knew how to use clay
2000–c. 1500 BCE	Phùng Nguyên culture. Pottery appeared; crudely made at first, it became more sophisticated later. The pieces were used to store, cook and serve food. Pollen analysis shows that the proto-Việt had plenty of greens, tubers, fruit and nuts to eat, as well as their traditional diet of meat, fish and shellfish. They had bamboo shoots, aubergines, lentils, green vegetables and watermelons
1000 BCE–c. 100 CE	Đông Sơn culture. Bronze artefacts and agricultural implements appeared. Images showing the growing and processing of rice were engraved on the tympana of the Đông Sơn bronze drums. Evidence of the Asian

	rice variety *Oryza sativa* dating from this time has been found underground, and glutinous rice is mentioned in historical documents. The traditional *bánh chưng* and *bánh dầy* appeared
2nd century BCE	Arrival of the first Chinese ruler in northern Vietnam. Rice was now the staple food, but hunting continued. Rice wine is mentioned in historical documents
257 BCE–938 CE	The Chinese millennium. Import of many Chinese ingredients, such as wheat, rice noodles, Chinese mushrooms, tea and soy products. Trading activities between the Han and the Roman Empire may have created the Roman fish sauce *garum* and Vietnamese *nước mắm*
939–1859 CE	Development of a specifically Vietnamese cuisine. Establishment of a specialized market in present-day Hanoi under the Lý (11th–13th centuries). Famines and feasts through the dynasties
Early 15th century	Pepper appears and both salt and pepper are tightly controlled under the brief Ming occupation of Vietnam
17th and 18th centuries	Adoption of Cham and Khmer foods as the Nguyễn dynasty moves southward. Development of the Mekong Delta with the help of the Ming refugees from Qing China
1859–1954	The French century. Import of dairy products, vegetables, coffee, pastries and charcuterie. Development of a French–Vietnamese cuisine and the rise of the French baguette (*bánh mì*) in Vietnamese food culture. Birth of the Vietnamese national dish beef *phở*
1945–54	The Great Famine. Anti-colonial war intensifies. The smokeless cooking system is invented in north Vietnam
1954–75	The Geneva Accord. Food problems arise in both north and south Vietnam
1963–73	Food problems continue in the north. Military rations of the three combat parties as war continues to rage in both north and south Vietnam. American foods, frozen foods and automatic rice cookers arrive in South Vietnam. Intense bombing causes food shortages in north Vietnam
1973–5	Fighting intensifies in south Vietnam and the north is bombed heavily until the country is reunified
1975–89	Post-war food problems throughout the country. Reinvention of Vietnamese food by refugees abroad
1989–present	Open-door policy brings in foreign investment and the return of many overseas Vietnamese. Private enterprise in Vietnam turns the economy around, and food becomes plentiful once more. Increased demand for better-quality food brings back many traditional recipes, and new ones are invented. Vietnamese cuisine becomes popular in cities around the world

References

ONE: From Molluscs to Venison

1 Tetzu Chung, 'Rice', in *The Cambridge World History of Food* (Cambridge, 2008), vol. II, 11.a.7.

2 Nguyễn Khac Vien, *Vietnam: A Long History* (seventh edition Hanoi, 2007), pp. 13–14; 'Thời Cổ Đại', http://dictionary.bachkhoatoanthu.gov.vn (accessed September 2013).

3 Stephen W. Solheim, 'Northern Thailand, Southeast Asia, and World Prehistory', *Asian Perspectives*, XIII/1 [12] (1972), p. 150.

4 Hà Văn Tấn, Nguyễn Khắc Sử and Trịnh Năng Chung, *Văn Hóa Sơn Vi (Sơn Vi Culture)* (Hanoi, 1999).

5 Ibid., p. 122.

6 'Ancient Calendar Unearthed', *VietnamNet*, 27 September 2012, http://english. vietnamnet.vn; '6,000-year-old Tombs Unearthed in Northeast Vietnam', *Thanh Niên News*, 20 December 2013, www.thanhniennews.com.

7 UNESCO, 'Con Moong Cave', http://whc.unesco.org (accessed 25 January 2015).

8 Madeleine Colani, *L'Âge de la pierre dans la province de Hoa-Binh (Tonkin)* (Hanoi, 1927); 'Stations Hoabinhiennes dans la region de Phu Nho Quan (Province de Ninh Binh)', *Bulletin du Service Géologique de l'Indochine*, XVII/1 (1928), pp. 1–47; *Thời Cổ Đại* ebook at www.lichsuvietnam.vn, September 2011.

9 Lich su Vietnam Toan tap, 'Prehistory', in official Vietnamese history online edition.

10 Solheim, 'Northern Thailand'.

11 Đỗ Đức Hùng et al., *Việt Nam Những Sự Kiện Lịch Sử (Từ Khởi Thủy Đến 1858)* (Hanoi, 2001), p. 8.

12 J. Eriksson et al., 'Identification of the Yellow Skin Gene Reveals a Hybrid Origin of the Domestic Chicken', *PLoS Genet,* IV/2 (2008).

13 Stephen W. Solheim, 'New Light on a Forgotten Past', *National Geographic*, 3 (1971), p. 333.

14 Ibid., p. 339.

15 *Thời Cổ Đại*.

16 Ibid., pp. 58–61.

17 Ibid.

18 Ibid.

19 Ibid.
20 Ibid., p. 46.

TWO: Towards a Cuisine

1 *Thời Cổ Đại*, ebook at www.lichsuvietnam.vn, September 2011.
2 Nguyễn Việt, 'Hoabinhian Food Strategy in Vietnam', in *SEA Archaeology*, ed. Stephen W. Solheim (Manila, 2004).
3 Kenneth F. Kiple, *A Movable Feast: Ten Millennia of Food Globalization* (Cambridge, 2007), pp. 38–9.
4 Ibid.
5 Ibid., pp. 57–9; Lam Thi My Dzung, 'Some Aspects of Vietnamese Bronze Age', in *The Final Research Results Supported by the KFAS International Scholar Exchange Fellowship Program (2001–2002)*, 2002, p. 230.

THREE: Agricultural Settlements, Animal Farms and Fisheries

1 Hà Văn Tấn and Nguyễn Duy Hinh, 'Kinh Tế Thời Hùng Vương', in *Hùng Vương Dựng Nước*, ed. Uy Ban Khoa Hoc Xa Hoi (Hanoi, 1973), pp. 145–6; K. W. Taylor, *The Birth of Vietnam* (Berkeley, CA, 1983), p. 12.
2 Trần Thế Pháp, *Lĩnh Nam Chích Quái*, trans. Lê Hữu Mục (Saigon, 1961), p. 44; *Thời Cổ Đại*, ebook at www.lichsuvietnam.vn, September 2011.
3 Vien Khoa Hoc Xa Hoi Viet Nam, trans., *Đại Việt Sử Ký Toàn Thư* (Hanoi, 1992), p. 61.
4 Trần Thế Pháp, *Lĩnh Nam Chích Quái*, p. 44.
5 Lê Tắc, *An Nam Chí Lược*, trans. Huế University (Huế, Vietnam, 1961), p. 12.
6 Viên Sử học, trans., *Khâm Định Việt Sử Thông Giám Cương Mục, Tien Bien*, vol. 1 (Hanoi, 1998), p. 4.
7 Taylor, *The Birth of Vietnam*, pp. 12–13.
8 Ibid., p. 417. The jar can be seen online in the Virtual Collection of Asian Masterpieces, available at http://masterpieces.asemus.museum (accessed November 2015).
9 Trần Thế Pháp, *Lĩnh Nam Chích Quái*, p. 44.
10 Ibid.
11 Ibid.

FOUR: The Chinese Millennium, 257 BCE–938 CE

1 Nguyễn Quang Ngọc, 'Việt Nam từ thời tiền sử đến thời dựng nước', in *Tiến trình Lịch sử Việt Nam* (Hà Nội, 2006), chap. 1, pp. 30–35.
2 Ibid., pp. 25–6.
3 See map in K. W. Taylor, *The Birth of Vietnam* (Berkeley, CA, 1983), p. 30.
4 Ibid.
5 Ibid.
6 Viện khoa học xã hội Việt Nam, trans., *Đại Việt Sử Ký Toàn Thư* (Hanoi, 1992), vol. 1, pp. 89–90; Viên Sử Học, trans., *Khâm Định Việt Sử Thông Giám Cương Mục, Tien Bien*, vol. 1 (Hanoi, 1998), pp. 22–3.

7 Hà Văn Tấn, ed., *Khảo Cổ Học Việt Nam*, vol. II (Hanoi, 1999), pp. 57–9.

8 Lê Tắc, *An Nam Chí Lược*, trans. Huế University (Huế, Vietnam, 1961), p. 66.

9 Kenneth F. Kiple, *A Movable Feast: Ten Millennia of Food Globalization* (Cambridge, 2007), p. 28; Joy McCorriston, 'Wheat', in *The Cambridge World History of Food*, vol. I (Cambridge, 2008), pp. 158–74.

10 Taylor, *The Birth of Vietnam*, p. 60.

11 Ibid.; G. Coedes, *The Indianised States of Southeast Asia*, trans. Susan Brown Cowing (Honolulu, HI, 1968), p. 60.

12 Thomas Suarez, *Early Mapping of Southeast Asia* (Singapore, 1999), pp. 89–99.

13 Author's own research in Rome.

14 Lê Tắc, *An Nam Chí Lược*, pp. 42 and 84–7; *Khâm Định Việt Sử Thông Giám Cương Mục*, pp. 71–2.

15 Taylor, *The Birth of Vietnam*, p. 60.

16 Andrew F. Smith, 'From Garum to Ketchup: A Spicy Tale of Two Fish Sauces', in *Fish: Food from the Waters*, ed. Harlan Walker (Totnes, Devon, 1998), pp. 299–302; David S. Reese, 'Fish: Evidence from Specimens, Mosaics, Wall Paintings, and Roman Authors', in *The Natural History of Pompeii* (Cambridge, 2002), p. 232.

17 Quoted in Barbara Flower and Elisabeth Rosenbaum, trans., *The Roman Cookery Book: A Critical Translation of the* Art of Cooking *by Apicius for Use in the Study and the Kitchen* (London, 1958), pp. 188–9.

FIVE: Independence Food, 939–1859

1 Đào Duy Anh, *Lịch Sử Việt Nam, Từ Nguồn Gốc Đến Giữa Thế Kỷ XIX* (Hanoi, 2002), p. 214; Viên Sử Học, trans., *Khâm Định Việt Sử Thông Giám Cương Mục, Tien Bien*, vol. I (Hanoi, 1998), pp. 281–7.

2 O. W. Wolters, *Two Essays on Dai Viet in the Fourteenth Century* (New Haven, CT, 1988), p. 16.

3 Ibid.

4 Ibid., p. 202.

5 Viện khoa học xã hội Việt Nam, trans., *Đại Việt Sử Ký Toàn Thư* (Hanoi, 1992), p. 322.

6 Ibid. Đào Duy Anh preferred to use the term *mắm*, which makes more sense since *mắm* signifies a product made with lots of salt to preserve whatever the bottle contains (vegetables, meat or fish), whereas *nước mắm* is a liquid extract of salted fish and as such does not contain such a high level of salt.

7 Vien Khoa Hoc Xa Hoi Viet Nam, trans., *Đại Việt Sử Ký Toàn Thư*, p. 326.

8 Trần Trọng Kim, *Việt Nam Sử Lược* (Hanoi, 2002), p. 254.

9 Viên Sử Học, trans., *Khâm Định Việt Sử Thông Giám Cương Mục*, pp. 446–8, 963.

10 Paul Pelliot, 'Le Fou-nan', *Bulletin de l'École Française d'Extrême Orient*, vol. III (1903), pp. 248–303.

11 Trần Trọng Kim, *Việt Nam Sử Lược*, pp. 208, 212 and 217.

SIX: The French Century, 1859–1954

1 L. Gilbert, 'Les Produits', *Bulletin des amis du vieux Hué* (January–June 1931), pp. 125–40.
2 See 'Effects of French Colonial Rule' in 'Vietnam: History', in *Encyclopaedia Britannica*, available at www.britannica.com (accessed December 2014).
3 Ibid.
4 Nguyễn Khac Vien, *Vietnam: A Long History* (seventh edition Hanoi, 2007), p. 153.
5 L. Gaide, 'Le Visage inconnu de l'opium', *Bulletin des amis di vieux Hué*, 2 and 3 (April–September 1938), pp. 87–102. The edition is devoted to opium, starting from p. 83.

SEVEN: Food at War

1 Ministère de l'Économie Nationale, Institut Nationale de la Statistique et des Études Économiques, Statistique Generale de la France, *Annuaire statistique*, LVI, 1940–45 (Paris, 1946), p. 360.
2 Author's interview with survivors.
3 War Office record WO 203/2336, South East Asia Command: Military Headquarters Papers, Second World War, Allied Land Forces South East Asia, British National Archives.
4 Hoàng Quốc Việt, 'Đẩy Mạnh Cải Cách Ruộng Đất Để Củng Cố Hoà Bình, Thực Hiện Thống Nhất Và Xây Dựng Đất Nước. Năm 1954', dossier 3908, Ministry of Interior, National Archives III, cited in Le Thi Quỳnh Nga, 'The Vietnam Communist Party's Views of the Land Reform Process as Seen from the Resolution of the Party Central Committee (1945–1956)', MA thesis, Lê Thi Quynh Nga University of Social Sciences and Humanities, Hanoi, thesis code: I VNH3. TB9. 115.
5 Nguyễn Khac Vien, *Vietnam: A Long History* (7th edition Hanoi, 2007), p. 480.
6 Author's interview with eyewitnesses.
7 Trương Như Tang, *A Vietcong Memoir: An Inside Account of the Vietnam War and its Aftermath* (New York, 1985), p. 158.
8 Bui Tin, *From Cadre to Exile: The Memoirs of a North Vietnamese Journalist* (Chiang Mai, Thailand, 1995), p. 51.
9 'Combat after Action Reports, December 1, 1967', Records of the U.S. forces in Southeast Asia, MACV, Assistant Chief of Staff of Operation (J3), Evaluation and Analysis Division (MAC J3-05), Reports 531–60, Box 9, Folder MAC J3 #544, National Archives.
10 Robert K. Brigham, 'The United States and the Army of the Republic of Vietnam', in *A Companion to the Vietnam War*, ed. Marilyn B. Young and Robert Buzzanco (Hoboken, NJ, 2006), pp. 150–4.
11 World Bank country data, available at http://data.worldbank.org (accessed May 2013).
12 Author's interviews with residents.
13 World Bank country data.

14 Trương Hữu Quýnh et al., *Đại Cương Lịch Sử Vietnam Toan Tap* (Hanoi, 2010),
    p. 1131.
15 UNHCR, *Yearbook of the United Nations 1979: Part 1*, 'Assistance to Refugees',
    p. 915.

EIGHT: From Traditional to Modern Vietnamese Food

1 Nguyễn Khuyến, 'Bạn Đến Chơi Nhà', available at http://vanhoc.xitrum.net
   (accessed June 2015).
2 Trương Đăng Thị Bích, *Thực Phổ Bách Thiên*, available at www.khamphahue.
   com.vn (accessed December 2014).
3 This is a Vietnamese play on words, and as such is impossible to translate
   adequately. This is a literal translation.
4 Lucy Siegle, 'Will Eating Insects Ever Be Mainstream?', *The Guardian*,
   6 July 2014, www.theguardian.com.
5 U.S. Food and Drug Administration, *Defect Levels Handbook*, available at
   www.fda.gov (accessed December 2014).
6 FAO Forestry paper, 'Edible Insects: Future Prospects for Food and Feed
   Security', 2013, www.fao.org.

Select Bibliography

'L'Annam', *Bulletin des amis du vieux Huê*, 1 and 2 (1931)

Barker, Randolph, Robert W. Herdt and Beth Rose, *The Rice Economy of Asia*, vol. 11 (Washington, DC, and Manila, 1985)

Brigham, Robert K., 'The United States and the Army of the Republic of Vietnam', in *A Companion to the Vietnam War*, ed. Marilyn B. Young and Robert Buzzanco (Hoboken, NJ, 2006)

Bui Tin, *From Cadre to Exile: The Memoirs of a North Vietnamese Journalist* (Chiang Mai, Thailand, 1995)

Coedes, G., *The Indianised States of Southeast Asia*, trans. Susan Brown Cowing (Honolulu, HI, 1968)

'Combat after Action Reports, December 1, 1967', Records of the U.S. forces in Southeast Asia, MACV, Assistant Chief of Staff of Operation (J3), Evaluation and Analysis Division (MAC J3-05), Reports 531–60, Box 9, Folder MAC J3 #544, National Archives

Vien Khoa Hoc Xa Hoi Viet Nam, trans., *Đại Việt Sử Ký Toàn Thư* (Hanoi, 1992)

Đào Duy Anh, *Lịch Sử Việt Nam, Từ Nguồn Gốc Đến Giữa Thế Kỷ XIX* (Hanoi, 2002)

Đỗ Đức Hùng, et al., *Việt Nam Những Sự Kiện Lịch Sử (Từ Khởi Thủy Đến 1858)* (Hanoi, 2001)

The Đông Sơn Collection, National History Museum, Hanoi

'Effects of French Colonial Rule' in 'Vietnam: History', in *Encyclopaedia Britannica*, available at www.britannica.com (accessed December 2014)

Eriksson, J., et al., 'Identification of the Yellow Skin Gene Reveals a Hybrid Origin of the Domestic Chicken', *PLoS Genet*, IV/2 (2008)

Flower, Barbara, and Elisabeth Rosenbaum, trans., *The Roman Cookery Book: A Critical Translation of the* Art of Cooking *by Apicius for Use in the Study and the Kitchen* (London, 1958)

Gaide, L., 'Le Visage inconnu de l'opium', *Bulletin des amis du vieux Huê*, 2 and 3 (April–September 1938), pp. 87–102

Gilbert, L., 'Les Produits', part III, ch. 1, *Bulletin des amis du vieux Huê*, January–June 1931, pp. 125–40

Hà Văn Tấn, ed., *Khảo Cổ Học Việt Nam*, vol. II (Hanoi, 1999)

——, and Nguyễn Duy Hinh, 'Kinh Tế Thời Hùng Vương', in *Hùng Vương Dựng Nước*, ed. Uy Ban Khoa Hoc Xa Hoi (Hanoi, 1973)

Hoàng Quốc Việt, 'Đẩy Mạnh Cải Cách Ruộng Đất Để Củng Cố Hoà Bình,
    Thực Hiện Thống Nhất Và Xây Dựng Đất Nước. Năm 1954', dossier 3908,
    Ministry of Interior, National Archives III, cited in Le Thi Quỳnh Nga, 'The
    Vietnam Communist Party's Views of the Land Reform Process as Seen from
    the Resolution of the Party Central Committee (1945–1956)', MA thesis, Lê Thi
    Quynh Nga University of Social Sciences and Humanities, Hanoi, Thesis code:
    IVNH3.TB9.115

Viên Sử Học, trans., *Khâm Định Việt Sử Thông Giám Cương Mục, Tien Bien*, vol. I
    (Hanoi, 1998)

Kiple, Kenneth F., *A Movable Feast: Ten Millennia of Food Globalization*
    (Cambridge, 2007)

Lam Thi My Dzung, 'Some Aspects of Vietnamese Bronze Age', in *The Final Research
    Results Supported by the KFAS International Scholar Exchange Fellowship Program
    (2001–2002)*, 2002

Lê Tắc, *An Nam Chí Lược*, trans. Huế University (Huế, Vietnam, 1961)

McCorriston, Joy, 'Wheat', in *The Cambridge World History of Food*, vol. I
    (Cambridge, 2008)

Ministère de l'Économie Nationale, Institut Nationale de la Statistique et des Études
    Économiques, Statistique Generale de la France, *Annuaire statistique*, vol. LVI,
    1940–45 (Paris, 1946)

Nguyễn Khac Vien, *Vietnam: A Long History* (7th edition Hanoi, 2007)

Nguyễn Khuyến, 'Bạn Đến Chơi Nhà', available at http://vanhoc.xitrum.net
    (accessed June 2015)

Nguyễn Việt, 'Hoabinhian Food Strategy in Vietnam', in *SEA Archaeology*,
    ed. W. Solheim (Manila, 2004)

Pelliot, Paul, 'Le Fou-nan', *Bulletin de l'École Française d'Extrême Orient*, vol. III
    (1903), pp. 248–303

Reese, David S., 'Fish: Evidence from Specimens, Mosaics, Wall Paintings, and Roman
    Authors', in *The Natural History of Pompeii* (Cambridge, 2002)

Siegle, Lucy, 'Will Eating Insects Ever Be Mainstream?', *The Guardian*, 6 July 2014,
    www.theguardian.com

Smith, Andrew F., 'From Garum to Ketchup: A Spicy Tale of Two Fish Sauces', in
    Fish: Food from the Waters, ed. Harlan Walker (Totnes, Devon, 1998)

Solheim, Stephen W., 'New Light on a Forgotten Past', *National Geographic*,
    no. 3 (1971)

——, 'Northern Thailand, Southeast Asia, and World Prehistory', *Asian Perspectives*,
    XIII/1 [12] (1972)

Suarez, Thomas, *Early Mapping of Southeast Asia* (Singapore, 1999)

'Sunda Shelf', in *Encyclopædia Britannica Online* (2011), available at www.britannica.
    org

Taylor, K. W., *The Birth of Vietnam* (Berkeley, CA, 1983)

'Thời Cổ Đại', http://dictionary.bachkhoatoanthu.gov.vn (accessed September 2013)

Tiến Trình Lịch Sử Việt Nam, ed., *Nguyễn Quang Ngọc* (Hanoi, 2000)

Trần Thế Pháp, *Lĩnh Nam Chích Quái*, trans. Lê Hữu Mục (Saigon, 1961)

Trần Trọng Kim, *Việt Nam Sử Lược* (Hanoi, 2002)

Trương Đăng Thị Bích, *Thực Phổ Bách Thiên*, available at www.khamphahue.com.vn
    (accessed December 2014)

Trương Hữu Quýnh et al., *Đại Cương Lịch Sử Vietnam Toan Tap* (Hanoi, 2010)

Trương Như Tang, *A Vietcong Memoir: An Inside Account of the Vietnam War and its Aftermath* (New York, 1985)

UNHCR, *Yearbook of the United Nations 1979: Part 1*, 'Assistance to Refugees'

U.S. Food and Drug Administration, *Defect Levels Handbook*, available at www.fda. gov (accessed December 2014)

Vu Hong Lien, *Royal Huế: Heritage of the Nguyễn Dynasty of Vietnam* (Bangkok, 2015)

Vu Hong Lien and P. D. Sharrock, *Descending Dragon, Rising Tiger: A History of Vietnam* (London, 2014)

War Office record WO 203/2336, South East Asia Command: Military Headquarters Papers, Second World War, Allied Land Forces South East Asia, British National Archives

Wolters, O. W., *Two Essays on Dai Viet in the Fourteenth Century* (New Haven, CT, 1988)

World Bank country data, available at http://data.worldbank.org (accessed May 2013)

www.lichsuvietnam.vn, *Thời Cổ Đại*, ebook accessed September 2011

Acknowledgements

I am indebted to a number of friends who helped to make this book great fun to write. My first thanks go to my dear friends in Vietnam Nguyen Ngoc Thanh-Quang and To Thi Hong Van-Khanh, who housed and fed me sumptuously while I was researching this book. Next, my thanks to all my London friends who have been my guinea pigs over the years, and who have shared many good meals with me all over Vietnam.

Photo Acknowledgements

Photo Aarchiba, adapted by Rama: p. 209; photo Claus Ableiter: p. 88 (this file is licensed under the Creative Commons Attribution-Share Alike 3.0 Unported license: any reader is free to share – to copy, distribute and transmit the work, or to remix – to adapt the work, under the following conditions: you must attribute the work in the manner specified by the author or licensor, but not in any way that suggests that they endorse you or your use of the work); photo Arvn: p. 138; photos author: pp. 12, 13, 15, 16, 17, 19, 21, 27, 28, 38, 45, 57, 59, 63, 66, 68 (top), 74, 75, 80, 81, 86, 90, 93 (foot), 133, 164, 168, 171 (top), 175 (foot), 177, 189, 193, 194, 196, 215, 227; from Samuel Baron, *Description of the Kingdom of Tonqueen* (London, 1746): pp. 99 (foot), 100, 101; from John Barrow, *A Voyage to Cochinchina, in the Years 1792 and 1793 . . .* (London 1806): p. 102; photo Biblioteca Nacional de Portugal, Lisbon: p. 102; photos Bình Giang: pp. 29, 36, 37, 40, 47; British Library, London: p. 85 (Harley MS 7182); British Museum, London: p. 22; photo Chaya Shinroku: p. 99 (top); photo d/k: p. 62; photo Jean-Pierre Dalbéra: pp. 190, 203 (these files are licensed under the Creative Commons Attribution 2.0 Generic license: any reader is free to share – to copy, distribute and transmit the work/s, or to remix – to adapt the work/s, under the following conditions: you must attribute the work/s in the manner specified by the author or licensor, but not in any way that suggests that they endorse you or your use of the work/s); photo Pierre Dieulefil: p. 201 (foot); photo Ron Diggity: p. 204 (this file is licensed under the Creative Commons Attribution 2.0 Generic license: any reader is free to share – to copy, distribute and transmit the work, or to remix – to adapt the work, under the following conditions: you must attribute the work in the manner specified by the author or licensor, but not in any way that suggests that they endorse you or your use of the work); photo Doremon360: p. 39 (this file is licensed under the Creative Commons Attribution-ShareAlike license versions 3.0, 2.5, 2.0, and 1.0.: any reader is free to share – to copy, distribute and transmit the work, or to remix – to adapt the work, under the following conditions: you must attribute the work in the manner specified by the author or licensor, but not in any way that suggests that they endorse you or your use of the work – permission is also granted to copy, distribute and/or modify this document under the terms of the GNU Free Documentation License, Version 1.2 or any later version published by the Free Software Foundation, with no Invariant Sections, no Front-Cover Texts, and no Back-Cover Texts); photo Everjean: p. 181 (this file is licensed under the Creative

suggests that they endorse you or your use of the work); photo Kham Tran – www. khamtran.com – p. 126 (this file is licensed under the Creative Commons Attribution 3.0 Unported license: any reader is free to share – to copy, distribute and transmit the work, or to remix – to adapt the work, under the following conditions: you must attribute the work in the manner specified by the author or licensor, but not in any way that suggests that they endorse you or your use of the work); photo Khamar: 85; photo Kingofthepings: p. 206 (this file is licensed under the Creative Commons Attribution-Share Alike 3.0 Unported license: any reader is free to share – to copy, distribute and transmit the work, or to remix – to adapt the work, under the following conditions: you must attribute the work in the manner specified by the author or licensor, but not in any way that suggests that they endorse you or your use of the work); photo Kowloneese: p. 71 (this file is licensed under the Creative Commons Attribution-Share Alike 3.0 Unported license: any reader is free to share – to copy, distribute and transmit the work, or to remix – to adapt the work, under the following conditions: you must attribute the work in the manner specified by the author or licensor, but not in any way that suggests that they endorse you or your use of the work); from *La Manche* (28 August 1926): p. 113; photo Larry: p. 188 (this file is licensed under the Creative Commons Attribution-Share Alike 2.0 Generic license: any reader is free to share – to copy, distribute and transmit the work, or to remix – to adapt the work, under the following conditions: you must attribute the work in the manner specified by the author or licensor, but not in any way that suggests that they endorse you or your use of the work); Library of Congress, Washington, DC (Geography and Map Division): p. 8; photo Lưu Ly: pp. 52, 171 foot (this file is licensed under the Creative Commons Attribution 2.0 Generic license: any reader is free to share – to copy, distribute and transmit the work, or to remix – to adapt the work, under the following conditions: you must attribute the work in the manner specified by the author or licensor, but not in any way that suggests that they endorse you or your use of the work); from Victor-Adolphe Malte-Brun, *La France Illustrée* (Paris, 1884): p. 110; photo Paul Mashburn: p. 154; photo Mini923: p. 68, foot (this file is licensed under the Creative Commons Attribution-Share Alike 3.0 Unported license: any reader is free to share – to copy, distribute and transmit the work, or to remix – to adapt the work, under the following conditions: you must attribute the work in the manner specified by the author or licensor, but not in any way that suggests that they endorse you or your use of the work); photo Mo Riza: p. 70 (this file is licensed under the Creative Commons Attribution 2.0 Generic license: any reader is free to share – to copy, distribute and transmit the work, or to remix – to adapt the work, under the following conditions: you must attribute the work in the manner specified by the author or licensor, but not in any way that suggests that they endorse you or your use of the work); from *Le Monde Illustre* (28 March 1891): p. 106; Museum of Custom-made China of the Nguyễn dynasty, Huế: p. 81; Museum of Royal Antiquities, Huế: pp. 57, 59, 80; Museum of the Western Han Dynasty Mausoleum of the King of Nanyue, Guangzhou, China: p. 62; photo National Archives and Records Administration, Washington, DC: p. 146; National History Museum, Hanoi: pp. 12, 13, 15, 16, 17, 19, 21, 27, 28, 36, 37, 40, 63, 133; National History Museum, Ho Chi Minh City: pp. 20, 38, 86, 90, 93 (foot); photo Ngô Trung: p. 182 (this file is licensed under the Creative Commons Attribution 2.0 Generic license: any reader is free to share – to copy, distribute and transmit the work, or to remix – to adapt the work, under the

Generic license: any reader is free to share – to copy, distribute and transmit the work, or to remix – to adapt the work, under the following conditions: you must attribute the work in the manner specified by the author or licensor, but not in any way that suggests that they endorse you or your use of the work); from Jean-Baptiste Tavernier, *Recueil de plusieurs relations et traitez singuliers & curieux de J. B. Tavernier chevalier, baron d' Aubonne [...] Relation nouvelle & singuliere du Royaume de Tunquin . . .* (Paris, 1692): p. 175 (top); photo Thang Nguyen: p. 200 (this file is licensed under the Creative Commons Attribution-Share Alike 2.0 Generic license: any reader is free to share – to copy, distribute and transmit the work, or to remix – to adapt the work, under the following conditions: you must attribute the work in the manner specified by the author or licensor, but not in any way that suggests that they endorse you or your use of the work); Trịnh Quang Vũ: p. 101; photo TURGAN: p. 111 (top); photo [Tycho] talk , http://shansov.net: p. 64 (this file is licensed under the Creative Commons Attribution-Share Alike 3.0 Unported license: any reader is free to share – to copy, distribute and transmit the work, or to remix – to adapt the work, under the following conditions: you must attribute the work in the manner specified by the author or licensor, but not in any way that suggests that they endorse you or your use of the work); image by uploader, based on Gryffindor's map (this file is licensed under the Creative Commons Attribution-Share Alike 3.0 Unported license: any reader is free to share – to copy, distribute and transmit the work, or to remix – to adapt the work, under the following conditions: you must attribute the work in the manner specified by the author or licensor, but not in any way that suggests that they endorse you or your use of the work): p. 103; photo U.S. Information Agency: p. 150; photos Viethavvh: pp. 51 (released into the public domain), 53 (this file is licensed under the Creative Commons Attribution-Share Alike 4.0 International license: any reader is free to share – to copy, distribute and transmit the work, or to remix – to adapt the work, under the following conditions: you must attribute the work in the manner specified by the author or licensor, but not in any way that suggests that they endorse you or your use of the work), 56 (this work is licensed under the Creative Commons Attribution-Share Alike 3.0 License – with no Invariant Sections, no Front-Cover Texts, and no Back-Cover Texts - permission is also granted to copy, distribute and/or modify this document under the terms of the GNU Free Documentation License, Version 1.2 or any later version published by the Free Software Foundation, with no Invariant Sections, no Front-Cover Texts, and no Back-Cover Texts), 172, top (released into the public domain), 214, 219 (these files are licensed under the Creative Commons Attribution-Share Alike 3.0 Unported license: any reader is free to share – to copy, distribute and transmit the work/s, or to remix – to adapt the work/s, under the following conditions: you must attribute the work/s in the manner specified by the author or licensor, but not in any way that suggests that they endorse you or your use of the work/s); photo (WT-shared) Shoestring at wts wikivoyage: p. 167; photo Yuchinkay: p. 192 (this file is licensed under the Creative Commons Attribution 2.0 Generic license: any reader is free to share – to copy, distribute and transmit the work, or to remix – to adapt the work, under the following conditions: you must attribute the work in the manner specified by the author or licensor, but not in any way that suggests that they endorse you or your use of the work); photo Yun Huang Yong: p. 222 (this file is licensed under the Creative Commons Attribution-Share Alike 2.0 Generic license: any reader is free to share – to copy, distribute and transmit the work, or to remix – to adapt the work, under the following conditions: you must attribute the work in the manner specified by the author or licensor, but not in any way that suggests that they endorse you or your use of the work).

Index

Page numbers in *italics* indicate illustrations

36 Streets 97, 100, *105*, 107

Agricultural Co-operative 145
Allies 137, 141, 152
American food 148–9, 151, 154, 216
amphorae 88–90, *88*
An Nam Chí Lược 42, 54, 63–4, 89
An Tiêm 34
anchovies 89–90
Annam 109
anniversaries of death 173, 208
ant larvae 65
areca nut 55–8, 83, 200
artichoke 118
ARVN 153–4
asparagus 119, 208
Âu Cơ 22, 41, 205
Âu Lạc 60–62, *61*
Aurelius, Marcus 85
Australia 21, 226–7

Bắc Ninh 30, 62
baked beans 148
bamboo 18, 25–6, 33–5, 38, 49, 52, 57, 95–
6, 119, 127, 143, 153, 164, 173, 177, 183,
187, 191–2, 199, 202, 212–13, 217, 221
banana 31–3, 46–7, 49, 51, 54, 95–6, 143,
165, 170–71, 176, 178, 183, 186, 196,
199, 204
banana heart *32*, 186
bánh bao 68, *69*
bánh bèo 198–9

bánh chưng 31, 49, 51–3, *51*, *52*, 79, 162
bánh cuốn 189–90, 220
bánh dầy 31, 49, 52–4, *53*, 162
bánh giò 198–9
bánh hỏi 181–2, *182*
bánh mì 9, 128–31, *130*, *131*, *160*, 161, 208,
227–9
bánh nếp 198–9
bánh tráng 190, 192–3
bánh xu xê 198, *199*, 200
Bát Trân 78
bear's hand 78
Beau, Paul 133
beef 33, 67, 104
beer 133, 151, 212, 219, 221
berries 31, 116
betel 54–9, *56*, *57*, 83, 180, 200
betel-chewing 56, 58–9
Beurre Bretel 112–13, *113*, 120, 151
bivalves 12, 14, 211–12
blood 55, 58, 180, 211, 213–15, 220–21, 228
blood clams *211*
boat people 157
bouillabaisse 122, 208
bronze 21, 35–40, 43–4, 66, 86, 168
Buddhism 73, 81, 92–3, 95
bún 47, 65, 104, 158, 181–90, 192–6, 198,
202, 220–21, 225
bún bò Huế 104, 158, 183, 188–9, *189*, 221
bún chả Hanoi 158, 186, *188*, 194–5
bún ốc 183, 185–6, 196
bún riêu 47, 183, 186

bún thang 183–5, *184*, 220
bún thịt nướng 183, 188, 193, 195
butter 110–13, 116–17, 128–9, 148, 154–5,
   165, 218–19

Cả river 9, 21, 119
cà bát 33
cà cuống 219–20, *219*
cà pháo 33
Cao Lang 58
Cao Tan 58
caramelized pork *206*
Carpinus 30
carrot 118–19, 129, 177, 186, 188, 191, 207–8
Cát Hải 91
Catholic missionaries 108
Cattigara 86–7
cattle 16, 18–9, 21, 49, 54, 64, 116, 152,
   179, 216
cauliflower 118–19, 207–8
celery 119, 207–8
century egg 71–2, *71*, 173
ceramic 56, 80–83, 90, 199
chả 78, 123, 129, 158, 170–71, 173, 183,
   186–8, 192–5, 203, 220–21
chả cá 183, 221, *222*
chả giò 123, 192–3, *193*, 227
Cham 44, 91, 102–4
Champa 42, 44, 60, *103*
charcuterie 110, 117–18, *118*
Cheddar 130–31
cheese 110–13, 130–31, 148, 151, 154–5,
   200, 219
chicken 19–20, 23, 26, 28, 37, 47, 67, 69,
   71, 75, 79–80, 95, 97, 104, 124–5,
   129, 148, 150–51, 158, 160, 162–5,
   164, 170, 173–4, 179–80, 183–4, 191,
   196, 198–9, 207–8, 215, 221, 225
Chinese sausage 69–70, *70*, 118, 165
Chiu Chow 105
chocolate 110, 148, 151
chopsticks 82, 164–5, 177
chuối ngự 31, 178
citrus 31, 212
clam 14, 25, 122, 185, 211–12
clay 23, 25–30, 34, 41, 72, 79, 82, 90,
   168–9, 178, 205

Cổ Loa 96
Coca-Cola 148, 150
Cochinchina 102, 109–11, 123, 208
cockles 12, 14, 176, 185, 211–12
coconut 30–31, 47, 49, 104, 165, 200, 212,
   216, 218–19
coconut worms 216, 218–19
cocoon 31, 71, *115*, 215, 217
coffee 79, 110, 113–17, 151, 154–5, 206–7,
   227, 229
collectivization 145
colonial cookery 121
cốm 46–7, *47*, 79
Con Moong 14–15
condensed milk 111, 113–14, 119, 150, 165
Convention of La Haye 134
cookbooks 109, 168, 178, 204–6, 208, 211
corner street market *121*, *166*
cornichons 119
crocodile meat 123
crustaceans 14
curries 103–4

Decoux, Jean 137
deer 13–14, 16, 18, 23, 37, 44, 64, 78, 124
Denis Frères 110–11, *111*, 133
dog 17–18, 23, 44, 151, 179, 198, 220
Doumer, Paul 133
drought 92, 97–8, 100, 106, 137
duck 20, 47, 69–71, 79, 97, 124, 170, 173,
   221, 228

Đại Việt 42, 57, 136
Đào Thịnh 43
Điện Biên Phủ 141–2, 144
Đồng Nai *20*, 21, 43–4
Đông Sơn 21, 28, 35, *36*, 36–7, *37*, *38*, *39*,
   40, 43, 45

earthquake 97, 100
East–West maritime route 85, 91
eel 47, 213
elephant 14, 16, 18–19, 21, 78, 99, 123
elephant's foot 78

famine 97–8, 106, 136–7, 139–42, *139*,
   147

fermented foods 65, 72–5, 87–8, 96, 103–4, 147, 164, 176, 178, 188–9, 192, 200–202, 204–5, 228
fermented tofu *74*
fertilized duck egg 221
fish herb 193, 198
fish sauce 51, 74, 79, 87, 89–91, 95–6, 101, 120, 124, 148, 155, 170, 182, 187–8, 195, 200, 202, 212–13, 217
flooding 97, 106
Fontaine 133
food rationing 156
food stamps 146, 152
foxes 14, 21
Fromageries Bel 112
frozen pork 150
Fujian 105
Funan 44, 60, 86, 104

gấc 172, 173
galangal 64, 198, 201–04
Gao Pian 96
garum 87–9
geese 20
Geneva Accord 128, 141–2, *142*, 144, 148, 152
Gia-Long 106, 136, 168, 176
ginger 64, 73, 79, 89, 104, 125, 184–5, 198, 201, 203–4, 212
giò 123, 129, 170–71, *171*, 173, 190–93, 198–9, 227
glutinous rice 31, 49–50, 54, 79, 116, 128, 165, 173, 181, 198–9, 204–5
goat 18, 38, 67, 104, 124, 174, 221
Gracey, Douglas 141
Great Famine of 1945 136–7, *140*, 142
Greeks 84
green rice 46–7, *47*, 95, 171
grubs 30
Guangdong 42, 60–61, 86–7
Guangxi 42, 61

Hạ Long Bay 13, 27, 35, 136, 212
Hà Tiên 105
Hà Văn Tấn 27
Hải Phòng 27, 30, 86, *201*
Hainanese 105

hamburger 151, 187, 224
Han 54, 61–5, *63*, 72, 76, 79, 82–6, 98, 220
Hanoi 27–8, 37, 39, 41, 43, 62, 96, 105–6, *105, 106*, 121, 126–7, 133, 139, 158–60, *159, 160*, 166–7, *167*, 186, 188, 194–5, 198, 201, 212, 217, 221–3
herbivorous 18
Hindu 104, 208
Hồ 42, 98
Hòa Bình *15*, 17–18, 20–21, 27, 144
Hoa Lư 96
Hoành Sơn 62
Hội An 102, *102*
hojiso 33
Hồng Bàng 39, 41, 44, 54, 60
hot dogs 151
Hsi Kuang 65, 72
Huế 56, 104, 108, 123–4, 158, 174, 176, 178, 182–3, 188–9, 198, 221
Hùng kings 31, 41–3, 49–50, 54, 59, 89

Ice Age 10, 13
Ikeda, Kidunae 147
inflation 156
insects 30, 73, 215–7, 220

Japanese 33, 69, 99, 137–41, *140*, 147, 158, 161, 198, 213, 225, 229
Java 13, 33, 103
Jen Yen 65–7, 72
Jiaoche 60
Jingdezhen 80
Jiuzhen 60
Juglans 30

Khmer 83, 102–5
kitchen gods 178–9
Kublai Khan 57, 84, 98

La Vache qui rit 112
Lạc 22, 41–5, 49, 54, 60–63
Lạc Long Quân 22, 41
land reform 141, 144, 147
lap cheong 70
larvae 30, 65, 218
Last Great Melt 13, 22

Lê court *99*
Lê Lợi 99
leeks 118–19, 207–8
Lepidoptera 30
lime pot 56–7, 59, *59*
Lĩnh Nam Chích Quái 25, 31, 49
Lipton tea bags 151
long braising 79
lotus 46–7, 79, 82, 92–5, *93, 94*
Luy Lâu 62, 73, 83, 86–7, 91
Lý 92–3, *93,* 95–7, 200

Mã river 60
MACV 153
madeleines 117
Maggi 120, 129, 165
Maison Bretel Frères 112
malnutrition 140, 156
mắm 87, 89–91, 99, 101–4, 119, 124, 147–8,
    155, 163–5, 170, 176, 183–4, 188–90,
    192, 194–5, 197, 199–203, *201, 203,*
    205, 220
mắm nêm 103
mắm pò hóc 104
mắm ruốc 104, 188–9
mắm rười 176, 202–3
mắm tôm 104, 183–4, 202–3
mắm tôm chua 203
mandarin 77, 100–101, 179
mango 33, 197
Mê Linh 41
Mekong Delta 30, 33, 60, 85–6, 91, 102–6,
    118, 132, 136–7, 147–8, 152, 176, *197,*
    202–3, 208, 218–19
Military Payment Certificates (MPCs)
    149, *149*
military plantation 107, 136
milk 67, 73, 104, 110–11, 113–14, 116, 119,
    125, 130, 150, 165, 207, 212
Ming 82, 85, 92, 98–9, 105
Minh Mạng 176
molluscs 7, 10, *12, 13,* 14, 21, 23, 26, 29, 185,
    211–12
Mongols 98, 136
monkeys 14, 21
monsoon 45, 85
morning glory 47, 186–8

Mount Đọ 13
MSG 147–8, 153, 225–6, 228–9
mulberry 133
mung beans 49, 52, 54, 165, 173, 199–200
Mường 44
Muslim 104
Mỹ Tho 105

Nam Giao 124, 174–5, *175*
Nan-Hai trade 86
Nan-Yueh 54, 60–62, *61, 62*
nem chua 204, *204,* 228
new economic zones 157
Nghệ An 12, 16
Ngô 92
Nguyễn 60, 78, 80, 92, 96, 102–3, *103,* 106,
    108–9, 134, 136, 168, 174, 176, 178,
    188, 197, 205
Nguyễn Ánh 102, 106, 136
Nguyễn Huệ 136
Nile delta 33
noodle 32, 47–8, 65–9, 104, 116, 120,
    125–7, 156, 165–7, 180–84, 186–7,
    189, 191–2, 194, 220, 223–5
nước chấm 176, 194–7, *194*
nước mắm 87, 89–91, 99, 102, 119, 128,
    147–8, 155, 163, 165, 190, 192, 194–5,
    197, 199, 202–3, 205, 220

Óc-eo, 30, 44, 85, *86, 87, 90,* 91
One Hundred Good Dishes 169, 202,
    204–5, 213
opium 134–5
orang-utan's lips 78
Oryza sativa 10, *11,* 35, 42, 49

paddy crab 32, 47–8, *48,* 183, 186
paddy fields 42, 46, 100, 158, 185, 200,
    219
paddy snail *185,* 211–12
Page, François 108
Panduranga 91
papaya 196–7, 203
Parmentier, Henri 26
pastries 116–17, 192
pâté 9, 116–17, 120, 129, 207
peacock 37, 63, 77–8

peanut butter 148, 154–5
pepper 51, 55, 89, 99, 117, 129, 153, 155, 170,
  186–7, 191, 202, 212–13, 217, 220–24
Phan Thiết 91, 212
pheasant 37, 63, 78
phở 65, 125–8, *126*, *127*, 161, 165, 180–81,
  225, 227–9
phoenix 55–6, 77–8, 178
Phong Châu 41
Phú Quốc 91
Phùng Nguyên *22*, 24, *27*–30, 33–5, 39
pickled foods 33, 72, 96, 101, 119–20,
  129–30, 164, 169, 178, 186–8, 207,
  222, 228
pickled vegetables 72, 96, 101, 119, 130,
  164, 169, 178
pig 13, 18, 21, 23, 33, 38, 46, 51, 179, 188–9,
  198, 221
pig's trotters 188–9
pigeon 20, 47, 97, 173, 207
Pius, Antoninus 85
plantation life *114*
polder 97–8
polder corvée 98
Polo, Marco 84
pomelo 33, 197–8
pop-up markets 97, 166
poppies 134
pork 20, 23, 32–3, 49, 51–4, 67, 69–71,
  75–6, 79, 104, 116, 118, 120, 124–5,
  129, 150, 163, 170, 173, 181–92, 194,
  196–7, 199, 203–7, 212, 225, 228
pork sausage 53, 184, 189–90
potato 96, 119, 169
potsherds 14, 23, 26, 28–9
pottery 23, 26–8, 35
pottery shards 23, 27–8
proto-Việt 10, 13–4, 16, 18–9, 21–30,
  35–6
Ptolemy 85–6, *85*, 91
pupae 30, 215, 217
PX 150, 152

Qing 78, 105, 136
Quảng Bình 21
Quảng Trị 17, 102–3
Quỳnh Lưu 12

ration 141, 146–7, 152–6, *153*
Red River delta 97–8, 145
rhinoceros skin 78
rice cooker 209–10, *209*
rice noodles *66*
rice planting *45*
rice stalks *168*
rice wine 49, 54, 64, 70, 72, 83, 133, 173,
  203–5, 212, 228
rice-paper wrapper 190–93, *190*
Rinan 62
roast meat 69, 173
Roman Empire 33, 83–4, 87–9, 91
royal cookbook 178, 204, 211
royal cuisine *77*, 176, *177*, 178
rubber 133, 137
rượu nếp 205
Russian 157–8

Sa Huỳnh 12, 28, *29*, 30, 43–4
Saigon 105–6, 108–11, *109*, *110*, *111*, 122–3,
  132–4, *150*, 158, *196*, 221
Salix 30
salt 46, 49, 63–4, *64*, 70, 72, 75–6, 87,
  89–91, 95, 98–9, 104, 120, 147, 153,
  155, 165, 186–7, 191, 201–5, 212,
  221–4
salted egg 71–2
sandwiches 53, 118, 120, 128–9, 151, 170,
  229
Sarraut, Albert 133
sausage 49, 53, 69–70, 117–18, 129, 165,
  170, 184, 189–90, 201, 207, 227
scallop 14
sesame 75–6, 96, 153, 165, 193, 204
shaking beef 224
Shanghai 105
shellfish 13, 21, 30, 35, 178, 185
Shennong 41
shiitake 73, 79, 212
silk 57, 72, 83–5, 215, 217
Silk Route 83–4, *84*
silkworm 72, 133, 215–18, *215*
silkworm pupae 217, *218*
slaked lime 55
Smokeless Cooking System, the 143
snacking 167, 210

snails 12, 14, 21, 32, 47, 185–6, 211–12
snake 213–15
snake wine *214*
soldier/farmer 97
Son of Heaven 108
Sơn Vì 14
sour cream 158
Southern Route 12
soybeans 67, 73, 76
spices 54, 63–4, 69–70, 79, 84, 102, 104, 106, 118, 125, 170, 196, 198, 208, 212
steam braising 79
steam-cup 80, *80*
stone grinders *15*
stone hoes 37
street food 68, 124, 127, 162, 181, *181*, 186, 227
subsidized 150, 152
suckling pig 21
sugar cane 133
summer rolls 192, *192*
Sunda Continent 13
swallow's nest 77, 79

Tang 62, 81, 86, 96
taro 30
tea 81–2, 95, 114, 116, 151, 164, 170, 194, 206
teapot *81*
termites 216
Tết 136, *171*, 204
Thăng-Long 96–8, 100, *100*, 166
Thanh Hóa 13–14, 23, 26–7
Thừa Thiên 102
Thục Phán 60
tía-tô 32–3
tofu 73–5, 95–6, 128, 156, 163, 170, 182–3, 191, 202, 207
tomato 9, 33, 47–8, 74, 118–19, 124, 129–30, 185–6, 207, 224
Tonkin 109
Trần 97–8, 100
Tràng Kênh 30
Trịnh lords *101*, 102
Trường Sơn 13, 25, 82
tubers 27, 30
typhoon 97, 139

Union Indochinoise, L' 109

Văn Lang 39, 41–4, *43*
Varenne, Alexandre 133
vegetarian 73–6, 95–6, 100, 170, 174, 191, 225
venison 10, 23, 78
Vichy 137
Việt-Minh 140–41
Vietnamized French 109, 120, 208
Villers, Charles Le Myre de 134
Vĩnh Phú 13–14, 35, 39, 41
vịt tiềm 79

Wandering Souls' Day 174
water buffalo 40, 64–7
wet-rice 41–2, 44–7, 61, 65, 186
wheat 7, 9, 67–9, 76, 116, 120, 128, 147, 156, 193, 228
wild boar 14, 18, 124
wildcats 14
wildfowl 19–20
wok 82
won-ton 68–9, *68*, 158, 180
wooden fish 100–102, 180
worm 89, 176, 202–3, 216–20

yam 30–32, 47, 95, 119, 169
Yangtze River 10, 41–2, 66
yếm 44
Yuan China 98, 136

Zhao To 54, 60–61, 220
Zheng He 85